Gender, Power,
and Persuasion

Gender, Power, and Persuasion

The Genesis Narratives and Contemporary Portraits

MIGNON R. JACOBS

Baker Academic
Grand Rapids, Michigan

©2007 by Mignon R. Jacobs

Published by Baker Academic
a division of Baker Publishing Group
P.O. Box 6287, Grand Rapids, MI 49516-6287
www.bakeracademic.com

Printed in the United States of America

Library of Congress Cataloging-in-Publication Data
Jacobs, Mignon R.
    Gender, power, and persuasion : the Genesis narratives and contemporary por-
traits / Mignon R. Jacobs.
      p.   cm.
    Includes bibliographical references (p.   ) and indexes.
    ISBN 10: 0-8010-2706-3 (pbk.)
    ISBN 978-0-8010-2706-2 (pbk.)
    1. Bible. O.T. Genesis—Criticism, interpretation, etc. 2. Sex role—Biblical teach-
ing. 3. Man-woman relationships—Biblical teaching. I. Title.
BS1235.52.J33 2007
222′.1106—dc22
                                              2007004995

In loving memory of
Jacintha

Contents

List of Tables and Diagram

Tables

Diagram

Acknowledgments

W hat started as a presentation at a Pacific Coast Regional meeting of the American Academy of Religion and Society of Biblical Literature became an opportunity to write this book. For that opportunity, I am indebted to Jim Kinney, editorial director at Baker Academic, who encouraged me to expand my presentation. Over the years that it took to write the book, I have grown to appreciate Jim and Baker Academic for their commitment, support, and vision.

Many persons have made the writing of this book an enlightening and enjoyable process. Some are the authors whom I had the pleasure to read. Most are family and friends. My brothers Carlos and Edwin listened and critiqued my ideas and perspectives. One person more than others challenged and transformed me and thus has been present throughout the book project. In her short life and death, my sister Jacintha taught me how to live.

I thank my God for all the blessings and challenges in my life.

June 2006
Pasadena, California

Abbreviations

ANET	*Ancient Near Eastern Texts Relating to the Old Testament.* Edited by James B. Pritchard. 3rd ed. Princeton, NJ: Princeton University Press, 1969.
ASV	American Standard Version
ESV	English Standard Version
JSB	Jewish Study Bible
JSOT	*Journal for the Study of the Old Testament*
JSOTSup	Journal for the Study of the Old Testament: Supplement Series
KJV	King James Version
NIV	New International Version
NRSV	New Revised Standard Version
TWOT	*Theological Wordbook of the Old Testament*. 2 vols. Edited by R. Laird Harris, Gleason L. Archer Jr., and Bruce K. Waltke. Chicago: Moody, 1980.
WBC	Word Biblical Commentary
ZAW	*Zeitschrift für die alttestamentliche Wissenschaft*

Introduction

Relationships define the well-being of a community and reflect its ideologies. For many, religious commitments inform or define their ideologies and their perspectives on female-male relationships. Furthermore, the assumption that the problematic aspects of female-male dynamics in the private and public domains have been resolved by including women in aspects of decision making and leadership is challenged by the continuing struggles to achieve, maintain, and advance equitable relationships between women and men. Not even the appeal to "biblical principles" has been successful in the constructive resolution of female-male dynamics. Instead, the appeal to biblical principles has contributed to the challenges and ambiguity concerning the nature and essence of female-male dynamics, specifically as these challenges relate to leadership and relational equity. As the church and society teeter on the brink of realizing the need for holistic models of human relationship, sociocultural realities continue to demonstrate the inevitability of synergistic leadership of both women and men.

There is no doubt that the Bible has had immeasurable effects on female-male relationships and female and male perceptions of each other. This book is proposed as part of the necessary conversation and realization of the significance that the Hebrew Bible/Old Testament (hereafter Old Testament) has had in shaping contemporary understandings of the female-male dynamics in all arenas where issues of gender, power, and persuasion are involved. There are many disciplinary perspectives from which such a book may be presented, but given my field of expertise and my interests, in this book I focus on Old Testament narratives. Using several Genesis narratives as the primary interpretive framework, I build on the proposition that even the understanding of the texts is

15

shaped by ideological commitments about female-male dynamics and the role of God (the Deity) in human relationships and behaviors. Additionally, I propose that investigating the Genesis narratives through the conceptual windows of gender, power, and persuasion will further illuminate (a) their relevance for understanding the particularities of the texts themselves and (b) the human dynamics within systems or domains that presuppose the presence and vitality of God as a defining principle (i.e., their views and treatment of persons).

The book is divided into three parts. Part 1, Divine and Human Dynamics in Genesis 2–3, consists of chapters 1–2. Both of these chapters examine the divine-human relationship, with chapter 1 focusing on God, the Deity's creation and orchestration of the various created elements, and chapter 2 focusing on the power of persuasion manifested in the relationships of the created beings vis-à-vis their relationship to the Deity. Part 2, Human to Human—The Conceptual Triad in the Genesis Narratives, consists of chapters 3–7. I examine five narratives that depict various configurations of gender involvement, namely, female-male (chapters 3 and 7), female-female (chapters 5 and 6), and male-male (chapter 4). While the primary focus in these chapters is on the particular gender configuration, the focus is instrumental and recognizes that gender roles in any domain are defined relative to each other and always include aspects of the other configurations. The other major organizational aspect of part 2 is its attention to each of the conceptual windows that define the goal of this book, namely, gender, power, and persuasion. Part 3, Female-Male Dynamics in Contemporary Contexts, consists of chapters 8–9. These chapters continue the summarizing observations of the chapters in parts 1 and 2 and use these observations as starting points for sketches of the contemporary issues. Chapters 8 and 9 are restricted to selected issues of female-male dynamics as viewed through the lenses of power and persuasion.

Ideological Starting Place

At the outset, a few preliminary comments will clarify the choice of texts, ideology, and approach used in this book. In particular, the legal corpus is excluded from this study, although it reflects many of the same dynamics of gender and power observed in the Genesis narratives (see the excursus following chapter 7).

First, as obvious as it may be at this juncture in the history of interpretation, one must be cognizant of the point of view that is encoded in the narratives and not take lightly the fact that language is power used to create and destroy perception. Those who control the use and normative formulation of language control the perception of reality of any linguistic representation. Consequently, any analysis of narratives must at least acknowledge the constraints and inquiries that are facilitated by the narratives. Such analysis must also recognize that no communication or interaction exists without underlying concepts. Every communication, whether conscious or unconscious, is shaped by beliefs, ideas, or assumptions. For example, a person may walk into a room and choose a seat directly opposite the door. When asked why, she may say that she wanted to see every person who enters the room. Whatever value she places on seeing persons who enter the room, she has put those values into action. Likewise, a man who greets all his colleagues when he enters the room but ignores the janitorial staff does so for a reason. He may say that he did not notice the staff or that he did not notice his behavior or even that the janitors are not part of his organization. Whatever his reasons, there is a conceptual basis for his behavior. Whether it originated with him or is incorporated from the domain, it regulates his behavior. Narratives are no different.

As products of their milieu, narratives are shaped by conceptual frameworks that also control what is said, how it is said, and why it is said. Without such frameworks, a narrative is neither coherent nor intelligible to its audience or readers. Presumably, the intended audience also controls the narrative's approach to its subject because the narrative regulates its use of language and portrayal to suit the audience's ability. Since their goal is to be intelligible and to persuade the audience of the validity of what is presented, narratives conform to normative ways of expression; for example, their portrayals must be plausible to the audience.[1] Another aspect of control is the assumption and knowledge shared with the audience. The narratives may include gaps that the primary reader simply takes as omissions of shared knowledge; however, other gaps may create ambiguity because these gaps are present only with certain characters (e.g., the male and female motivation for deceit).

Second, the view of the dynamics is a product most often of the male perspective, reflecting male ideologies about females. Power and weakness belong to the narrative—the power of portrayal, of ambiguity, of exoneration, and weakness as a characteristic of the marginalized "other." As a product of a milieu, the narrative views women as the source of contamination or chaos yet valuable for procreation and the survival of the family. Consequently, her "otherness" in and of itself is presented as a point of difference between her and the male. In such perspectives,

1. We are in essence dealing with the meta-reality to which the narrator belongs and the reality portrayed by the text. For the most part in this book I deal with the realities portrayed by the text as the first point of contact to the socioconceptual matrix in which the narrator operated. I do not intend to reconstruct the social setting or historical milieu.

the narrative portrayal of the female includes her relative value as compared to the male. She, while human, is seen to be less valuable than her male counterpart. Such valuation is therefore variously reflected in her functional and relational identity relative to the male. As an adult, she is the property of her father until he consents to her marriage, whereupon she becomes the property of her husband.

Her status is further typified by the regulation of her sexual practices. While she is a sexual being and the existence and viability of the lineage depends on her, consent to engage her sexually belongs to the male—her father and her husband. Outside of these sanctioned modes of consent to sexual expression she is deemed unacceptable and thus marginalized. Likewise, in the narrator's view of the female-male dynamic, the male is the dominant sanctioned power. The female often resorts to alternative expressions of power that are unsanctioned by the community. In the family domain, the narrator does not appear to mind the woman's expression of her power and thus readily depicts that manifestation (Sarah, Rachel, and Leah). Consequently, more often than not, in female-male dynamics the male narrative perspectives are windows through which women are viewed. This tool thus creates for the reader the image of women consistent with the ideologies of the male system. One cannot minimize the effects of these portraits on modern views of women.

Third, the narratives also show that when left on their own, women will usually dominate one another and behave toward one another as men behave toward them. Even in these female-female relationships (e.g., mother-daughter, co-wives, sisters), the nature of the relationship presupposes male influence. Some view Ruth and Naomi as the exception. However, other examples define the matriarchy as being a feminized patriarchy, for example, Sarah and Hagar, Rachel and Leah, Hannah and Peninnah. Thus the narrator paints women as their own adversaries. Like males, females will seek their own interests and wield their power to maintain their privilege. The fallacy of gender alliance is that women will support women simply because they are women. Rather, lines of loyalty are blurred when self-interest becomes a priority. In her place as matriarch over Hagar, Sarah instigated the situation that resulted in Hagar being the mother of Sarah's surrogate. Yet her interest or concern for a mother (Hagar) and her son (Ishmael) pales in comparison to her concern and her willingness to oppress Hagar to maintain her own status within the family.

Fourth, one of the aims of this book is to consider various nuances of characters and events, including both humans and the Deity. This is not an effort to portray any one in a more favorable light than another. Consequently, I consider various dimensions of the narratives for their contributions to the portrayal of relational dynamics. I presuppose that the narratives already reflect their preferred portrait of the events and agents/persons even to the point of being reticent on issues or events that may modify the overall portrayal.

Methodological Concerns

I have several points to make about methodology. First, in this investigation of the narratives I focus on the narrative portrayals rather than a reconstruction of the historical background of each narrative. I include the details of the analysis to illustrate the basis of the various observations. Second, this is a multicritical approach to the narratives that attempts to maximize the insights into the text rather than to demonstrate faithfully the principles of a specific approach. Accordingly, I incorporate the insights from a variety of methods—including historical, literary, concept analysis, feminist, form, psychological, postcolonial, and ideological criticism. This approach is an invitation to enter the narratives through the eyes of the narrator, to interact with the dimensions of the actions, behavior, reticence, and so on, and to discern the presuppositions of the narratives and the larger literary and conceptual contexts. Third, this book is intended to facilitate further insights into the relevance of the Old Testament narratives to discussions about female-male relational and behavioral dynamics. Finally, the mechanics of the presentation include the following:

- Translation and transliteration of terms are provided where references to the Hebrew text are noted, for example, the "dust" (*'āpār*) of the ground. Likewise, limited grammatical analyses are included (especially for readers who wish to investigate the text further).
- The variations in the designation for God are recognized (God, Yhwh, Lord, etc.), but instead of attempting to account for the various designations in each narrative, "the Deity" is used interchangeably with "God" to speak of the divine agent vis-à-vis humans.
- The quotations from the Bible are from the New Revised Standard Version (NRSV) unless otherwise indicated.
- Summary observations are included in parts 1 and 2. Therefore, the reader is encouraged to engage the analysis in these parts as preparation for the discussion in part 3.

Divine and Human Dynamics
in Genesis 2–3

Interpretations of Gen. 2:4b–3:24 (hereafter Gen. 2–3) have defined modern perspectives on gender roles and identity in communities around the world. These interpretations have been used to argue for a system in which human history and relationships in particular are orchestrated and perpetually influenced by the Deity. Furthermore, the interpretations of Gen. 2–3 are also used to sustain a system of male domination and female subjugation. Understanding this text is therefore fundamental to discussions of human relationships and the role of the Deity in them.

The goal of part 1 is to delineate an understanding of two types of dynamics involving the Deity and humans. Accordingly, I assert in part 1 that the behavioral and relational dynamics characterized by the text are fundamental to the discussion of gender, power, and persuasion. Consequently, in this section I examine these three aspects of the narratives as portrayed in the Deity's construction of female-male dynamics.

In chapter 1, I examine Gen. 2 by looking at the Deity's power in creating and addressing the needs and functions of the created beings.[1]

---

1. In this examination I recognize that Gen. 1 and 2 are two distinct creation narratives and I do not harmonize the two accounts. I treat the Gen. 2 narrative as a discrete whole with its own perspective on the creation process, intent, and outcome.

I focus on the interaction between the Creator and the created (Deity vis-à-vis human, animals). In chapter 2, I examine Gen. 3 in light of the relationship between the Creator and created beings and the challenges of authority, persuasion, and the power of choice. I focus on the dynamics among the created beings (i.e., humans, animals, plants).

1

Setting the Stage

God and Human (Genesis 2)

Introduction

The narratives of the book of Genesis build on the assumption of a domain defined by the presence of God, the Deity. While this presence is noted through God's specific actions apart from and in relationship to human beings, the absence of the presence also contributes to the portrayal of the divine-human relationship. Genesis 2 presents this divine-human relationship from the perspective of the starting point and the establishment of behavioral and relational parameters. Through the representation of these parameters, aspects of the Deity's power are highlighted, revealing a power manifested in the purposeful creation, control of the creation, and issues of human power. In this chapter I explore the behavioral and relational dynamics of the divine-human relationship as depicted in Gen. 2. The behavioral parameters are viewed through the Deity's creation activities and rationale, and the prohibition regarding the tree of knowledge of good and evil. Accordingly, I propose that the purposefulness of the creation is evidence of the Deity's power, and that the Deity is acting on a plan in progress in which the prohibition is a decisive element. The prohibition sets the stage for a test. The behavioral dynamics are also depicted in the Deity's intention and effort to find a suitable companion for the human; likewise, the relational parameters are viewed through the concern about solitude and the subsequent efforts to resolve it. I propose that the text represents solitude as a precursor to companionship, while indicating that companionship does not obliterate solitude. The narrative raises several issues, namely, human solitude in God's presence, types of solitude, and a resolution that assumes compatibility criteria.

Behavioral Parameters of Power

Purposeful Creation

God's intentionality is observed in the creative act of "shaping" (*yāṣar*) "the human" (*hā'ādām*) from the dust of the ground (Gen. 2:7).[1] Both the action and the material used constitute the essential part of the Deity's intentionality. As in other instances, the shaping includes a skill and a vision of what is to be shaped (cf. 2:19; Isa. 44:2, 24; Ps. 104:26).[2] The material used is what the Deity previously created (Gen. 2:4–5) with the resultant barren land caused by two complementary components—one from the Deity and the other from an undefined agent. Likewise, the cause-effect sequence is noted with reference to two topographical areas and the reason for their condition—the "field" (*śādeh*) and the "ground" (*'ădāmâ*).[3] It is reported that the field was without plants or shrubs because the Deity had not caused it "to rain" (*māṭar*).[4] Elsewhere "rain" (*gešem*) is associated with God's act of punishment or blessing (7:12), and the withholding of it is accomplished by closing the windows of heaven.[5] In 2:5 the withholding of rain is not a punitive measure but part of the starting condition of the earth that would be resolved by the Deity's intentional act. On the other hand, the condition of the ground is

1. Victor P. Hamilton, *Genesis 1–17*, New International Commentary on the Old Testament (Grand Rapids: Eerdmans, 1990), 159–60. He proposes that when the term appears with the definite article (*hā'ādām*) it is translated as "human"; without the article ('*ādām*) it is translated as a personal name, Adam. Unfortunately, the uses in Gen. 2–3 do not conform to this pattern, thus leading to the idea of combined sources. The occurrences are noted as follows: *hā'ādām* (Gen. 2:7, 8, 15, 16, 18, 19, 20, 21, 22, 23, 25; 3:8, 9, 12, 20, 22, 24; cf. 1:27); and '*ādām* (2:5, 20; 3:17, 21; cf. 1:26).

2. Contrast Isa. 44:9–10 where humans shape idols. See Gordon J. Wenham, *Genesis 1–15*, WBC 1 (Waco: Word, 1987), 59.

3. Wenham (*Genesis 1–15*, 58) identifies distinctions between "field" (*śādeh*), "the wilderness fit only for animal grazing," and "the ground" ('*ădāmâ*), "where agriculture is possible with irrigation and human effort."

4. The verb *māṭar* (to rain) and its noun form are used of precipitation, of water or other elements (Gen. 7:4; 19:24; Exod. 9:18, 23, 33; 16:4; Deut. 11:1–17; 28:12).

5. Cf. Deut. 11:11–14; 1 Kings 8:35–36; Isa. 5:6; Jer. 14:4; Amos 4:7.

attributed to the lack of an unspecified agent (*'ādām*) to work the ground
(*'ǎdāmâ*). Thus the starting condition is characterized by nonproductiv-
ity of both field and ground, and the resolution would be a cooperative
effort of the Deity and the other agent.[6] In this instance, the Deity could
send the rain to water the earth while the other agent tills the ground.
While the divine agent already exists, to resolve the other part of the
deficiency another agent is needed to till the ground. The exigency is
therefore not a relational one but rather a functional one defined by the
particular stage of the creation activity.

For his functional role, the human is shaped from the material that
he is to tend—the "dust" (*'āpār*) of the ground. The use of the material
signals the affinity between the human and the ground. But neither the
formation nor the material affinity is sufficient for the functioning being.
The progressive activity continues, and the decisive stage of the shaped
entity is finalized through another creative act of the divine agent. God
blows[7] the "breath of life" (*nišmat ḥayyîm*) into the shaped entity and
that entity becomes a "living being" (*nepeš ḥayyâ*).[8] This living being
begins as a product of the Deity's power to shape it and to decide the
nature of its existence. It is distinct from the plants and the dust from
which it is made because of the breath of life that alters it from entity
to living being.[9] Furthermore, the material makeup of the being is not
necessarily responsible for the nature of the being.

Second, the Deity's intentionality is presented in "planting" (*nāṭaʿ*)
the garden and placing the human in it.[10] The narrative that gave an
indication of the Deity's evaluative power in saying that the garden
had no one to work it (Gen. 2:5) now states that the intent is for the
human "to work" (*'ābad*) the garden. The planting of the garden thus
addresses the lack of plant life (2:5) and the progression from the
starting place of desolation to the earth's productivity in much the

6. Cf. Hamilton, *Genesis 1–17*, 152–53.

7. The act at this stage of the process is signified by the verb *nāpaḥ* (to blow, breathe).
Along with its representation of the life process, it is also used of revitalization, as in the
case of returning life to dry bones (Ezek. 37:9). Cf. Milton C. Fisher, "נפח," *TWOT* 2:586.

8. Genesis 7:22 combines both "spirit" (*rûaḥ*) and "breath" (*nĕšāmâ*) to speak of animals
and humans. Joshua 11:11 and Isa. 2:22 use "breath" (*nĕšāmâ*) and suggest that the breath
is the distinguishing aspect of a human that constitutes its life. Cf. Milton C. Fisher, "נשם,"
TWOT 2:605. In the story of *Aqhat*, Paghat is invigorated by the breath of life. See *ANET*,
155; Victor H. Matthews and Don C. Benjamin, *Old Testament Parallels: Laws and Stories
from the Ancient Near East* (New York: Paulist Press, 1991), 92–93.

9. That is, living as compared to a corpse (e.g., Lev. 22:4; Num. 5:2; 6:6, 11; 9:10, 13);
but the entity is not named until it is called "living being."

10. In Gen. 2–3 the Deity is designated as "YHWH God" (*yhwh 'ĕlōhîm*). This epithet is also
used elsewhere, including Exod. 9:30; 2 Sam. 7:25; 2 Kings 19:19; 1 Chron. 17:16; 2 Chron.
6:42; 29:1; Ps. 59:6 (NRSV 59:5); 72:18; 80:20 (NRSV 80:19); Jer. 10:10; Jonah 4:6.

same way as the transformation of the human from entity to living being (2:7). God caused every kind of "tree" (*'ēṣ*) to grow from the ground with two conditions—the trees were visually pleasant[11] and good for food. The latter condition presupposes that one could eat from the trees and thus be satisfied with their fruits. They are all deemed "good" (*ṭôb*) not simply for the visual effect but potentially for the sustenance that they provide (*ma'ăkāl* "food"). These qualities are part of the intentionality of the Deity in causing the tree to grow, just as the inclusion of the tree of life[12] and the tree of the knowledge of good and evil[13] are part of the effort to grow the garden. Whatever additional properties these trees possess, the starting point of their existence reflects the sustaining and appealing qualities of all the trees in the garden with the location of the named trees as their distinguishing feature—in the midst of the garden (2:9).[14] That these two trees are named apart from the other trees also signals their importance to the narrative, an importance that is first noted in the prohibition concerning the tree of knowledge (2:17).

The "river" (*nāhār*) flows through the garden "to water" (*šqh*) it, and the tributaries sustain the garden (Gen. 2:10). Here the created symbiosis is depicted through the provisions for the garden itself; provisions for the human are juxtaposed—water for the garden, the human to work the ground, and food for the human. The success of the symbiosis is not that it was structured as such but that it meets the exigencies of the various created elements and processes. It was already anticipated that the lack of plants was due to the lack of water and the cultivation of the ground. Therefore, the presence of both of these elements addresses the perceived deficiencies. Placing the human in the garden indicates the progression in the creative activity as well as the power of the Deity

---

11. The formulation "pleasing to look at" (*nehmād lěmar'eh)* uses the verb *ḥāmēd* (to take pleasure in, desire). It also depicts the woman's perspective on the desirability of the tree of the knowledge of good and evil (Gen. 3:6), thus affirming God's success in producing a tree of such visual quality. Likewise the verb *ḥāmēd* is also used in various prohibitions about desires, namely, "do not covet" (Exod. 20:17; 34:24; Deut. 5:21; 7:25).

12. The tree of life (*'ēṣ haḥayyîm*) also occurs in Gen. 3:22, 24, and elsewhere metaphorically of wisdom (Prov. 3:18; 11:30), fulfilled desire (13:12), and a gentle tongue (15:4). Cf. Wenham, *Genesis 1–15*, 62; Hamilton, *Genesis 1–17*, 162–63; Roland E. Murphy, *The Tree of Life: An Exploration of Biblical Wisdom Literature*, 2nd ed. (Grand Rapids: Eerdmans, 1996), 136–37, 145. The sustaining quality of a tree is also noted.

13. On the tree of the knowledge of good and evil (*'ēṣ hadda'at ṭôb wārā'*), cf. Hamilton, *Genesis 1–17*, 163. He prefers "tree of the knowledge good and evil."

14. The location of both trees in "the midst of the garden" is represented by the use of the formulation *bětôk-haggān* in Gen. 2:9 and 3:3. See Wenham, *Genesis 1–15*, 62. Using the location of the tree as evidence, he proposes that the text was reworked. Genesis 2:9 locates the tree of life at the center of the garden, while the tree of knowledge is placed in that location in 3:3.

to define the human's role in the creative order (2:8, 15).[15] The stated purpose of the human in the garden is to "work" it (*'ābad*) and "guard" it (*šāmar*) (cf. 3:24).[16] Already the functional aspect of the human identity is set to include work without any suggestion of a punitive nuance to that work. It is therefore suggested that work is an essential part of the identity established by the Deity in response to a perceived functional deficiency of the creation. Consequently, as long as the human tills the ground and guards the garden, his functional purpose within the created order is fulfilled.

Power of Prohibition

Having placed the human in the garden, God communicates with the human (*hā'ādām*) about the parameters of his behavior relative to the plants in the garden.[17] The act of speaking to the human at this point indicates the ability of the human to comprehend what is said, even if the total ramification of the behaviors addressed is not understood. The mode of the communication is to "command" (*ṣāwâ*) the human, thus suggesting that this is not intended as a dialogue between the giver of the command and the receiver. The command includes the preparatory component establishing the permissible aspect of the behavior, the command itself establishing the proscribed aspects relative to the tree of knowledge (Gen. 2:16–17) and a stated consequence. First, the preparatory component of the command indicates the parameters of possible actions and points of differentiation between what is and is not permitted. It recalls the reference in 2:9 to "all trees" (*kol-'ēṣ*) in identifying the range of possibilities for eating and affirming that the trees were in fact for food. Second, the command defines the range of acceptable behavior by noting the action and the proposed consequence of a particular course of action. The alternatives indicated are eating and not "eating" (*'ākal*) from the trees within the garden.[18] It is inconsequential to the

15. While Gen. 2:8 uses the verb "to place" of God's action in establishing the contact between the man and the garden, 2:15 uses the verb *nûaḥ* in the Hiphil (cause to settle). Both have the idea of depositing the human in the garden. Both verses give the same information, but 2:15 specifies the reason that the man is placed in the garden. Cf. Hamilton, *Genesis 1–17*, 171–72.

16. The sense of *šāmar* is often "to guard" with the nuance of protecting, but here it may simply mean careful tending of the garden. Cf. Hamilton, *Genesis 1–17*, 171; Wenham, *Genesis 1–15*, 67.

17. At this point the woman was not yet created; cf. Gen. 2:21.

18. The nuance of the formulation is "you may definitely eat" (*'ākōl tō'kēl* —infinitive absolute followed by the imperfect form of the same verb). The same verbal construction is also used in the stated consequence of eating from the proscribed tree—thus *môt tāmût* (you will definitely die).

narrative whether there are other trees outside the garden from which the human may eat. Instead, the human is told that he may eat from all the trees in the garden with one exception: he may not eat from the tree of the knowledge of good and evil.[19] The prohibited action is eating, with no mention of "touching" (*nāga'*) or "looking" (*nābaṭ*)[20] at the tree, or any other possible actions (cf. 3:3). The possibilities also indicate that the ability to discern is a required asset of one who is to adhere to the prohibition. The human must discern among the trees to determine at each act of eating whether to choose one tree or another, and with that choice whether to include the proscribed tree as an option. Since the Deity did not prohibit looking at the tree and made the tree "pleasant to the sight" (2:9), the human may choose the proscribed tree for its visual qualities and not be in violation of the prohibition. Third, the command also identifies a consequence of eating from the proscribed tree—death (*môt tāmût*).[21] There are no explicit statements about the consequences of refraining from eating of the tree of knowledge like those seen in identifying the positive outcome of keeping the commandments (cf. Deut. 4:1; 6:3, 24; 28:9; Lev. 20:22; 26:3–4).[22] Rather, the stated consequences resemble the death sentences found elsewhere and usually translated "you shall surely die" (cf. Gen. 20:7; 1 Sam. 22:16; 1 Kings 2:37; 2:42; 2 Kings 1:4; Jer. 26:8; Ezek. 3:18; 33:8, 14–15). Notably, 1 Kings 2:37 also uses the temporal formula *běyôm* "on the day" to indicate the time frame of the actualized consequences.[23] In Gen. 2:17, the temporal formula is followed by a verb, "you eat" (*'ăkolěkā*),[24] designating the prohibited action as the catalyst that would bring the consequence into actualization within the same time frame.[25]

19. The form of the prohibition is typical of the Decalogue: the particle of negation plus the imperfect of the verb, namely, *lō'*+ *tō'kal* (Qal imperfect second masculine singular of *'ākal* "to eat"; e.g., Exod. 20:13–15: "You shall not murder. You shall not commit adultery. You shall not steal"). The difference between the Decalogue and the prohibition in Gen. 2:17 is that the consequences are stated in Gen. 2:17 and absent from Exod. 20:3–17.

20. Cf. God's command to Abram to look at the stars (Gen. 15:5); the command not to look back (19:17); fear associated with looking at God (Exod. 3:6); looking at an object as restorative (Num. 21:9). Cf. other occurrences in the Pentateuch: Exod. 33:8; Num. 12:8; 23:21.

21. The infinitive form (*môt*) is followed by the finite form of the verb (*tāmût*—Qal imperfect second masculine singular of *mût* "to die"). The death penalty is also indicated by the formulation *môt yûmāt* (infinitive + finite form [*yûmāt*—Hophal imperfect third masculine singular of *mût* "to die"]; Gen. 26:11; Exod. 19:12; 21:12–18; 31:14, 15; Lev. 20:2, 9, 10, 15; 24:15–17; 27:29; Num. 35:16–18, 31; Ezek. 18:10–13).

22. Cf. the stated consequences of not obeying, e.g., Lev. 26:14; Num. 15:22.

23. 1 Kings 2:37; cf. Isa. 10:3; Amos 3:14; Zeph. 1:8.

24. Infinitive construct form of *'ākal* (to eat) plus the second masculine singular suffix (*kā*), referring to the human. Cf. Isa. 30:26; Ezek. 16:5.

25. Wenham, *Genesis 1–15*, 67–68, 73–74. The formula "on that day" may also be rendered "when," but in several of the noted texts (e.g., 1 Kings 2:37, 42) it designates the

The Power Dynamics of the Prohibition

A command can be issued by anyone who has the capacity to communicate. The power to effect adherence to the command, however lies in the nature of the command, in who commands, and in the ability of the one commanded to obey. Consequently, the prohibition implies the power of choice. While it does not give power, it signals its presence and its ability to be manifested. Through the presentation of alternatives the prohibition indicates possibilities for the future, each possibility engendering a different course of action and presumably different sets of outcomes. In this instance, power, the ability to effect change, is part of the Deity's and the human's repertoires of behavior. The prohibition reflects various components of the Deity's choices as the one who designed the situation and the relational system of created being and creator. First, the design of the garden provides the elements that are to be distinguished, namely, the trees. Given the intentionality of the Deity in creating and addressing the perceived deficiencies, the Deity could have omitted these entities. That they exist is a manifestation of the Deity's choice to create them whether or not the act of creating them already presupposed using them, for example, toward the specific purpose as alternatives in a prohibition and in addition to producing a fertile garden. Second, the communication with the human being about what is permissible establishes the boundaries of acceptable behavior and eliminates ignorance as a justification for doing what is prohibited. One may therefore see this command as the Deity establishing the parameters for future dealings with the human should he opt to violate the Deity's prohibition.[26] Third, the articulation of the consequence indicates the possibility of choosing between the alternatives. Fourth, basic to these choices is the decision to give humans the power of choice in contrast to no decision-making capacity. Accordingly, the stated consequence of eating from the forbidden tree is death (*môt tāmût*) as a real possibility rather than an exaggerated threat.[27]

Power of Choice

Several issues are raised by the prohibition with reference to the power of choice and the possibility of altering the future by this manifested power. At issue is whether the decision-making power also implies an

---

immediacy of the consequence. Wenham also indicates the ambiguity of the formulation, reflecting both the immediacy and the eventual death. In contrast to this are those who propose ultimate rather than immediate death, e.g., Hamilton, *Genesis 1–17*, 172; E. A. Speiser, *Genesis*, Anchor Bible (Garden City, NY: Doubleday, 1964), 15.

26. Cf. Ezek. 33:18–21 regarding punishment of the wicked with and without warning.

27. Speiser, *Genesis*, 17. He proposes that the phrase be translated "you shall be doomed to death" rather than "you shall surely die." His rationale is that the narrative intent was to communicate "ultimate punishment rather than instantaneous death."

open system wherein decisions can lead to possibilities and actualizations other than those envisioned by the Deity. Here the stated consequence defines the extent of the punishment envisioned. The narrative offers two possibilities—to eat or not to eat. In giving the prohibition and the consequence, does the Deity already show the limitations placed on the human? Does the prohibited act necessarily lead to the cited outcome? And which is favored by the Deity—eating or not eating from the tree (i.e., its fruits, leaves, etc.)? Is eating the only avenue for manifesting the power of decision making? It would appear that not eating is a default position since it is the starting position at which the prohibition is given. Thus the prohibition in this instance is not to correct a behavior but to prevent a behavior. If eating was the plan and the prohibition the mode of implementing its possibility, the Deity was effective through the motive. But the motive in giving the prohibition and achieving the outcome are ambiguous at best. If the plan or favored position was that the human would not eat, then the Deity's plan failed. This failure would indicate the Deity's lack of power to control the choice of the human.[28]

As seen in the test, the power of choice is set. But what is the goal of this test? Certainly, the Deity's purpose is manifested through the evaluation and identification of exigencies (Gen. 2:5–15). The conceptual tension of the narrative is the dual perspective of the Deity's actions. On the one hand, the narrative implies that the prohibition may also have a purpose within the Deity's plan. On the other hand, the Deity's trial and error in the latter part of the narrative suggests that the design is a work in progress not predetermined before it is implemented (2:18–23). Still the question of the prohibition is haunting. If the narrative sequence is followed and hence the progression of action recognized, then the prohibition articulated an alternative that may be as understandable to the human as explaining death to an infant. If, as is most likely the case, the ramifications of the choice are not outside the ability of the human to comprehend, then the prohibition itself indicates the functional cognitive acuity of the human. The human is fully capable of discerning the choices and is cognizant of the ramifications expressed in the prohibition.

Additionally, the prohibition and evaluation of the human's relational status are manifestations of the Deity's power to determine what is good and what is not. The Deity's power is evident in creating possibilities for

28. Cf. Shimon Levy, "The Performance of Creation, Creation in Performance," in *The Creation of Man and Woman: Interpretations of the Biblical Narratives in Jewish and Christian Traditions*, ed. Gerard P. Luttikhuizen (Leiden: Brill, 2000), 190. Levy argues that the Deity is portrayed as a "frustrated theatre director, dissatisfied with his actors who do not properly perform their roles, yet he does not seem to know in advance the final format of the play."

the human without consulting with the human before embarking on the course of action. This is clearly not a relationship of equals. Rather, the stratification of the relationship is encoded in the Deity's design. The human's comprehension of the choices is one side of the Deity's attempt to persuade the human that one course of action is more desirable than another. As with any prohibition, the articulation of the alternatives and consequences reveals the perspective of the one who formulates the prohibition. In this case the Deity's perspective is that death will come from following one course of action. Notably, it is implied that life will follow the other course as a product of maintaining the status quo. This is precisely the quandary that the serpent expresses in Gen. 3:4–5. The power of the Deity is manifested in the ability to create and to control the human, to experiment with life, and to distribute power, allowing humans and animals some control over their existence. Still the Deity's motive in this particular design is shrouded in ambiguity, including a portrait of a deity who is discovering how to make things work, namely, a deity who does not know what the outcome will be until the outcome is actualized, or a deity who deliberately creates but does not anticipate deficiencies such as aloneness.

Another alternative is that the portrait of the Deity is itself part of a ruse. In this scenario, the Deity simply articulates the rationale for various components of the plan and is in control of all aspects of the plan. Accordingly, the prohibition is part of the plan to ensure a desired outcome. The prohibition and declaration are manifestations of the Deity's plan to assist the human in discerning, but the Deity already knows what the human chooses and needs. If everything is under the Deity's control, then the human is not designed to choose among alternatives since the choice is already encoded in the human. What appears as a choice is simply a manifestation of the programmed behavior. The human would then be functioning as designed, every choice a matter of hardwiring, every consequence an orchestrated sequence. This would mean that one being—the Deity—has ultimate power and the other being—the human—is ultimately powerless. Yet for both to have a measure of power would mean that the outcome is unknown. Though not necessarily so, it would also mean that the plan may be affected by the divine-human power dynamics. One simply cannot have both a Deity with absolute control and a decision-making human in the same system. Where a decision-making human exists, part of the Deity's power is surrendered to human participation in the plan. Here the human has a will that is also controlled, but the human is allowed some latitude in manifesting that will. The question is how much latitude. If the Genesis narrative is the basis of the response, there is no simple answer. Apparently the Deity has a master plan and allows contingencies as long as the master plan stays on course. In this case the human has some ability to affect the future, but the parameters for human expression are limited. While human will is present, it is not free to choose among infinite possibilities. Rather, the choice may be among a finite set of options defined by the relational dynamics of all involved. Likewise, the powerful Deity does not have total control of all that happens but has an unfolding plan that adjusts particular aspects while maintaining the major focus of that plan.

Relational Parameters of Power

The Gen. 2 narrative defines the divine-human relational dynamics of the participants. These dynamics indicate the three elements of the conceptual triad: the power exemplified in the creative act and the regulation of that created order; the persuasion of the humans regarding the prohibition; and the commonality and differentiation of the humans in their relationship with God and each other. Furthermore, there are several definitive aspects of the relational dynamics, including the prohibition concerning eating from the tree (Gen. 2:16–17), the Deity's evaluation of the human (2:18), and the ensuing intent and actions that address the perceived need of the human—that is, creation of a companion to address the human's solitude (2:18–23).

Solitude

After shaping "the human" (*hā'ādām*), God assesses the creation and deems that it is "not good" (*lō'-ṭôb*).[29] The evaluation, however, does not cover all aspects of the creation, or even the entity that was created. Other aspects are also evaluated and deemed good, for example, the trees (Gen. 2:9). In both the negative and the positive cases, the evaluation is further modified through an expansion that specifies the aspect being evaluated.

EVALUATING AND DEFINING SOLITUDE

The evaluation does not address the physical constitution of the human or his ability to meet his functional role of caring for and guarding the garden. Instead, it focuses on solitude. Basic to an understanding of this evaluative declaration, "it is not good that the man should be alone" (*lō'-ṭôb hĕyôt hā'ādām lĕbaddô*), is the idea that there are various

29. Note this in contrast to God's observation and evaluation: "God saw that it was good" (Gen. 1:4, 10, 12, 18, 21, 25), and "very good" (1:31). Cf. Beverly J. Stratton, *Out of Eden: Reading, Rhetoric, and Ideology in Genesis 2–3*, JSOTSup 208 (Sheffield: Sheffield Academic Press, 1995), 35–36.

types of solitude. Yet at this point in the narrative, the man is not alone; the Deity and the plants are present. This fact raises a few questions, including: What are the implications of human solitude in God's presence? Whether or not the Deity is a companion, the Deity/Creator is not seen as the solution to the human's solitude.[30] This is not to say that the Deity's companionship with the human does not fulfill an essential human need. Rather, aloneness may mean being (a) without other created beings, (b) in the company of incompatible beings (e.g., the Deity), or (c) with other created beings who are incompatible (i.e., animals, Gen. 2:20).[31] Consequently, using specific categories of distinction, one may be described as "alone" (*lĕbaddô*) while with others. Thus Jacob says Benjamin is alone after he thinks Joseph has died, even though his other brothers are still alive. Benjamin is one remaining entity of a set—one of Rachel's children (42:38; 44:20). Moses is depicted as alone in the midst of the people (Exod. 18:14). There are also other instances when one is physically alone, as when David appears before Ahimelech the priest (1 Sam. 21:2 [NRSV 21:1]; cf. 2 Sam. 18:24–26).

CHARACTERISTICS OF THE HUMAN'S SOLITUDE

In Gen. 2 the wholeness of the man is dependent on the woman, and physical isolation is not a criterion for solitude.[32] First, solitude exists in the presence of beauty, sustenance, and nonanimal life (Gen. 2:9). That the garden is beautiful and has the resources to sustain the human

30. Cf. Walter Brueggemann, *Genesis*, Interpretation: A Commentary for Teaching and Preaching (Atlanta: John Knox, 1982), 47. He argues that in contrast to such passages as Ps. 121:1 and Isa. 41:10, "God does not intend to be the *man's* helper."

31. Note that in the case of the animals the following formula for incompatibility is used: "there was not found a helper as his partner" (Gen. 2:20b). This formula concludes the first sequence of creative effort to find the man a helper and introduces the necessity for further creative effort. In so doing the formula also suggests the investigative/experimental effort of God the Creator in contrast to the decisive results achieved in the creation of the garden for human existence. The narrative does not depict this experimentation as the Deity's intent to find a helper; rather, this experimentation is depicted as the result of that intent. Furthermore, the investigative effort is portrayed as incorporating trial and error. Perhaps the effort was to demonstrate to the man the "suitable" counterpart.

32. The term *bādād* "isolation, alone" has various nuances. Cf. Louis Goldberg, "בדד," *TWOT* 1:90–91. He notes that the negative connotation of the word indicates Israel's isolation from God because of God's judgment on Israel (Isa. 27:10; Lam. 1:1; Mic. 7:14). It may also indicate the abandonment by God and community (e.g., Lev. 13:46; Ps. 102:2–8 [NRSV 102:1–7]; Jer. 15:17, the prophet sees isolation as imperative to his call; cf. 2 Sam. 17:20). A positive connotation is the idea of "incomparability and uniqueness" in reference to God (Deut. 4:35; 32:12; Neh. 9:6; Job 9:8; Ps. 72:18; 148:13; Isa. 44:24). See G. Sauer, "אחד," in *Theological Lexicon of the Old Testament*, ed. Ernst Jenni and Claus Westermann, trans. Mark E. Biddle, 3 vols. (Peabody, MA: Hendrickson, 1997), 1:78–80, esp. 80. He discusses the semantic relationship of בדד and אחד, noting examples such as 1 Kings 8:39//2 Chron. 6:30; 2 Kings 19:15, 19//Isa. 37:16, 20; Isa. 2:11, 17.

suggest that solitude is not determined solely by one's surroundings and the availability of basic means of sustenance.

Second, solitude in the midst of the divine presence is a significant part of the relational aspects portrayed by the narrative. Inasmuch as God makes the pronouncement, the question arises as to the suitability of the Deity as an answer to human solitude. Yet the fact of the divine pronouncement is significant because the Deity formed the human (Gen. 2:7). By citing the reason for creating the human as functional rather than directly relational, the narrative portrays the Deity as deliberate about aspects of creation. Genesis 2:5 gives a clue as to the order of creation. Thus the garden is created after the human, that is, when there is someone to care for it.[33] The narrative portrays an unfolding plan and its contingencies seen in reference to the creation of the garden. If the garden is not created as a preparatory measure for the human's well-being, it would be invalid to argue that the Deity has anticipated the needs of the human at this point. If, however, the human is created for the garden (cf. 2:5, 15)[34]—thus the priority of the garden rather than the priority of the human—then one must observe here an unfolding plan. The plan is made on the basis of observations to address anticipated needs (someone to care for the garden); however, the exigencies associated with solitude ensue from the creation of the human being.

Third, solitude in relation to functional existence suggests that functional identity and purpose do not deter solitude. The human's place in creation is juxtaposed to the Deity's as both contribute to the vitality of the earth. Thus God causes the plants to grow and provides water sources to sustain the plants and a human to cultivate the garden. Yet the magnitude or nature of the human task does not distract from the need for companionship. In this case the Deity creates a being, then observes a deficiency in that being—the being is "alone" (*lĕbaddô*). The functional intent of the human is evaluated apart from the relational,

33. Note the sequence of subordinate clauses in Gen. 2:5–6. Verse 5a consists of two conditional statements, which are explained by the conditional statement in v. 5b, then followed by another conditional statement in v. 6. The main clause begins in v. 7, indicating the creation of man. Cf. Gerhard von Rad, *Genesis*, rev. ed., trans. John H. Marks, Old Testament Library (Philadelphia: Westminster, 1972), 76.

34. Cf. David Carr, "The Politics of Textual Subversion: A Diachronic Perspective on the Garden of Eden Story," *Journal of Biblical Literature* 112 (1993): 578–80, esp. 580. He observes the differences in focus between the creation materials in Gen. 2:4b–5, 7–8, 15bβ (early material) and the redactional levels in 2:6, 9–15abα. The earlier material shows a progression from the lack of garden and man to the supplying of these, whereas the redactional materials anticipate Gen. 3 by depicting the nature of the garden. Cf. Howard N. Wallace, *The Eden Narrative*, Harvard Semitic Monographs 32 (Atlanta: Scholars Press, 1985), 69. He notes that man's purpose was to till the land.

thus denoting two domains of existence. On the one hand, the human is functionally complete, having been given a purpose for his existence. This is quite different from whether the human is able to till the ground alone. On the other hand, the human is deemed relationally deficient, and the narrative illustrates the Deity's efforts to address the exigencies or deficiencies resulting from accomplishing one aspect of creation. In a sense the narrative portrayal depicts the unfolding of the creative process by indicating the Deity's thoughts. The creation of animals and woman are part of the contingency plan to address the deficit, thus indicating that both the animals and the woman were created within a relational framework. Consequently, the Deity is portrayed as completing creation by creating after the human is placed in the garden to work it (Gen. 2:15). All subsequent acts of creation are therefore to correct the completed work.

Presumably, the human is formed to be autonomous and functional. The completed being, however, reveals a deficit. When the plants and trees are made to grow, they come forth with others of their kind. Likewise, the tree that is named is accompanied by another named tree—the tree of life and the tree of the knowledge of good and evil (Gen. 2:9). Even the river that is made to water the garden forms tributaries, indicating that it also has entities similar in kind (2:10–14). When the human is shaped, he is formed by himself (2:7). The question of suitability is further raised in relation to the animals that God deems unsuitable for the human although they are created to be his "helper as his counterpart" (*'ēzer kĕnegdô*).[35] The animals and birds are nondivine and, like the human, are formed from the "ground" (*'ădāmâ*) (2:19). They are created by the same process of being shaped (*yāṣar*) by the Deity into the beings that they become.[36] Notably, the Deity does not blow the "breath of life" (*nišmat ḥayyîm*) into the animals and birds. Rather they are brought to the human, who names them, and God sanctions the names by which they are designated (2:19). In this way the Deity also sanctions the human in

---

35. Ed Noort, "The Creation of Man and Woman in Biblical and Ancient Near Eastern Traditions," in *Creation of Man and Woman*, ed. Luttikhuizen, 11–13. He notes the experimentation of the Deity in making the animals and concludes that God did not anticipate a female creature. He bases this conclusion on the use of the masculine noun *'ēzer* (helper) rather than the female noun *'ezrâ* (helper) (Gen. 2:18). Cf. Lyn M. Bechtel, "Rethinking the Interpretation of Genesis 2:4b–3:24," in *A Feminist Companion to Genesis*, ed. Athalya Brenner (Sheffield: Sheffield Academic Press, 1993), 113–14.

36. Hamilton (*Genesis 1–17*, 176) argues that this is not the first instance of animals being created. Rather the created beings in this instance are for the specific purpose identified—to find a helper. These creatures are the only ones brought to the human to be named. Hamilton is attempting to reconcile Gen. 1:24–25 and 2:19. In his argument, however, he overlooks the conceptuality of each narrative as an independent representation of the creative process.

his functional status in relation to the animal. Yet this status of "namer" and the named does not constitute an inherent superiority over the animals.[37] Like the human, they are also designated as "living beings" (nepeš ḥayyâ), thereby suggesting that the suitability is not constituted by the creative process or the common creator. Not even the material determines suitability. The suitability comes from the formation out of one's own being such that the essence of the being formed and the one from which it is formed are one. Perhaps the suitability pertains to the status of the human (hā'ādām) in relation to Yahweh God (yhwh 'ĕlōhîm), the Creator.

Fourth, solitude in Gen. 2:18 may indicate uniqueness. It is possible that the pronouncement is speaking about the "uniqueness and incomparability" of the human as a created being without another entity of matching quality, form, or function. As this uniqueness may be considered a divine trait, one may see why the Deity deemed it "not good" (lō'-ṭôb) to have that trait.[38] If the uniqueness of the human is at issue, it is legitimate to see the unsuitability of the animals and the Deity for human "companionship." Having been presented to the human and named by him, none of the living creatures on the land and in the air[39] is deemed a suitable helper. The Deity's attempt to find a suitable helper for the human among the animals is thus futile and stimulates additional effort to find a helper.[40] What is "not good" is the isolation and the incomparability of the human. The suitability of the woman then is constituted in that she is comparable to the man (hā'ādām) because she shares his essence and distinction from other living beings (nepeš ḥayyâ). Perhaps the male is like God in uniqueness and having the breath of life (nišmat ḥayyîm) from God (2:7). The creation of woman limits the uniqueness of the man and leaves the breath as the connection to God. Thus the words of the snake in 3:5 may not be as insidious

37. Contrast Wenham, Genesis 1–15, 68.

38. Although it has its weakness, the view is noteworthy. It does not give a justification of the "helper." However, it may illuminate the snake's claims and the apparent heightened chagrin that "the man has become like one of us" (Gen. 3:22). Cf. David J. A. Clines, What Does Eve Do to Help? and Other Readerly Questions to the Old Testament, JSOTSup 94 (Sheffield: JSOT Press, 1990); cf. Karen R. Joines, "The Serpent in Gen. 3," ZAW 87 (1975): 1–11, esp. 7; J. van Seters, "The Creation of Man and the Creation of the King," ZAW 101 (1989): 335–41.

39. The fishes of the sea are not noted as having been created or as being brought before the human. Cf. Wenham, who notes that the fish are not identified because they "could not qualify as man's helpmeet" (Genesis 1–15, 69).

40. This interpretation presumes that the Deity is the subject of the verb māṣā' (to find) rather than the human. Cf. Hamilton, Genesis 1–17, 174–75n3. He cites the alternative for understanding the subject-verb-object elements of Gen. 2:20. Cf. Nahum M. Sarna, Genesis, Jewish Publication Society Torah Commentary (Philadelphia: Jewish Publication Society, 1989), 22. He presumes that the human is the one in search of a helper.

as most believe them to be.⁴¹ What is not good is for the human to be
without a corresponding being. No rationale is given about why that is
not good, but then again none is given when things are deemed good.
The pronouncement suggests two things: work, basic sustenance, and
beauty are not sufficient for the well-being of the human; and, an existence constituted by uniqueness and solitude is not the ideal for the
human.

God's response to the futile effort to find a helper for the human
among the animals is to "construct" (*bānâ*) a woman using the man's
"side" (*ṣēlā'*).⁴² This divine act is a revisionist effort born out of the
experience of failure to achieve a goal. The material correspondence is
deemed inadequate in producing a corresponding being; yet the breath
is not used as a corrective in the animals. The revision is the material
used to create a suitable helper, the unique material constituted by the
entity formed from dust fused with the breath of life from the Deity.
For this construction, God uses one of the man's sides (*ṣēlā'*) as the
starting point of the woman (*'iššâ*). Rather than a "rib," as it is usually
interpreted,⁴³ the term denotes in all its other uses the side of an object and in relation to the human body an "undesignated part."⁴⁴ God
takes one of the man's sides and closes the opening (Gen. 2:21). The
Deity alters the man's being by taking a side and constructing (*bānâ*)
woman from this vital part.⁴⁵ Even the act is depicted as different from
that used in shaping (*yāṣar*) the man, presumably because this is not a
first effort to form a human.⁴⁶ Rather the repetition of the effort aims
at achieving a bond through common material essence and relational
correspondence. Although the man exists, he is made unconscious and
is not given a part in constructing the woman lest he be placed in a
role as her creator. After the Deity's construction is finished, the man

41. Cf. R. N. Whybray, "The Immorality of God: Reflections on Some Passages in Genesis, Job, Exodus, and Numbers," *JSOT* 72 (1996): 89–102.

42. The noun *ṣēlā'* is usually translated "side." It occurs in several passages, including
those concerning the tabernacle and its implements as well as the placement of various
implements in the tabernacle (Exod. 25:12, 14; 26:20, 26–27, 35; 30:4; 36:25, 32; 37:3,
5, 27; 38:7). In other instances, it denotes the "side" of a hill (2 Sam. 16:13), chambers
(1 Kings 6:5; Ezek. 41:5–9, 11), the side of a building (1 Kings 6:15, 34; Ezek. 41:26). Cf.
Hamilton, *Genesis 1–17*, 178.

43. Wenham, *Genesis 1–15*, 69; cf. modern translations: NRSV, NIV, and JSB.

44. Hamilton, *Genesis 1–17*, 178; Trevor Dennis, *Sarah Laughed* (Nashville: Abingdon,
1994), 13–14.

45. Dennis, *Sarah Laughed*, 14. He disagrees with the translation "rib bone," which he
sees as an attempt to relegate the woman to a subservient status.

46. Levy ("Performance of Creation," 189–90) proposes that three different verbs are
used to denote "hierarchically linked types of creation": *bārā'* (to create, Gen. 1:27), *yāṣar*
(to shape, form, 2:7, 19), and *bānâ* (to build, 2:21). Levy suggests that the process of bringing the woman into being was more biological and surgical than the other processes.

responds to the woman by affirming that she is "bone of my bones and flesh of my flesh" (*'eṣem mē'ăṣāmay ûbāśār mibbĕśārî*)—an expression that confirms in this instance the material affinity of the man and woman (2:23). Furthermore, as in its other occurrences, it may also denote a relationship bond constituted by sharing a common bloodline (cf. 29:14; 37:27).[47] Both the man and the woman share the same essential characteristics. So if the flesh connotes weakness and the bone strength, then both the man and the woman have both weakness and strength as part of their humanity.[48]

Resolving the Solitude

COMPANION AND HELPER

The nature of the solitude also defines the solution to it. There are several interpretive trends concerning the female-male relationship in Gen. 2–3 that have thus far defined understandings of these texts and their implications. These trends are based in part on the interpretation of two words, *'ēzer* (helper)[49] and *negdô* (his companion).[50]

First is the interpretation that the woman was created for the man as his "helper" (*'ēzer*). One aspect of this interpretation is espoused by David Clines, who argues that the woman was necessary to carry out the imperative to be fruitful and multiply (Gen. 1:28).[51] Accordingly, her functional status within the created order is to procreate. By contrast, Beverly Stratton argues that "procreation alone is an insufficient explanation of the woman's help in Genesis 2–3."[52] In Stratton's view, procreation is not an issue in the Gen. 2 account since in this account there is no imperative to be fruitful and multiply.[53] Yet another perspective is

---

47. Other occurrences include Gen. 37:27, of Joseph, "he is our own flesh" (*bĕśārēnû hû'*); Laban says to Jacob, "you are my bone and my flesh" (*'aṣmî ûbĕśārî'attâ*) (29:14; cf. Judg. 9:2; 2 Sam. 5:1; 19:13).

48. It may be a statement of covenant and loyalty representing a commitment that remains unaltered between those who make it because of the nature of the bond. Hamilton (*Genesis 1–17*, 179–80) believes this statement to be the counterpart to contemporary marriage vows. Cf. Walter Brueggemann, "Of the Same Flesh and Bone," *Catholic Biblical Quarterly* 32 (1970): 532–42.

49. U. Bergmann, "עזר," *Theological Lexicon*, ed. Jenni and Westermann, 2:872–74; cf. von Rad, *Genesis*, 82.

50. Literally: his opposite. This is usually translated as "corresponding to him." Cf. Speiser, *Genesis*, 17; Sarna, *Genesis*, 21.

51. Clines, *What Does Eve Do*, 33–34.

52. Stratton, *Out of Eden*, 98n2.

53. Stratton, *Out of Eden*, 36–37. She considers the possibility of an absent-minded God who is making up the plan as God goes along. Note this in contrast to God as portrayed in the Gen. 1 narrative.

that woman was created to meet man's sexual needs.[54] This interpretive trend makes sexual needs and their fulfillment fundamental to human existence and defines human sexual relationship with either the Deity or an animal as an unsuitable mode of human fulfillment (cf. 6:4; Lev. 20:5–16).

Another aspect of this interpretive framework of woman as helper is that she is created within an agricultural setting in which the demands of cultivating the land are central to existence. She is therefore created to assist in the tasks of cultivating the land.[55] Stratton endorses the validity of this observation that a farmer would need assistance in farming, and goes on to question why the narrative does not indicate this in conjunction with Gen. 2:18.[56] Clearly, the creation of the woman and the animals is an afterthought. Even so, both the animals and the woman are created with a definite purpose, just as the man was created for a purpose. Stratton would agree with this since she recognizes what she refers to as the "priority of the man."[57] Certainly, one sees a plan unfolding where the focus is the earth and its vegetation; all other aspects ensue from the status of the earth. It is therefore possible for man to be given a helper for tending the garden. Even so, this interpretation does not address why the animals would be unsuitable for that task. Thus one may further suggest that suitability for labor may mean more than mere assistance to lighten the workload.

Third, the relational and the inherent value of the helper are not determined by the status of the helper. God is identified as a helper[58] and in that role is not inferior to those who are helped. Phyllis Trible argues that "since the creature [hā'ādām] is not only of the earth but also other than the earth, it needs fulfillment from that which is other than in the earth."[59] She contends that "helper" is not an accurate translation since that term connotes inferiority and the text indicates

54. Francis Watson, "Strategies of Recovery and Resistance: Hermeneutical Reflections on Genesis 1–3 and Its Pauline Reception," *Journal for the Study of the New Testament* 45 (1992): 99.

55. Thus Carol Meyers, *Discovering Eve: Ancient Israelite Women in Context* (New York: Oxford University Press, 1988). She proposes that the woman was created to assist in farm labor. Cf. Stratton (*Out of Eden*, 37), who cites Gen. 2:5, 8, and 15 as the basis of her observation that man was created to work the land.

56. Stratton, *Out of Eden*, 102–5.

57. Stratton, *Out of Eden*, 102–5.

58. Phyllis Trible, *God and the Rhetoric of Sexuality*, Overtures to Biblical Theology (Philadelphia: Fortress, 1978), 90. Stratton's (*Out of Eden*, 96) assertions about Trible are inaccurate, since Trible does not argue at that point in her book for the superiority of woman. Trible argues for mutuality and equality. Cf. Exod. 18:4; Deut. 33:7, 26, 29; Ps. 33:20; 70:6 (NRSV 70:5); 115:9, 10, 11; 121:1, 2.

59. Trible, *God and Rhetoric*, 90.

identity, mutuality, and equality. When used in reference to God, Trible notes, *'ēzer* (helper) indicates superiority. Accordingly, the connotation of superiority is tempered in the present text by pairing *'ēzer* and *kĕnegdô* (corresponding to him).[60] Carlos Masters shares Trible's view, though not her translation of the term. He translates *'ēzer* as "helper" but notes that "the wife is not dominated by the husband but is his equal companion."[61]

Purpose of the Helper

Endemic to the interpretive framework that posits an inferior role to woman is the idea that to be a "helper" is to be inferior. The presupposition is used to ascribe subordination and inferiority to the female. Part of the divergence of the views concerning the female-male relationship is due to the different questions that interpreters ask. Thus while Trible contends that the woman is "one who alleviates isolation through identity,"[62] others ask questions about the functional identity of the woman. For example, Stratton affirms that "she is not created for her own sake, but in order to meet some divinely discerned needs of the man."[63] Clines argues that the role of helper connotes inferiority regardless of the status of the person who is so designated.[64] He examines the role in light of what the woman does (to procreate) and based on the nature of the punishment after the sin further contends that her role is not intellectual.[65] One also sees in this interpretive trend the tendency to assign quality to functional identity. Thus, the helper is usually deemed inferior even though the Deity is also depicted as a helper.

One cannot deny that in the conceptuality of the narrative the nature of the woman is directly connected to the purpose for which she was created. The ambivalence about the role of the woman lies in the understanding of the text's multivalence. Whether or not she is a helper, she is

---

60. Trible, *God and Rhetoric*, 90; cf. 140n13, where she cites the references to God as *'ēzer*—Exod. 18:4; Deut. 33:7, 26, 29; Ps. 33:20; 115:9–11; 121:2; 124:8; 146:5. Cf. Helen Schüngel-Straumann, "On the Creation of the Man and the Woman in Genesis 1–3: The History and Reception of the Texts Reconsidered," in *Feminist Companion to Genesis*, ed. Brenner, 53–76, esp. 66. She shares Trible's view and further notes that the text does not speak of an inferior or subordinate role of woman in reference to procreation.

61. Carlos Masters, *Eden, Golden Age or Goad to Action?* trans. Patrick J. Leonard (Maryknoll, NY: Orbis, 1974), 25, 91, 93; Cf. Bechtel, "Rethinking," 77–117, esp. 113.

62. Trible, *God and Rhetoric*, 90.

63. Stratton, *Out of Eden*, 96; cf. P. E. Jongsma-Tielman, "The Creation of Eve and the Ambivalence between the Sexes," in *Creation of Man and Woman*, ed. Luttikhuizen, 181–82. Jongsma-Tielman explores the hypothesis that Gen. 2–3 is a matriarchal context in which the dominant sex is the female.

64. Clines, *What Does Eve Do*, 30.

65. Clines, *What Does Eve Do*, 33–34.

essential to the well-being of the man out of whom she is "constructed" (*bānâ*). She is neither inferior nor superfluous because of her order or purpose in creation.[66] Likewise her designation as "helper" does not automatically signify her superiority or inferiority to man.[67] The man is central in that the creation even of the animals is done for the man. However, this in and of itself does not challenge the essential quality of the animals.

Part of the problem in the history of interpretation involves the modern notions of a helper.[68] Most assume that to be a helper is to be subordinate and inferior in essence to the one being helped. This notion makes light of the fact that without the helper the one who is being helped has *less than* full potential. Needing help is a subjugation of need to a larger purpose. Likewise to help is a subjugation and redirection of power to embrace a purpose. As God is not subordinated by helping humans, and as the king is not subordinated by helping others, neither is the woman subordinate in her relationship to the man by being designated a helper. To the extent then that the helper enhances the well-being of the helped, the helper is a source of power to the helped—regardless of the status of the helper (cf. Ps. 121:1; Isa. 30:5). Furthermore, if one is compelled to help another, one is subjected to the power of that need; that is, someone's need predisposes the helper to behave in a particular way and thus affects the future. For as long as one depends on someone else for the actualization of one's totality, that dependence creates a measure of equality of purpose that transcends status. If a deficiency persists without the involvement of the helper, then the helper is essential, and that which is essential is not inferior to the exigency.

Accordingly, concerning the nature of the pronouncement "it is not good for the human to be alone," some propose that the nature of the woman's presence is that of companionship. First, the purpose of the companionship is to resolve the uniqueness of the human being, a uniqueness that engenders an irrevocable solitude apart from the creation of the woman. Thus the female is more than a physical presence. Her presence further differentiates the male created being from the Creator. The human was already differentiated from the other living beings. If indeed the essence of the woman supersedes her order in creation and the need she addresses, her presence invalidates any assertion of her inferiority. Consequently, her subordination is in relation to the Creator, not to the man, with whom she is comparable.

---

66. Wallace, *Eden Narrative*, 69.
67. Cf. Bechtel, "Rethinking," 112–13; Hamilton, *Genesis 1–17*, 175–76; contrast Clines, *What Does Eve Do*, 30, 33–34.
68. Clines, *What Does Eve Do*, 25–48.

Conclusion

The starting place of the human relationship is defined by the Deity's power to determine the behavioral and relational parameters of the humans. The behavioral parameters establish a pattern in which the Deity defines the limits and imposes penalties on transgressing those limits. In this behavioral domain, the lines are blurry between the Deity's control of the human and the possibility of the human affecting the Deity's plan. To the extent that the Deity created a system that allows for the power of human choice, humans have real power. On the other hand, if the Deity's plan involves the orchestration of set choices that the humans are directed into, humans have no real power. Rather, the humans in the latter scenario are simply playing out the functional role to which they have been assigned.

As with the behavioral parameters, the relational parameters are also defined by the Deity, who places man and woman into relationship. Nonetheless, the nature of the relationship is also perplexing given the efforts of the Deity to find a suitable helper. The man affirms that he and the woman are one and suggests a mutuality evident in the way that creation functions. At issue is whether the relational parameters are also part of the functional identity of the humans defined and maintained by their physical bond. Ideally, if indeed man and woman are of the same substance, their relationship may be shaped by that mutual dependence wherein support or violation of the one is experienced by the other.

The Ultimate Test

Created versus Creator (Genesis 3)

Introduction

The Gen. 3 narrative presupposes Gen. 2 as the basis of its conceptual unity. Thus one cannot understand the significance of the serpent-female dialogue apart from Gen. 2:16–17, nor can one understand the significance of the punishment to expel the humans from the garden apart from 2:5, 9, 15. The female-male dynamics occur within the framework of God's creative plan. The central points in the plot are the prohibition about the tree of knowledge of good and evil, and the contingency plan that results in the creation of animals and the woman. This representation of the conceptual unity in no way suggests or denies that the man may have persisted through his existence without succumbing to the same fate of eating from the tree. The tree is part of the framework of the garden and the humans' relationship to the garden. In this chapter I propose that the Gen. 3 narrative depicts a domain in which both male and female participate and are conscious of their choices. Within this domain, the presence and influence of the Deity are evident through the dialogue about the Deity's prohibition and response to human choices. Fundamentally, the narrative is about persuasion, power, and the consequences of both.

Since the Deity created the exigency and the solution for that exigency, the Deity knew that the human needed companionship and the necessary type of companionship. Consequently, the human's response to the animals (unsuitable) and to the woman (suitable) was already encoded in the design and plan. The portrait is of a powerful Deity who is in control of the design and enjoys the successful execution of a plan. Nonetheless, the portrait leads to various questions, including the following: Given the power of the Deity as creator, could the design fail? Could humans make choices apart from the Deity's design for them?

Apparently, all aspects of the creation (including gender) have a purpose. Accordingly, gender is the product of a plan to resolve an unanticipated "human" (*'ādām*) need. As a mode of differentiation and identity, gender is not primary to the creative effort[1] but results from the effort to establish behavioral and relational parameters, including finding a suitable helper for the human. Humans are thus differentiated from plants and from the Deity, who orchestrates their functional identity. Thus it is with the creation of the woman that gender is differentiated.[2] Identity is further defined by the fact that the humans share one substance. Yet they are differentiated in that they are distinct beings created for different purposes and through different processes.

Like gender, power dynamics are also part of the purposeful design of the creation. What constitutes power in the narrative? Power is the ability to influence the future and others.[3] Thus within the narrative "the human" (*hā'ādām*) is given the choice to partake of all the trees in the garden except the tree of knowledge of good and evil (Gen. 2:16–17). This choice is indicative of power, and the prohibition indicates that the human is not autonomous or self-determining. Although the human is given power through choices, the human's power is regulated by limited options: to obey or to disobey. The human also has another power constituted by the Deity's allowance, that is, the power to name the animals (2:19). The human's first power then is not that of domination but of choice and, by implication, of discernment.[4] Genesis 3 is thus a narrative about the interplay of persuasion and power as manifested in human choice.

1. Bechtel ("Rethinking," 85–86) argues that there are various levels of differentiation. The first of these is an awareness of differentiation. It is at this level that one learns to distinguish between self and others. The second level is that of sexual deferential, which Bechtel identifies with the creation of the woman. Cf. Charles Ess, "Reading Adam and Eve: Re-Visions of the Myth of Woman's Subordination to Man," in *Violence against Women and Children: A Christian Theological Sourcebook*, ed. Carol J. Adams and Marie M. Fortune (New York: Continuum, 1995), 102–12.

2. Cf. Bechtel, "Rethinking," 85–86.

3. Cf. George W. Coats, "The God of Death: Power and Obedience in the Primeval History," *Interpretation* 29 (1975): 227–39.

4. Hamilton, *Genesis 1–17*, 177. He sees naming as an act of discernment.

Persuasive Dialogue

Laying the Foundation

The foundation of the persuasive dialogue lies both outside and inside the Gen. 3 narrative. Outside the narrative, the foundation is the prohibition articulated to the human before the creation of the female counterpart (Gen. 2:17). Within the prohibition, the behavioral parameters are defined relative to the trees in the garden, particularly the tree of knowledge of good and evil. Inside the narrative, foundational aspects facilitate the progression of the dialogue, including the identity of those involved and the conditions for persuasion.

IDENTITY OF THOSE INVOLVED

The identity of those involved in the persuasion process defines the nature of the persuasion and the outcome. Within the persuasive dialogue there are two distinct sets of agents, the primary and the secondary participants. Here the primary participants are defined as those who are involved in the conversation through an exchange of speech (the serpent and the woman). The secondary participants are those who are involved through indirect means, either through observation or by references to them within the speech exchange (the man and the Deity). Table 1 depicts the agents according to their involvement in conversations (see page 46).

The serpent. As the first primary agent, the "serpent" (*nāḥāš*) is identified by its function, type, and origin. Regarding its function and type, it is more "cunning" (*'ārûm*) than all the animals. Its acuity is the first aspect of its identity that is mentioned, signaling it as possibly the most significant quality in the subsequent interactions. The serpent is cunning, denoting a form of valued "wisdom" (*ḥokmâ*) but also suggesting that it is perhaps something other than wisdom.[5] As a positive quality, wisdom is contrasted with being a "fool" (*'ĕwîl* or *kĕsîl*, Prov. 12:16, 23; 13:16; 14:8) or being "simple, naïve" (*petî*, 14:15, 18; 22:3; 27:12).[6] The cunning person also possesses wisdom that helps to direct her/his decisions (14:8). Most modern translators agree that the same term, *'ārûm*, is used for the serpent as well as for clever and prudent persons;

---

5. Another comparable term is *śākal* (prudence, understanding) (cf. Gen. 3:6; Ps. 53:3 [NRSV 53:2]; 111:10; Prov. 1:3; 16:22; 19:11). Hamilton (*Genesis 1–17*, 187–88) identifies the reasons the neutral term "cunning" (*'ārûm*) is used for the snake. He proposes that "it appears best to take 'astute, clever' as an appropriate descriptor of the snake, one that aptly describes its use of a strategy of prudence when it engages the woman in dialogue" (188).

6. Ronald B. Allen, "ערם," *TWOT* 2:697–98. Cf. Job 5:12 and 15:5, where it is usually translated as a pejorative, "crafty."

Table 1: Communication Processes in Genesis 2–3

Type of communication	Agents		Text
	Primary [spoken or addressed]	Secondary [mentioned]	
Prohibition	God ⇒ Man	—	2:16–17
Evaluation	God	Man Helper	2:18
Evaluation and response	Man	Woman	2:23
Persuasion dialogue	Serpent ⇔ Woman	God Man	3:1–5
Confrontation	God ⇔ Man	Woman God	3:9–12
	God ⇔ Woman	Serpent	3:13
Announcement of consequences	God ⇒ Serpent	Animals Woman Offspring (*children and serpent*)	3:14–15
	God ⇒ Woman	Children Man (*husband*)	3:16
	God ⇒ Man	Woman (*wife*) God	3:17
Reflection and decision	God	Man God	3:22

however, most prefer a pejorative nuance to the word by referring to the snake as "crafty."[7]

Whether applied negatively or positively, the quality includes discernment and skill and signifies no less when applied to the serpent. The serpent's interaction with the woman illustrates that being cunning entails power, that is, to understand a situation and the influential forces that define its existence, and to foster the choices made in response to that understanding. Additionally, that power includes the capacity to nuance language and perception as tools that alter another's perception, understanding, and actions. The description facilitates a portrait of the serpent's power by identifying the serpent's acuity and habitat as compared to the "animals" (*ḥayyâ*) of the "field" (*śādeh*). Part of the inherent challenge of the serpent as described is that it demonstrates a capacity beyond that of its fellow creatures, among whom it excelled

---

7. Cf. NIV and NRSV "crafty"; JSB "shrewd."

in being cunning. The question that therefore plagues the narrative is, How does the serpent's cunning compare to the humans' and even the Deity's? This question may be addressed in light of the serpent's origin and function.

Regarding its origins, it is reported that God "made" ('āśâ) the serpent (Gen. 3:1; cf. 2:19), a claim that discounts any idea that the serpent originated on its own. Furthermore, it also challenges any notion of the serpent's mental acuity as the product of its supernatural origin. That God made the serpent also discounts any suspicion that the serpent's insight about the Deity derives from a prior relationship with the Deity while the serpent was in a supernatural form. Likewise, nothing in the narrative suggests that the serpent is the devil or a preconfiguration thereof.[8] From the perspective of the text, the serpent's qualities are the result of the Deity's design and its animal rather than supernatural essence. Even so, that the Deity made the animal generates some unresolved tensions. While it is apparent that the design may have unanticipated challenges (as the man's solitude reveals), the Deity's purposefulness also indicates the intentionality of the design and presence of the creatures. So one may not assume or discount that all aspects of the serpent's behavior or manifestation of its qualities are predetermined. The Deity made the serpent in an effort to find a suitable helper for the man, but it was deemed unsuitable along with the other animals. Yet there is no noted corrective purpose assigned to the animals as there was a corrective process in choosing the material used to construct the woman. Consequently, part of the serpent's relational and functional identity is represented in its interaction with the humans, the disclosure of information about the Deity, and a challenge to the Deity's trustworthiness. With all these components, the narrative raises the question of the source of the serpent's ability and the Deity's relationship to the serpent's persuasion process.

The woman. The second primary agent in the persuasion process is "the woman" (hā'iššâ). The serpent speaks directly to her rather than to the man, to whom the prohibition was articulated (cf. Gen. 3:6 with 2:17). Thus at the outset the woman is addressed about a subject of which she herself was not informed (in the text), and immediately the discrepancies about the subject begin to present themselves. On the one hand, the man and the Deity constitute the primary agents of the first conversation, where the prohibition was articulated. That conversation established the behavioral parameters of the human relative to the vegetation in the garden. The Deity and the human together formed the contingent that

8. Cf. Wenham for his discussion of the various arguments regarding the serpent's role as evil and shrewd (*Genesis 1–15*, 72–73). See Joines, "Serpent in Gen. 3," 1–11; von Rad, *Genesis*, 87–88.

would mutually sustain the earth and its vegetation. On the other hand, the serpent addresses the woman, who was not present at or even presupposed by the first conversation. Nonetheless, in addressing her, the serpent presumes the first conversation and another mode of transmitting the prohibition to the woman—either as part of her biological makeup or, more likely, through communication with the man. Whether or not he is present from the beginning of the persuasion process to its culmination, the man is a secondary agent in the serpent's conversation with the woman (see table 1). The conversation is distinct because of the agents involved—the serpent and the woman, both brought into existence to address the need of the man and both named by him.[9] This is not to argue their inferiority to the man, but simply to highlight that there may be an affinity between the serpent and the woman constituted by their prospect as man's helper. Yet they are differentiated from each other by their material essence and relational correspondence to the man: the woman of the same flesh as the man and suitable; the serpent presumably of the same soil or ground (*hā'ǎdāmâ*) as the man but unsuitable.

The conversation between the serpent and the woman opens a world of possibilities constructed by the serpent's cunning and the loose end represented by a creature whose functional identity is undefined yet devalued with reference to the human. The serpent's conversation with a human suggests that whatever the source of the incompatibility, it is not in the area of mental acuity. Furthermore, to test the boundaries of the human's mental acuity would further disprove any lingering impression of the serpent's inferiority. The conversations in Gen. 2–3 suggest that both the Deity and the humans recognized the ability of the serpent to comprehend (see table 1).

Conditions of Persuasion

The persuasion of the humans to eat or not is attributed to the serpent and the Deity, respectively. As noted above, the Deity threatens the human with death as the consequence of eating from the proscribed tree (see chapter 1). The serpent's persuasion process initiates a test to ascertain whether the Deity was effective in persuading the human to adhere to the behavioral parameters designed for him (Gen. 2:16–17). The process also initiates an awareness of human consciousness and the ability to discern and make choices, all necessary conditions for persuasion. Even so, the persuasion entails an attempt to convince another to act or think in a particular way. In this respect, the act of persuasion is tied to the goal of persuasion and inevitably to the participants in the communication process.

9. Cf. Meyers, *Discovering Eve*, 85.

Notably, the conditions for persuasion include the awareness of alternatives (usually by the one who instigates the process) and the plausibility of the alternatives (whether perceived or real).[10] Whether the communication is one- or two-way, it includes a measure of persuasion.

First, everyone involved in the persuasion process is aware of the alternatives. The Deity first articulates the alternatives in permitting all trees for food except the tree of knowledge of good and evil (Gen. 2:16–17). In this permission, nothing is said that excludes the tree of life, and thus allows that it too was permissible for food (2:17). Whether by design or by accident, the humans are granted permission to eat from the tree of life. Their access to the tree, however, is later corrected by expelling them from the garden (3:22–24).[11] Additionally, the permission builds on the ability of the human to comprehend the permission and to discern which of the identified objects are permissible. Fundamentally, it presumes the mental acuity of the human to comprehend and discern between the concepts of permission and prohibition. Thus the permission and prohibition already signal that the human is a reasoning being capable of understanding the identified alternatives and of distinguishing between them.

Second, the plausibility of the alternatives ensues from the first condition of being aware of them. Whether or not that awareness coheres with what is manifested or real, in speaking of the plausibility of the alternatives one already presumes that there is a perception of what is valid. Plausibility here is more a function of process than of an inherent quality of the alternatives. Furthermore, plausibility involves the correlation between the alternatives and the anticipated outcomes. The prohibition expressed that if the human should eat of the tree of knowledge of good and evil, then he would die. It assumes a correlation between the act of eating and death without specifying the mode of death. Consequently, it is left open as to whether the act of eating or the inherent quality of what is eaten would result in death. At issue is whether the consequence ensues from the disobedience, such that the proscribed tree could have been any other tree and would therefore lead to the same consequence, or whether the disobedience would lead to consumption of a lethal substance.[12] In the latter instance, the prohibition is motivated

10. Cf. Kathleen Kelly Reardon, *Persuasion in Practice* (Newbury Park, CA: Sage, 1991), 48–60, who discusses attitude changes in the persuasion process.

11. Notably, nothing is said about the consequence of eating of the tree of life until after the disobedience (Gen. 3:22). Cf. James Barr, *The Garden of Eden and the Hope of Immortality* (Minneapolis: Fortress, 1993), 57–58. He explores several questions, including whether the humans had already eaten from the tree of life, and concludes on the basis of 3:22 that they had not.

12. This is a consideration of whether the fruit of the tree of knowledge of good and evil was poisonous. If it was, that fact would contradict the representation of all the trees as being good (*ṭôb*) for food (Gen. 2:9).

by protection of the humans against a poisonous element but suggests nothing about immortality.[13]

Like the Deity, the serpent posits two alternatives, assumes that they are plausible, and presents a different outcome of eating from the tree of knowledge of good and evil. While the consequence stated by the Deity focuses on death, the serpent focuses on status elevation, the continuation of life, and thriving within that life. In the latter case, the presented plausibility is not simply "being like" the Deity but that possibility vis-à-vis death. Not eating, then, is presented as a choice to remain human and to forfeit becoming like God. By contrast, in the Deity's alternative, not eating means maintaining the mode of existence, the status quo. The serpent does not discuss the probability of the status elevation for the humans but only its possibility, namely, knowing good and evil. The perception that the human being may become like the Deity defines the plausibility of the serpent's argument. Nonetheless, the nature of any alternative is that it incorporates limitations such that one alternative may exclude another—eating excludes not eating. Further serving as a catalyst for the choice between the alternatives, the mutual exclusiveness of the alternatives may also contribute to their plausibility.

In her presentation of the alternatives, the woman recognizes the Deity's as well as another possibility (Gen. 3:3). For the Deity there are two behavioral choices, eating and not eating. For the woman, there are at least four choices: touching; not touching; touching and eating; or touching and not eating. She also perceives possibilities that were not articulated about the tree. While the narrative regards the tree as pleasing and good for food, the woman perceives these qualities and one other—it is desirous "to make one wise" (śākal, 3:6).[14] Like the serpent, she also introduces an alternative that the Deity did not specifically mention. Whether or not wisdom is already implied in the serpent's alternative, she does not mention status elevation per se—at least not in the way that the serpent envisions it. Her reported thoughts reflect her awareness that she does not possess all the wisdom that may still be acquired. Consequently, that she alters her behavior may illustrate that she has been persuaded, although not completely for the alternatives presented by the Deity and the serpent. The persuasion ultimately is effective in that it affirms to the woman that she can become other than what she is—namely, wise. Since the narrative is silent about the man's reasons for eating, one cannot posit that this too is his reason. The eat-

---

13. Cf. Wenham, *Genesis 1–15*, 67. He asserts that the tree was not poisonous. Barr (*Garden of Eden*, 8–9) asserts that since the humans did not die as indicated by the Deity, the serpent was right in saying that they would not.

14. Wenham, *Genesis 1–15*, 75; Trible, *God and Rhetoric*, 112; Hamilton, *Genesis 1–17*, 190.

ing alone says nothing about his reason, only about his choice. Clearly, the serpent not only introduces alternatives but also plants the seed of "longing to be something else." In that seed is also a latent myopia in one's understanding of the alternatives and how they actually compare to each other. Nonetheless, the seed may generate changes that allow further communication and persuasion.

Persuasion Process

With the various conditions in place, the process through which the humans are persuaded to eat from the tree of knowledge of good and evil is illuminated. Persuading the humans to eat also attests to the serpent's power to convince them to disobey the Deity. This assertion presumes that the Deity's preference for them is not to eat of the proscribed tree. It further presumes that the preference signals a particular plan for the humans maintained by their choice to adhere to the prohibition. Accordingly, the persuasion process includes several components: the serpent's argumentation, the woman's response (verbal), the serpent's rebuttal, and the actions of the woman and the man. While the Deity is absent as a primary agent in the conversation, the Deity is nonetheless present as a secondary agent in the dialogue, as the articulator of the less favorable alternatives—that is, from the serpent's perspective (Gen. 3:1–6; see table 1).

THE SERPENT'S INITIAL ARGUMENT

The serpent establishes a common subject for dialogue and thus places the woman on familiar ground (Gen. 3:1). It engages her thoughts about a subject matter that is of concern to the Deity and that is the focus of the Deity's first conversation with the man (2:16–17). The serpent begins with a searching question that picks up two crucial aspects of the woman's existence—physical sustenance and obedience to the Deity. First, the matter of physical sustenance enters the conversation. Along with these aspects of the initial question, one must also be aware of the mode of inquiry as a significant part of the persuasion process. The serpent does not articulate a consequence in the opening formulation, but communicates a measure of disbelief about the content of the prohibition.[15] The incredulity stems not from the existence of a prohibition but from

15. There are at least two interpretive trends regarding the translation of the particle 'ap kî and consequently the mode of expression. First, the particle is interrogative and the opening formulation of a question that the serpent asks the woman. See Wenham, *Genesis 1–15*, 45, 47. Second, the particle is exclamatory, expressing the serpent's surprise at the content of the Deity's prohibition. See Hamilton, *Genesis 1–17*, 186n1; contrasted with von Rad, *Genesis*, 86.

the objects proscribed. The serpent presumes that the Deity prohibited the humans from eating of any of the trees of the garden. The inquiry therefore suggests that while they were prohibited from eating of the trees in the garden, they may eat of the trees outside the garden. Like the prohibition, here too the serpent does not directly consider the possibility of the domain outside the garden. It thus represents the totality of the domain as the garden. If the Deity prohibited eating of the trees inside, there would surely be alternatives, one of which would have been trees outside the garden.

Another alternative (based on the serpent's inquiry) could have been food other than fruits, namely, animals. This seems unlikely, since at the point of the articulated prohibition the animals were not in existence but were subsequently formed as potential helpers for the man (Gen. 2:19). The third understanding of the serpent's argument, reflected in the inquiry and the basis of the perception of incredulity, is that through the prohibition the Deity was forcing the humans to choose between life and death.[16] One must ask how the serpent acquired the knowledge about the prohibition and whether that acquisition is responsible for the distortion of the information. Even so, the narrator's characterization of the serpent as the most cunning creature may already suggest that any distortion is due not to the acquisition of misinformation but rather to the use of that information toward a desired outcome.

Table 2: Perspectives regarding the Proscribed Tree (Genesis 2–3)

	God's	Serpent's	Woman's
Permission	And the Lord God commanded the man, "You may freely eat of **every tree** of the garden; (2:16)	—	The woman said to the serpent, "We may eat of the **fruit of the trees** in the garden; (3:2)
Prohibition	but of the *tree of the knowledge of good and evil* you **shall not eat**, for in the day that you eat of it you shall die." (2:17)	He said to the woman, "Did God say, 'You **shall not eat** from *any tree* in the garden?'" (3:1b)	but God said, 'You **shall not eat** of the *fruit of the tree* that is *in the middle of the garden*, **nor shall you touch** it, or you shall die.'" (3:3)

On the issue of obedience, through the serpent's representation, the Deity did not grant permission to eat of any tree. The serpent's designation of the Deity is conspicuous among the other references in Gen. 2–3. While

---

16. Cf. Hamilton, *Genesis 1–17*, 189. He contends that part of the serpent's effort is to show God as malevolent and oppressive rather than as a benevolent provider. Cf. Danna N. Fewell and David M. Gunn, *Gender, Power, and Promise: The Subject of the Bible's First Story* (Nashville: Abingdon, 1993).

most of the narrative refers to the Deity as Yʜᴡʜ God (*yhwh 'ĕlōhîm*), the serpent simply refers to the Deity as "God" (*'ĕlōhîm*), a reference taken by some to signify distance or even disregard.[17] The serpent exaggerates by extending the scope of the prohibition from a proscribed tree to all trees and by omitting the fact that permission was granted. Since the trees are the only source of food noted in the narrative (Gen. 2:9), if the humans obey the Deity by not eating, they would deprive themselves of sustenance and die. If the Deity were to set up such a scenario, the default option would be death since to live would presume disobedience and eating (see table 2). Additionally, in this characterization, the Deity does not look out for the well-being of the humans but by design sets them up for failure whether or not they obey. Herein lies the insidious nature of the serpent's inquiry and the aspect that the woman appears to address.

Tʜᴇ Wᴏᴍᴀɴ's Vᴇʀʙᴀʟ Rᴇsᴘᴏɴsᴇ

In responding to the serpent, the woman both corrects the serpent's apparent misconception and embellishes the prohibition. The first noted aspect of the woman's involvement in the persuasion process is that she "speaks" (*'āmar*) and responds to the serpent. While that response creates a dialogue, it also acknowledges that the serpent has addressed her and that it is worthy of a response. Note that there is no suggestion that she ask the man about the matter, either to verify that the Deity issued a prohibition or to ascertain the specific content of any prohibition that may have been issued (see table 1). Rather, her response suggests her awareness of a prohibition and her knowledge of its details (Gen. 3:2; cf. 2:17). Even so, she speaks for both herself and the man in using the plural forms—"*we* may eat" (3:2), "*you* [pl.] will die" (3:3).[18]

The narrative therefore presents a competition between the created beings: the serpent (of unmatched cunning among the creatures) versus the humans (of latent mental acuity). In this competition, the serpent appears to have the advantage over the humans, who may be unaware of their ability and of what is at stake. At stake is the ability of the serpent to outwit the humans and thus to be seen not only as the most cunning "creature of the field" (*ḥayyat haśśādeh*) but as the most cunning of all living beings. By implication, the serpent would be second only to the Deity, having surpassed the humans' ability. However, if it fails, the serpent would simply affirm its status as most cunning among the animals but not as cunning as the

---

17. E.g., Wenham, *Genesis 1–15*, 73. Note that the woman also uses this designation in her response (Gen. 3:2).

18. The Hebrew terms are the first person plural form of the verb *'ākal* (to eat) and the second masculine plural form of *mût* (to die). Cf. Hamilton, *Genesis 1–17*, 188.

humans. Similarly, the serpent also sets up a competition between it and the Deity by testing the ability of each to persuade the humans to follow a course of action. Thus in using the humans as the basis of confronting the Deity, the serpent also puts the humans in tension with the Deity. The choice is to trust the serpent, a fellow creature, or God, the Creator.

Second, the woman identifies the "fruit" (pĕrî) of the trees as part of the permission. However, the Deity simply says "from the trees"—whether its leaves, bark, or roots (Gen. 2:16). The woman's representation specifies fruit (3:2) and is thus more restrictive. Additionally, she differs in the extent of the permission by not specifying "all the trees" (kōl 'ēṣ).[19] As to the prohibition, she represents it with as much accuracy as she does the permission (see table 2). She continues to speak for both herself and the man, presumably representing their perspectives and their agreement on the details she articulates.[20] The woman also adopts the serpent's designation of the Deity as God ('ĕlōhîm).[21] This adaptation may reflect agreement with the serpent. Although her language still attempts to reflect and even defend the Deity, her response may already indicate the attitudinal alignment with the serpent. Even in her defense, she misrepresents the Deity to be more restrictive than the Deity's own representation. First, she focuses on the fruit of the tree and further identifies the location (in the midst of the garden) rather than the name of the tree. Two trees are indicated in that location, namely, the tree of life and the tree of knowledge of good and evil (2:9).[22] This is not an instance of the woman's misrepresenting the location of the proscribed tree, but her representation creates ambiguity about the tree she perceives as proscribed. The woman also cites the Deity as saying that they should not eat the fruit or even "touch" (nāga') the tree. Yet the only proscribed behavior relative to the tree was eating (see table 2). Intriguingly, the woman also identifies the consequence relative to both touching and eating by adding some elements and distorting others.

19. Cf. Wenham, Genesis 1–15, 73.
20. Cf. J. M. Higgins, "The Myth of Eve: The Temptress," Journal of the American Academy of Religion 44 (1976): 639–47. On the basis of Gen. 3:3b he argues that the man was with her during the dialogue. He also offers several other reasons for this understanding of the woman's role in the presence of the serpent and the man. Hamilton (Genesis 1–17, 188) acknowledges that there are various possibilities for understanding why the serpent conversed with the woman (her sexual vulnerability and weakness); however, he denies that any of them "can be proved." Phyllis Trible ("Depatriarchalizing in Biblical Interpretation," Journal of the American Academy of Religion 41 [1973]: 40) argues that the woman is more appealing, intelligent, and aggressive and also possesses "greater sensibilities."
21. Wenham, Genesis 1–15, 73.
22. While he does not adhere to that perspective, Wenham (Genesis 1–15, 62) mentions the view that perceives redaction of an older version in which there was only one tree, i.e., the tree of life (Gen. 2:9; cf. 3:3).

THE SERPENT'S RESPONSE

The persuasiveness of any argument is not directly related to the truthfulness of it. Rather, truth in persuasion is relative to the understanding of the hearer (see chapter 7). Persuasion is a product of appeal, but being persuaded is also dependent on one's beliefs. In Gen. 3 the situation is dependent on the serpent's representation of the truth in conjunction with other forms of appeal. One may note a plethora of interpretations regarding the truth of the serpent's claim. While these will not be discussed at this point, it is worth noting that for the woman the serpent's appeal constitutes the truth versus death.[23]

The woman's response is a gallant effort to defend against the serpent's representation of the Deity as a malevolent being. As part of her strategy, she exaggerates the Deity's prohibition and in so doing presents a more restrictive prohibition. While her motive is apparent, her success at achieving it places her on tenuous ground. The serpent, the cunning creature, does not miss the various loopholes in her defense. In challenging the woman, the serpent introduces additional doubt about the Deity's perspective on the consequence of the eating, making no mention of "touching." If the woman is not already aware of her exaggeration, the serpent's clarification may alert her to it. Even so, the serpent does not contest whether the Deity included touching the tree in the prohibition, but focuses on the consequence of eating. At this point, the serpent does not inquire about what God "said" (*'āmar*), as in the initial inquiry (Gen. 3:1). Instead, the serpent presumes to build on the woman's representation of what God said. Furthermore, the serpent presumes not only to know what God said, although it was not present when the first Creator-creature dialogue took place, but also presumes to know what God "knows" (*yāda'*; see table 1).

Additionally, the serpent purports to have inside knowledge about God that God had not communicated to the humans. That information is represented as God's knowledge of a reality that may contradict what God said. In essence, the serpent argues that the Deity articulated a cause-effect sequence that does not match reality.[24] While the cause (catalyst) is the act of eating, the effect is not death but status elevation. The serpent introduces an alternative that has not been within the sphere of alternatives for the humans. It affirms that the choices are eating and not eating, but from the serpent's perspective, eating leads to becoming like the Deity, while not eating means stagnation as a human being.

---

23. For an extensive discussion, see Whybray, "Immorality of God," 89–102; cf. Barr, *Garden of Eden*, 8–11.

24. Cf. D. R. G. Beattie, "What Is Genesis 2–3 About?" *Expository Times* 92 (1980): 10.

The appeal is to be more like the Deity and by implication less like the humans that they are. Inherent in this alternative is also the introduction of dissatisfaction with oneself in favor of a longing to be someone else.[25] In another sense, it is a quest to be undifferentiated in a particular area and thus be more homogeneous. Unfortunately, being differentiated in at least one area—shared ability, function, and so on—would disallow homogeneous manifestation. This was part of the discovery in searching for a helper for the man, namely, the presence of any difference results in difference (see chapter 1). Consequently, even if they were to become like the Deity in knowing good and evil, the manifestation of that ability or essence would be filtered through their humanity. In this respect, their quest to be undifferentiated from the Deity is futile. The humans are essentially differentiated, namely, from other beings (humans vis-à-vis the Deity and the animals) and from each other (male vis-à-vis female). Any commonality would be filtered through their difference and hence manifested according to the particular being.

Power of Choice

The Deity had been active in designing humans and animals and their function; however, while this persuasion process is transpiring, the Deity is noticeably silent. In the Deity's absence, the serpent—the being deemed unsuitable—appears to be powerful and in charge (Gen. 2:7), that is, as compared to the first living created being. Consequently, both of the beings who were formed to address man's need are active in determining the future within their domain. However, the one who is entrusted with the care of the garden, including all the trees, does not speak. The silence of the man and of the Deity raises questions about their awareness of what is happening. If the man is present with the woman at the time of the dialogue, is he involved and responsible for the outcome (3:6)? If the Deity is aware, is the Deity involved in the persuasion process and its outcome? Strikingly, the Deity who was so hands-on has become hands-off during a crucial process that decides the fate of the humans. After the humans exercise their power to choose, the Deity suddenly reappears and punishes them for their choices. Apparently, those choices do not align with what the Deity wants for them.

While the reticence of the Deity may indicate a lack of control, this control may have been conferred on the humans to allow them the power to exercise their choices. In this domain, the humans are not powerless, and power is not monopolized by either gender. Instead, each gender

25. See chap. 6—Rachel and Leah, Gen. 29–30.

has power that may be peculiar to that gender or shared by both; but the power itself does not determine the gender role. What determines the man and woman's power? Do limitations on choices constitute the limitations of power?[26] Likewise, is superiority power?[27] While superiority may suggest power, it does not guarantee effectual power. Superiority is the product of incompatibility such that beings of the same essence cannot be legitimately deemed superior or inferior to one another. The Deity as creator is superior to the creatures, and the animals are inferior to the human. But in terms of their human essence, humans cannot be inferior to one another. Accordingly, power in relation to gender may have more to do with function than essence. Hence one may speak of functional identity, including dominance and subordination, without suggesting the inferiority or superiority of the beings involved.

The danger of any power is the unrealistic assessment of that power. Many have conceded the trickery of the serpent without noting the relative status of the serpent. Thus some affirm that man's naming of the animals constituted a measure of control over them and thereby minimize the serpent.[28] Yet it is the named creature, the one deemed unsuitable for the human, whom the narrative depicts as powerful. Within Gen. 3, the power lies in both the means of persuasion as well as the status of the serpent. If the serpent is deemed inferior or weak because of its status as an animal, it demonstrates that weakness is a type of power since weakness has the potential to determine the future and affect another being.[29] The narrative shows that functional equality is unnecessary to persuade someone.

The narrative tension consists of an anomaly, namely, the Deity's inability to persuade the humans to obey the command and to refrain from eating from the forbidden tree. Furthermore, the serpent uses persuasion as a vehicle to disclose alternatives. By giving humans choice, the Deity limits its means of control and permits the possibility that the humans may not conform to the Deity's desires for them. Yet it is that choice that allows the serpent's persuasion to challenge the Deity.[30] In this instance,

26. Von Rad, *Genesis*, 80.

27. John J. Schmitt, "Like Eve, Like Adam: *mšl* in Gen. 3, 16," *Biblica* 72 (1991): 1–22. Cf. Peter Morriss, *Power: A Philosophical Analysis* (New York: St. Martin's Press, 1987), 29–35.

28. Trible, *God and Rhetoric*.

29. Cf. Carol Smith, "Samson and Delilah: A Parable of Power?" *JSOT* 76 (1997): 45–57. For further discussion of the role of the serpent, see Philip R. Davies, "Women, Men, Gods, Sex, and Power: The Birth of a Biblical Myth," in *Feminist Companion to Genesis*, ed. Brenner, 194–201; Adrien Janis Bledstein, "Binder, Trickster, Heel and Hairy-Man: Rereading Genesis 27 as a Trickster Tale Told by a Woman," in *Feminist Companion to Genesis*, ed. Brenner, 282–95.

30. Joines, "Serpent in Gen. 3," 7.

power is the ability to persuade as much as it is the ability to choose to act or to refrain from a particular action.

Some have argued that the male and the female in Gen. 3 are naïve and still maturing.[31] Being persuaded to eat the forbidden fruit is therefore seen as a manifestation of their immaturity. Would maturity have prevented persuasion? Since persuasion has to do with appeal and representation of a way of thinking, it follows that all levels of maturity are open to persuasion. One must at least consider that the effectiveness of persuasion is not nullified by one's level of maturity. Instead, at any level of maturity the effectiveness of persuasion is dependent on plausibility and the awareness of choices.

First Choice

Some argue that the original sin occurred because of the woman's weakness, namely, that she was gullible and thus succumbed to the trickery of the serpent.[32] This interpretation loses sight of the fact that the man too was persuaded to eat from the proscribed tree. It further raises the question: Is persuasion a function of gender? Traditional interpretations have presumed so. Yet to argue that the woman (Eve) seduced the man (Adam) is to admit (willingly or unwillingly) that she exerted power over him. It further affirms that gullibility is not monopolized by the female but is shared with the male. Consequently, male and female would be equal even in their gullibility, immaturity, and pliability.

Gender does not determine the ability to persuade or to be persuaded. The neutrality of the serpent (not designated as male or female but as animal) suggests that. Likewise, naming does not limit the named in relation to the namer. In this respect, naming is not a way of controlling or subordinating the named.[33] Clearly, neither the serpent nor the woman seeks the man's authorization before assuming their course of action. What is exemplified is the power of the created beings to exercise their choices even to the extent of pushing the boundaries of the imposed behavioral parameters. Nonetheless, the interpretive framework of gender and persuasion has been defined by the association of woman's persua-

31. Cf. van Seters "Creation of Man," 339–40; Bechtel, "Rethinking," 85–87; Reuven Kimelman, "The Seduction of Eve and the Exegetical Politics of Gender," *Biblical Interpretation* 4.1 (1996): 23–25.

32. Cf. Schüngel-Straumann, "Creation of Man and Woman," 67–69. Several other views are noteworthy: Trible ("Depatriarchalizing," 40) argues that she is more intelligent and appealing than the male. Hamilton (*Genesis 1–17*, 188) argues that these representations about the woman are not verified on the basis of the narrative. Barr (*Garden of Eden*, 6–8) argues against the notion of "original sin."

33. Contrast Trible (*God and Rhetoric*, 9), who sees the naming of the woman as an act of reducing her to the status of the animals.

sion with seduction and man's persuasion as normative. This framework assumes the vulnerability of the man and further suggests the power of the woman over him. This is a double-edged sword in that the power attributed to the woman is likewise deemed her weakness insofar as it is beyond her control. Even so, any suggestion that the woman is a seductress by virtue of her gender does not come from Gen. 3.

While using a series of verbs, the narrative indicates an action sequence in which the man is a willing participant. The woman "took" (*lāqaḥ*) the fruit, "ate" (*'ākal*), "gave" (*nātan*) it to her husband, and he ate (*'ākal*) what was given to him (Gen. 3:6). She was persuaded to eat and her reasons for eating are clear—the appeal of the tree and the possibility of becoming wise (3:6). If he simply ate in conformity to her action, he displayed no judgment in the matter and would appear more pliable than the woman.[34] It is the same pattern seen elsewhere in the book of Genesis, depicting the compliance of the male in response to the female. Thus wives give their maids to their husbands as surrogates in the family domain. The husbands in turn take the maids and bear children through them. For example, Sarah "gave" (*nātan*) Hagar to Abraham and "he went in to her" (16:3–4), and Rachel gave Bilhah and Jacob "went in to her" (30:4).[35] In these examples, the male's action indicates his willingness. Certainly, the husbands in these situations may have refused to take a maid as surrogate, but they complied with their wives' wishes for them (cf. Onan, 38:9).[36] Similarly, in this pattern, Adam ate the fruit that was given to him without any noted refusal or resistance (3:6).

In Gen. 3:6 the male is depicted not as one who was seduced but as one persuaded to act. The man was part of the same persuasion process as the woman (3:1–5). Other examples suggest that persuasion is a neutral act that is given specific nuance by its content and intent. Hence any neutrality in the male's use of persuasion is such because of the act, not the content. Instances of sexual assault, for example, cannot be termed instances of persuasion and are subject to different rules.[37] Yet within the Tamar story, Tamar attempts to persuade her brother Amnon not to rape her (2 Sam. 13:12–13). This example raises the question of the

34. Hamilton, *Genesis 1–17*, 191. He argues that the woman's "is a sin of initiative. His is a sin of acquiescence." Cf. Barr, *Garden of Eden*, 12–13.

35. In both of these instances, the formulation "he went in to her" (*wayyābō' 'ēlêhā*) is used of sexual encounter, the result of which is conception and the birth of a son. See chap. 5 for further discussion of the use of this formulation.

36. The refusal as well as the compliance would have consequences. In Onan's case, his noncompliance resulted in his death.

37. See Dinah (Gen. 34) and Tamar (2 Sam. 13). Cf. Exod. 22:15–16 (NRSV 22:16–17); Deut. 22:28–29: a woman is violated and the law specifies marriage to her assailant.

relationship of persuasion and coercion and suggests that Gen. 3 is not an example of coercion.

It is upon the simple statement "that she also gave some to her husband, who was with her, and he ate" (Gen. 3:6) that centuries of misinterpretation have persisted and have been codified within the Scriptures themselves.[38] Did the woman by the act of giving the fruit to the man persuade the man to eat? If this interpretation is endorsed, then the man is portrayed as gullible, and he enhances the portrayal by his attempt to exonerate himself before God (3:12). Moreover, his attempt depicts him as incapable of standing by his choice to eat. Although it is a true statement, by saying that she gave him the fruit the man admits to relinquishing his power of choice to the woman. Gender then may be seen as a factor in persuasion only to the extent that the participants are differentiated beings. This is not to deny the particularity of gender in persuasion; there are situational particularities that must be considered in evaluating the role of gender in persuasion.

According to Gen. 3, the persuasion of the male and the female was already affected by the inherent appeal of the proscribed tree—it was pleasing to the eye and readily available (Gen. 2:9). Rather than hide it in the garden and safeguard it from the humans, or locate it outside the garden away from the humans' immediate domain, the Deity chose to place the tree in a central location. So while the prohibition imposed behavioral restrictions relative to the tree, it did not restrict physical access to the tree or diminish its visual appeal. One must therefore consider that the basis of the persuasion was already in place for both the man and the woman and that the serpent was only the catalyst that actualized the dormant choice to eat from the tree.

Second Choice

After eating the fruit of the tree, the man and the woman's eyes were opened and ensuing aspects of the outcome took effect. Consequently, they "knew" (*yāda‘*) that they were naked. Thus knowledge became the first element that they gained after eating the fruit. Their response to their nakedness suggests clear thought about a solution (Gen. 3:7). Like the Deity, who identified a need and took measures to address it, the humans took measures to address their perceived need. It was also the first time that the humans acted to resolve a deficiency on their own. Acting together to find a workable solution, they sew fig leaves together and clothe themselves. Amazingly, although they had not experienced

38. There are common misconceptions, including: that the woman seduced the man into his behavior; that the woman's choice reflects her weakness.

the challenge of resolving difficulties, the man and woman find a solution, presumably on their first attempt.[39] Furthermore, the man and the woman's cooperation with each other is represented through the harmony of their effort. While the woman ate and gave to the man, who then ate, the text represents the harmonious effects of their eating: *they* knew (*yāda'*) and *they* sewed (*tāpar*) coverings to resolve their nakedness. Notwithstanding their disobedience, their action also shows their ability to make a choice and assume the risk of the unknown.

Implications of the Choices

The punishments in Gen. 3 suggest that being persuaded does not nullify one's responsibility. Likewise, the textual constraints compel a distinction between persuasion and coercion in the assessment of responsibility. It further suggests that the subject of praise and blame may be one and the same. Thus a few questions arise: When one is persuaded to do something, is it valid to blame another for the action and outcome?[40] Are persuasion and coercion the same thing? Is blame appropriate in coercion? If coercion is the imposition of another's will on a person, it may allow blame. Not so with persuasion. Blame belongs to situations where another person does something that is beyond one's control and that alters one's behavior. Thus, in any situation where someone acts, whether she/he was persuaded to do so, the responsibility for the action is hers/his. To blame another as a way of exonerating oneself is to acknowledge a forfeit of one's personal power of choice, and this forfeit is itself a choice.

Choice and Responsibility

DEITY'S ABSENCE (CHOICE OR IGNORANCE)

The extent of the Deity's power is represented through the narrator. Therefore, the metalanguage of the text contributes to the understanding of that power. The humans "heard" (*šāma'*) the Deity walking and "hid" (*ḥābā'*) (Gen. 3:8). The explanatory statement functions on several levels. First, it gives insights into the behavior of the man and woman. Their action was a response to the Deity's presence evidenced through the sound produced by the Deity. As in making coverings for themselves,

39. This is in contrast to the trial and error seen in the Deity's attempt to find a suitable helper for the man. Wenham (*Genesis 1–15*, 76) suggests that making the loincloths was a quick but somewhat ineffective action because of their skimpy nature.

40. Deryn Guest, "Hiding behind the Naked Women in Lamentations: A Recriminative Response," *Biblical Interpretation* 7.4 (1999): 413–48.

their concealment is done together and shows no sign of tension between them. In addition, neither takes the lead to present a case to the Deity about their nakedness or disobedience. Strikingly, the serpent's perspective is muted in their response to the Deity's presence. One would think that if they had become like the Deity (and believed it) they would have welcomed an audience with their new counterpart. Instead, they avoided such an audience.

Second, the Deity's return forms a transition from their situation to a new one characterized by the interaction between the Creator and created beings. Up until now the humans have interacted with other created beings, especially the serpent.

Third, the absence and return also absolves the Deity of direct participation in the sequence of events that transpired prior to the walk in the garden. By absolving the Deity in this way, the narrator also leaves open the question of the Deity's awareness of the events, suggesting that only when the man and woman chose physical isolation and hid from the Deity did the Deity become aware of their disobedience.

The last point fits with the trial-and-error mechanism employed by the Deity and further suggests the Deity's ignorance of the events and lack of control over the creatures. Yet to posit the Deity's awareness and absence as strategies that permitted the events to occur is to portray a Deity who through silence and absence allowed humans to break a prohibition. The portrait is obscure about whether the Deity's actions represent the willingness of the Deity to give humans their freedom. The absence of the Deity at crucial moments may be a deliberate narrative strategy to depict the centrality of the human power of choice and action.[41] Apparently, the Deity introduces a particular course of action or trajectory and leaves the humans the freedom to live out their choices within set parameters. Finally, whereas the serpent addressed the woman, the Deity inquires about the whereabouts of the humans by addressing the man. Addressing the man utilizes established lines of communication and presumes his ability to provide a response.[42] In keeping with this narrative pattern, more two-way conversations ensue, namely, God and man, God and woman (see table 1).[43]

41. See Gen. 38:12–30 (Judah's neglect of Tamar), where actions are no longer attributed to the Deity, as was previously done to explain the death of Er and of Onan. Other examples include Sarah in the house of Pharaoh and of Abimelech (Gen. 12; 20) and Sarah's mistreatment of Hagar (Gen. 16).

42. Sarna, *Genesis*, 26. He proposes that God addressed only the man because only the man heard the prohibition directly from God. This would presume that the man is held primarily responsible for the disobedience.

43. Cf. Dennis (*Sarah Laughed*, 24), regarding the two-way conversations in Gen. 2–3.

BLAME AND PERSUASION (THE HUMANS' ARGUMENT)

In his response to the Deity, and defending his actions, the man first clarifies the reasons for his action. He speaks only of his actions—"*I* heard the sound of you in the garden, and *I* was afraid, because *I* was naked; and *I* hid myself" (Gen. 3:10).[44] Any depiction of the concerted effort of the man and woman is hidden by his communication with the Deity and by his presentation of himself as a solitary being.[45] The irony is evident in that he was given a companion with whom he acted in concert in the realization of a new state of existence, but he denies that companion when he first resumes communication with the Deity. Furthermore, when asked about his location, the man responds by revealing the reason for his concealment. Diagram 1 shows the centrality of knowledge and fear in the humans' choice to conceal themselves. There is no indication that the man has come out from hiding while speaking to the Deity, but some suggest that the inquiry "Where are you?" is an invitation to come out from hiding.[46] Even so, in representing his reason for hiding, he also reveals an altered state of existence.[47] The man identifies the cause-effect of all his actions, namely, hearing the Deity leads to fear, fear results from awareness of his nakedness, and fear leads to concealment. In this articulation of the connections, the man fails to mention how he became aware of his nakedness.

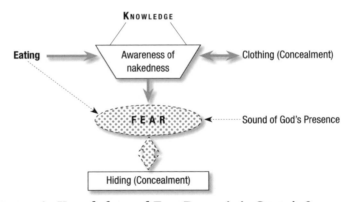

Diagram 1: Knowledge and Fear Dynamic in Genesis 3

44. The series is three first person common singular verbs and a personal pronoun: *šāma'tî* (I heard) + *wā'îrā'* (I was afraid) + *'ānōkî* (I) + *wā'ēḥābē'* (I hid).

45. From another perspective, the Deity may have assumed that he was the responsible party, with the action becoming part of his responsibility. See Hamilton, *Genesis 1–17*, 193.

46. E.g., Wenham, *Genesis 1–15*, 77.

47. Wenham, *Genesis 1–15*, 77.

Given that he presents the stimuli of all the other actions, it is striking that he omits the catalyst to his awareness of his nakedness. The Deity therefore responds by asking how the man knew that he was naked (Gen. 3:11). The man shifts responsibility for his action by implicating the woman. He claims that the woman gave him fruit of the tree and that he ate. He does not specify which tree, but the Deity is aware of the tree in question. His response further assumes that he ate because the woman gave him the fruit and that he would not have otherwise eaten. His power to articulate also implicates the Deity in that the woman is identified as "the woman whom you gave to be with me" (3:12). Again, the man places the responsibility for his actions on another, the Deity, and implies that the whole situation could have been avoided if the Deity had not given him the woman and the woman had not given him the fruit. The only other known intelligent being that he does not mention is the serpent.

Nonetheless, the Deity does not address the man's responsibility. Instead, the Deity addresses the woman for the first time. During this first reported communication, they are involved in a confrontation in which the Deity blames the woman for her role in the man's action (Gen. 3:13; see table 1). It appears that the Deity is persuaded that the man is telling the truth, but the Deity ignores part of the man's response, namely, the Deity's role. One cannot miss the quality of the exchange as the man blames his wife, and without the consolation of his solidarity or companionship, she is forced to address the Creator to defend herself. Understandably, when the woman speaks, she blames the serpent, thus averting blame—just as the man had done. She claims that she was "deceived" (nāšāʾ) and consequently yielded her judgment to another. Her response to the Deity seems like a regression to a point prior to the dialogue with the serpent. In that conversation, she appears strong and keenly aware of herself and the realities available to her. Showing her creative thought and acute reasoning, she also envisions a reality that was not presented to her. Yet in speaking with the Deity, she does not cite any of the reasons for her decisions but in essence claims to be coerced into her behavior. She thus misrepresents her decision-making process and ability. However, she does not implicate the man or the Deity by highlighting the Deity's role in constructing the relational parameters between the created beings (3:13). Likewise, she does not accuse the man of not helping her. Nonetheless, her response suggests that if one is deceived and acts while deceived, then one is not responsible for that action. However, the punishment suggests that since one has the power to choose one's behavior, being deceived does not absolve one of responsibility.

The responsibility also extends to the serpent. In this scenario the Deity treats the serpent as a nonentity by choosing not to hear its version of the events (Gen. 3:14–15). The serpent is not asked about its involvement but is told the consequences of its actions. It is curious that there is no dialogue between the Deity and the serpent, especially since the serpent's representation of the Deity challenges the character of the Deity (see table 1). One would think that the Deity would call the serpent to task and demand that the serpent defend itself.[48] However, it may not have been in the best interest of the humans to disclose what the serpent discovered about the Deity's design or secrets. That the serpent is stripped of its connection to the woman indicates no further collaboration between them. This is not surprising since in the aftermath of the eating the serpent does not praise their achievements or affirm that they did not die. It therefore appears that whatever the serpent's motive, it was not to help the humans in their status elevation, but to challenge the Deity's authority. They became the first pawns who are used against themselves to fulfill another being's motive. It is possible that the serpent more accurately represented their situation and disclosed to the humans more than the Deity intended them to know.[49] In any event, the serpent is "cursed among all the animals" and goes from the most cunning to the most debased (3:14).

Consequences of the Choices

All are punished, and a series of consequences are expressed, including those involving creatures and different aspects of the garden. The first point to note is that the various consequences do not include immediate death within the temporal framework of their eating. Indeed, the man lived to be nine hundred thirty years old (Gen. 5:5). For this reason some have presumed that the death sentence (2:17) addressed an eventual rather than an immediate death. Others have argued that since humans are mortal, death would have occurred whether or not they had disobeyed. Still others suggest that the serpent was telling the truth and thus exposed the Deity's lie about the consequences.[50] Regardless of who was lying or telling the truth, the serpent succeeded in raising doubt about the Deity's trustworthiness. If the serpent's depiction is contiguous with reality—eating leading to becoming like the Deity—then at best both the serpent and the Deity reveal only part of the consequences. In any case, neither the serpent nor the Deity fully disclosed to the humans what to

---

48. One must also consider that such a confrontation may reveal a scene more like that of the meetings in the heavenly realm concerning Job (Job 1) and Micaiah the prophet (1 Kings 22) than one may be comfortable with or expect.

49. Barr, *Garden of Eden*, 8–9; Beattie, "What Is Genesis 2–3 About?" 8–10.

50. See Beattie, "What Is Genesis 2–3 About?" 8–10; Barr, *Garden of Eden*, 8–12; contrast Hamilton, *Genesis 1–17*, 172–74.

expect from their actions. Consequently, the perpetual dilemma for the humans is whether to trust the Deity—their Creator—and if so to what extent. No agents escaped this test unscathed. The relational dynamics were redefined through the doubt and the suspicion about whether and when the humans would again transgress. The woman's attempt to defend the Deity demonstrated her trust in the Deity, but the serpent succeeded in challenging her perception of the Deity's trustworthiness. Her defiance of the Deity thus evidences her change in attitude toward the Deity. Whether momentary or continual, it shows a shift from implied trust to nurtured doubt.

Although exonerated by the absence of an immediate death, the serpent is demoted. While it offered status elevation to the humans as an alternative, it receives demotion as a punishment. Even so, the Deity's place in orchestrating the test remains an enigma. The punishment illustrates an attempt to suppress the power and initiative of the woman; therefore, the punishment is designed to maintain an order that is inconsistent with the capacity of those involved. The Deity's order includes the mutual coexistence of male and female and a yet-to-be-defined functional and relational role for the animals.

One of the serpent's characteristics is that it demonstrates a capacity beyond that of the other animals. Yet to be explored, however, is the permissible use of that capacity in the garden and in relation to the humans. Furthermore, it is also yet to be explored how all of the creatures would function together in the garden without the immediate organizing and controlling presence of the Creator. The loose end in the design was formed by the animals. If they are unsuitable helpers for the man, then what is their role? Is it left up to them to find their counterpart(s) and function? Is there a possibility that they might be suitable for the woman? The disobedience forced the Deity to define the relational parameters at least in one case—the serpent vis-à-vis the woman (Gen. 3:16). It also was a test for the Deity to decide the range of choices allowed for the humans and the availability of various alternatives.

Second, the tree of life was available to the humans for food and within the range of permissible food sources (Gen. 2:9). Nonetheless, neither the Deity nor the serpent presented it as an alternative. Yet the tree of life was as appealing and readily available to the humans as the prohibited tree. Clearly, the serpent would not have gained an advantage by starting a conversation about a matter that was not of significance to its conversation partner. Its strategy was to focus on the tree that the Deity had already highlighted. Once the humans disobeyed, the Deity decided to safeguard the tree of life to prevent them from eating from it (3:22–24). That decision apparently came from the realization that the Deity could not control the choices of the humans, but more directly that there was no obstacle in exercising their power of choice. It also seems an afterthought to safeguard the tree of life and its qualities of immortality. Notably, the Deity does not issue another prohibition that includes the tree of life. Rather, the Deity imposes physical restrictions by expelling the humans from the garden and setting up guards for the tree of life. Nothing is said about the animals' access to the tree and the benefits that they may gain by eating from it. Rather, the restrictions signal a double barrier between the humans and the tree of life: the distance and guardians (should they erase that distance). Thus while the Deity previously limited the domain of the created beings to the garden, the expulsion reveals that there was a reality beyond their first physical and mental domains. The delimiting phrase within the prohibition and permission (in the garden) reinforces the differentiated realities—in and outside the garden domain (see table 2).

The functional identity of the humans then pertained to a defined domain and provided no insight into a larger reality. By its preview of a reality outside the garden, the expulsion suggests a domain where the previous behavioral and relational dynamics are challenged (at the least) or obsolete (at most). There are no articulated parameters for life outside the garden. The expulsion and punishment are the Deity's attempt to control an order or address a deficiency—the creatures' transgression of the previously designed order.[51] Nonetheless, the Deity was already aware that the created system still may have unexpected challenges similar to the challenges previously addressed, namely, someone to till the ground and a suitable helper for the tiller of the ground. In the expulsion, one sees that an emergency measure became a permanent solution in an effort to anticipate the challenge of immortality.

While it is a possible interpretation, it may not be the best representation of the text to say that God was in complete control of all aspects of what happened in the garden, including the choice to transgress. To attribute complete control to the Deity would be to portray a being who had set up the created beings with encoded decisions and outcomes (see diagram 1). Consequently, what appears as choices would be manifestations of programmed behavior, speech, and attitudes. This would also mean that the punishments are simply the expression of the programming to adhere to a plan and ensure its predetermined outcome down to the smallest details.

Third, both the man and the woman will endure the difficulties of "toiling" (*'iṣṣābôn*) for sustenance as part of their normative existence (Gen. 3:17). The Deity's curse on the ground would cause the increased

---

51. Ess ("Reading Adam and Eve," 95–98) presents the chaos/order theme in many of the creation stories in the ancient Near East, e.g., *Enuma Elish*, *Gilgamesh Epic*.

difficulty. Thus the consequence envisions the existence of the humans beyond the initial modes in the garden. The toil will encompass the lives of the male and the female in similar ways, though the woman's toil (*'iṣṣābôn*) in her "pregnancy" (*hērôn*) will be quantitatively increased. The narrative presumes that both would have been part of their existence and that the change is that they would increase.[52] It does not suggest that prior to the Deity's pronouncement humans would not have toiled. Their new existence is thus described for the woman as one of hardship in her work, pregnancy, and pain in "bearing children" (*yālad*).[53] The term *yālad* is also used for men to signify fathering children and thus includes more than the actual birth process (e.g., 5:3, 4, 6, 7; 6:10; 10:15). The woman is to be frequently pregnant, enduring the pain of childbirth, and should she and her children survive, she would endure the challenge of rearing children in addition to her work responsibilities. Consequently, her dual function will constitute an extremely difficult life. To add to this, she will find her husband irresistible to the point of being dominated by that "longing" or "desire" (*tĕšûqâ*) for him. A similar desire is depicted between lovers in Song of Songs 7:11. In Gen. 4:7 the term refers to sin's desire or longing to dominate Cain, a desire that he must "control" (*māšal*).[54] The situation for Cain is that sin is poised to dominate him, and he must gain mastery over it. Thus the reference is broader than sexual desire but may include an intensified level of compulsion for someone. In 3:16 a similar perspective exists in that a woman's desire for her husband may consume and control her. It is not a pronouncement or prescription for the man to dominate the woman, or for husbands to subjugate their wives.[55] Unfortunately, in many instances, Gen. 3 is used to justify violence against women and to sustain the perception of an infantile adult who must be controlled.

Conclusion

If Gen. 2–3 is the interpretive framework of a valid understanding of gender and power, one must come to terms with the mutual yet dif-

---

52. Meyers, *Discovering Eve*, 104–6. She argues that this refers to extreme physical labor rather than distress. Cf. Kimelman, "Seduction of Eve," 21–22.

53. Dennis, *Sarah Laughed*, 27; Meyers, *Discovering Eve*, 105–6; Wenham, *Genesis 1–15*, 81.

54. Hamilton, *Genesis 1–17*, 201–2; Meyers, *Discovering Eve*, 110–12.

55. Thus Wenham (*Genesis 1–15*, 81) argues: "Women often allow themselves to be exploited in this way because of their urge toward their husband: their sexual appetite may sometimes make them submit to quite unreasonable male demands." Ess ("Reading Adam and Eve," 95–98) notes the tendency to view women as chaos agents who may be controlled through violence.

ferentiated power of each gender. Several concluding observations are in order.

First, in and of itself gender is not an indicator of power or weakness.[56] To equate gender and power is also to equate gender and weakness. Yet it is commonplace to equate females with weakness while extolling male supremacy as the divinely created relational order. Furthermore, one must recognize domination as an aberration of the normative ideal of relational dynamics. The man did not have the power to meet all his own needs. While his sustenance was within his power, finding a suitable companion was beyond his power. His naming the animals and the woman is indicative of his discernment, not of the inherent subordination of what he names. If the serpent and the woman were subordinate, their subsequent activities would show that the named surpassed the initial subjected status to rival the male's discernment and his ability to exercise his choices.

By contrast, the woman's power is her purpose in creation. She was created for the man because the man was deemed deficient apart from the woman. The man was not an autonomous, self-sufficient being; consequently, the woman has the power to complete his status as a created being. The formulation "bone of my bones" (ʿeṣem mēʿăṣāmay, Gen. 2:23) suggests her equality with the man rather than her deficit.[57] Her power is also that she has the ability to choose among options—power that the man also has. This power is a product of choice that the Deity allowed the created beings. Likewise, this power is not absolute but is defined within the boundaries of the Deity's specification. Within those boundaries, the woman has the ability to bear children. Since this is a means of determining the future, she is powerful.

Second, persuasion and the persuasion process are products of preconditions. The success of persuasion depends on the readiness to be persuaded. This readiness is constituted by the disposition to be convinced or to change the behavior as prescribed by the persuasion process. Even so, persuasion is part of a larger system that makes sense of the alternatives presented or suggested by the process.

Third, since power is defined by function rather than the essence of the beings that manifest it, all beings have a measure of power. Consequently, it would be an error to overlook the persuasive power of the relatively weak by predetermining that their status makes them inferior. Those who assign the serpent to the category of the subordinate because it was presumably named miss much. The same is true in relation to

56. Kimelman, "Seduction of Eve," 1–39.
57. The occurrence of the formulation "bone of my bones" is unique to this context. Similar formulations include "my bone and my flesh" (ʿaṣmî ûnĕśārî, Gen. 29:14; 2 Sam. 5:1; contrast 2 Sam. 19:13); "your bone and your flesh" (ʿaṣmēkem ûbĕśarkem, Judg. 9:2).

the woman, and thus her role is often recast as that of a seductress or a nebula of chaos. Her innovation and courage to venture into the unknown have been viewed as troublesome. The result is that she is seen as one who needs to be monitored or parented to prevent her from bringing chaos into an otherwise ordered existence.[58] Instead, one may appreciate her courageous attempt to achieve a different form of actualization than that imposed on her by her domain. She is audacious in her attempt to defend the Creator and, like Job's friends, believes herself equipped to do so. She, like them, presumes to speak for the Deity without understanding the totality of the being about whom she speaks.

Finally, the relationship of Creator and created beings is an open system. In that system, human choices contribute to the ongoing manifestation of the Deity's power within the divine-human relationship. Neither the male nor the female has a more intimate relationship with the Deity. Rather, their status with the Deity is a definite point of equity between them whereby both are isolated because of disobedience and the Deity's choice to punish them. Through punishment, the Deity reclaims some of the authority over human existence and reinforces that humans are responsible for their behavior.

---

58. Cf. Ess, "Reading Adam and Eve," 95–98.

Human to Human—The Conceptual Triad in the Genesis Narratives

The Genesis narratives portray various relational configurations, power dynamics, and modes of persuasion. All these portrayals are manifested within domains that are decisive to them. In part 2, I focus on human-human dynamics as the framework of power and persuasion, and this focus necessitates several definitions. First, a domain is defined by people's status, awareness of others, contact, and interaction within a time frame, relationship, or location. While all share power within a domain, typically the persons of the higher status tend to dominate by initiating and maintaining actions, purposes, and ideologies that define the domain (e.g., Abraham over Sarah, Gen. 12:10–20). The domain sets priorities and uses them to regulate and evaluate behavior and persons. Consequently, where private and public domains conflict, either domain may define the priorities. In issues where the rights of a person compete with the family, the domains may give priority to the individual's rights (e.g., Judah and Tamar, Gen. 38).

Additionally, where purpose defines a domain the purpose and plan of those involved define the priorities. Thus the Deity's specific plan may define the domain such that the Deity's purpose triumphs by making the human purpose and efforts secondary and even unrealized. For example, Hagar chose obedience to the Deity and with it oppression within the family domain rather than survival apart from it. In Hagar's judgment,

71

some things were more valuable than others, namely, the absence of home was more valuable than her presence in a home where there was deliberate and sustained abuse. Yet when she was told to return to the abusive situation, she complied with the Deity's command. Her compliance would mean that she must trust in an authority who sided with her oppressor and thus condoned her oppression. This is a conflict of domains in which the wishes of the human and the Deity conflict.

The second definition is the relational configuration, namely, human relationships that are designated by gender identity and manifested in various domains, for example, female-male (Sarah-Abraham), female-female (Sarah-Hagar), male-male (Isaac-Jacob). These configurations are essential aspects of human interaction and are understood through various conceptual models, including cultural, place, and occupational models.[1] I incorporate aspects of the cultural and place models in suggesting that female and male together define the essence of any domain. Thus whether or not they are physically present, female and male variously affect the domain by trying to exclude or control a person on the basis of gender or by simply trying to define oneself as different from or similar to the other gender.

Part 2 consists of chapters 3 through 7. When a particular chapter focuses on either power or persuasion, that focus is for the sake of organization of thought rather than a suggestion that power and persuasion are mutually exclusive. One disclaimer is necessary to clarify the discussions within this book, namely, that these discussions of the text do not equate the modern situations with those of the Old Testament. Rather the discussions are used to illuminate an interpretive domain of the texts. This book builds on a fundamental principle of *limited hermeneutical applicability*,[2] which holds that not all aspects of a text are necessarily understandable, directly pertinent to, or harmonious with the context of its modern interpreters.

In chapters 3 and 4, I focus on persuasion, examining the persuasion dynamics in female-male relationship in chapter 3 and persuasion in a male-male relational configuration in chapter 4. The remaining chapters focus on power: the examination of the power dynamics among females (in chapters 5 and 6) and the exploration of power within a female-male relationship (in chapter 7).

---

1. Jessie Bernard, *The Female World: A Brilliant Exploration of a Previously Uncharted Region—the Special World of Women* (New York: Free Press, 1981), 20–23.

2. Mignon R. Jacobs, "Methodological Challenges and Necessities of Diaspora Studies: Some Preliminary Observations," in *Institute for the Study of Religion and Culture in Africa and the African Diaspora*, ed. Carol Duncan and Hugh Page (South Bend, IN: University of Notre Dame, 2005), 23–25. See part 3 for further discussion and elaboration of this principle.

3

Persuasive Appeal

Abraham and Sarah (Genesis 12 and 20)

Introduction

Persuasion is a normative element of communication and manifests itself according to the relational dynamics in which it occurs. As such, persuasion in female-male dynamics is both intriguing and challenging. In this chapter I look at the anatomy of persuasion, including the power dynamics of those involved and the nuances of persuasion, for example, appeal, coercion, and perception. I presuppose that there are differences between intentional persuasion (where the parties are aware that they are being persuaded to engage in a particular behavior) and deception (where the parties are unaware of the goal of the persuasion). In deception, they may be misguided regarding how a particular speech or behavior is intended to persuade them. Of the three narratives that depict sister-wife stories, the focus here is Gen. 12:10–20 and 20:1–18, both portraits of power and persuasion within a female-male relationship.[1] In

---

1. Two of these stories include Abraham and Sarah (Gen. 12:10–20; 20:1–18) and the third includes Isaac and Rebekah (26:1–11). Notably, Gen. 12 uses the personal names Abram and Sarai while Gen. 20 refers to them as Abraham and Sarah. For the sake of consistency within this chapter, the names Abraham and Sarah are used to discuss both narratives.

particular, in this chapter I look at Abraham and his ability to persuade others in his domain to behave as he wishes. I argue that persuasion is a basic element of communication and human interaction that shapes and is shaped by the relational dynamics in which it occurs.[2]

Genesis 12:10–20: Persuasion as Power

Anatomy of Persuasion

As part of the anatomy, a basic definition of persuasion includes the following: "to successfully urge somebody to perform a particular action, especially by reasoning, pleading, or coaxing; and to make somebody believe something, especially by giving good reasons for doing so."[3] The persuasion process includes attitudes,[4] perception, plausibility, and trust that the information being received is accurate and accurately presented. With all of these, persuasion is also the product of opportunity.

Circumstances as Opportunity

Genesis 12:10 reports that there was a famine in the land and sets up a scenario for the subsequent events. This is a "type-scene" where a famine is the catalyst for leaving one's location (cf. Gen. 26).[5] Abraham had been an itinerant since journeying with his father from Ur to Haran (11:31). Terah, his father, took him to Haran, and they remained there until Terah died (11:32). Afterward Abraham assumed the role that his father had played, journeying from one location to another with Lot and Sarah in tow (12:4–5).[6] Along with these persons, he took the possessions acquired in Haran (12:5). Responding to the Deity's promise and command, Abraham went from Haran through Shechem into the

2. Cf. Reardon, *Persuasion in Practice*, 4–20.
3. *Encarta World English Dictionary* (Microsoft, 1999), s.v.
4. Reardon, *Persuasion in Practice*, 32–60.
5. Robert Alter, *Genesis: Translation and Commentary* (New York: Norton, 1996), 52. He offers the following definition of a type-scene: "It is a scene in which the writer invokes a fixed sequence of narrative motifs, familiar as a convention to his audience, while pointedly modifying them in keeping with the needs of the immediate narrative context." In Gen. 12 the land is Egypt, Pharaoh is the ruler, the occasion is a famine; in Gen. 20 and 26 the land is Gerar and the ruler is Abimelech the king. In Gen. 26 the occasion is also a famine; but in Gen. 20 the itinerant lifestyle takes Abraham to Gerar.
6. The text reports that Lot went with Abraham and also that Abraham took them with him, much like Terah had taken them from Ur (Gen. 11:31). The double formulation leads some to propose that there are two juxtaposed sources: "he went with him" (*wayyēlek 'ittô*), 12:4a (J), as compared to Abraham took (*lāqaḥ*) Sarah and Lot, 12:4b–5 (P). Hamilton (*Genesis 1–17*, 376) points out that the formulations may represent the latent tension between Abraham and Lot that will surface later in their journeys.

land of the Canaanites and on to the Negeb (12:1–2, 9). Each leg of the journey was an opportunity for future events. Even so, the narrative signals a new and different opportunity when it reports a famine as a catalyst for Abraham's journey to Egypt, a location outside the land of Canaan. Additionally, the narrator reports Abraham's purpose for going to Egypt, namely, "to live as a resident alien" (*gûr*, 12:10). Because the narrator already emphasizes that the reason for his journey to Egypt is the severity of the famine in the land, it leaves open the idea that the duration of his stay in Egypt would be contingent on the length of the famine. In other words, the length of the stay in Egypt is indefinite to the extent that the duration of the famine is indefinite; yet if the famine is temporary his stay there will likewise be temporary. Nonetheless, by saying that Abraham intends to reside there, the narrator also suggests that there were competing reasons for the journey to Egypt. In the Joseph narrative, the duration of the famine was seven years, though even then the famine was "severe" (*ḥāzaq*) in Egypt and in the entire region, including Canaan (41:56–57). Jacob sent his sons to Egypt to obtain food and eventually moved his entire family to Egypt with the assurance that God had a plan "to make [them] a great nation there" (46:3). In that case the catalyst was the famine, but the journey to Egypt itself was a catalyst for God's plan for Jacob's family.[7] In Abraham's situation, the journey to Egypt is not depicted as a foundation to an alternate divine plan. Even so, the move to Egypt fosters circumstances that become expedient for Abraham and an opportunity for his behavior.

Aspects of Abraham's Argument

Using his life as the basis of his argument, Abraham appeals to Sarah by proposing that she is key to his safety (Gen. 12:13). His incessant focus on his well-being versus Sarah's gives the impression that Sarah has power to control the course of his life. She could make it go well for him; she could spare his life in that situation.

His life versus hers. In the book of Genesis, famine in Canaan is a common reason for journeying to Egypt; however, this threat to life appears to be remote for Abraham. Instead, he perceives the threat to life as the Egyptians' desire for Sarah. For this reason he is willing to jeopardize Sarah to spare his life. Whether or not she was his sister, why would the Egyptians spare Abraham? He would be her male guardian and could restrict the Egyptians' access to her. In the narrative, Sarah has no voice either to comply or to resist. Furthermore, by preserving his own life, Abraham is apparently attempting to assist in God's plans

---

7. Cf. Mignon R. Jacobs, "Conceptual Dynamics of Good and Evil in the Joseph Story," *JSOT* 27.3 (2003): 309–38.

to make him into a great nation.[8] Through its interpretation of her, the narrative minimizes Sarah's role while reporting Abraham's view of her importance.

Within Gen. 12:12–15, two elements come into focus: the appeal to Sarah and the narrator's observation about how Abraham prospered. Ironically, although she is depicted as key to Abraham's survival, Sarah is identified only by the feminine pronoun, not by name. While Abraham cites his survival as the rationale for compromising her, his economic prosperity results from the ruse's effectiveness and the compromise. Nothing is said of any further threat to his or Sarah's life. On the contrary, the threat is to Pharaoh and his household, whom the Deity afflicts because of Sarah. Consequently, Pharaoh confronts Abraham by asking about the deception and the reason for lying about Sarah's identity. The narrative does not assign blame to Sarah for consenting to the ruse, and Abraham does not blame or implicate her. It is clear that Pharaoh's behavior hinges on the relational status of Sarah and Abraham. In other words, the perceived relationship leaves open the possibility that she has been sexually intimate with Pharaoh, and his generosity to Abraham does not diminish that possibility.

Life versus wealth. Since he had already acquired "possessions" (*rěkûš*) during his time in Haran, Abraham is by no means a poor man when he journeys to Egypt. Naturally it was typical for a people to take property with them when they moved from one location to another (e.g., Jacob, Gen. 31:18; 46:6; Esau, 36:6).[9] On the one hand, one may presume that Abraham entered Egypt with Sarah and others, including Lot, and whatever possessions they had were not diminished by the famine. On the other hand, one cannot presume that every person who entered Egypt was received in the manner that Abraham and Sarah experienced in securing the attention of Pharaoh's officials. Abraham's possessions would have already placed him in a position of status even if that status was not the highest in the land. It is precisely because of his low status compared to Pharaoh's that the threat Abraham perceives seems plausible. However, Abraham, even in the foreign domain, is not powerless or as powerless as his appeal to Sarah suggests. As one who owns property, he has power over his household and a measure of status in the community. The famine, therefore, creates an opportunity for Abraham to be in Egypt and have access to a different economy. But is the threat to

---

8. Hamilton, *Genesis 1–17*, 383.

9. William White, "רכש," *TWOT* 2:848. The noun *rěkûš* includes transportable property, animals, and spoils of war (see Gen. 14:16, 21; 31:18; 46:6; 2 Chron. 20:25; 21:14). The amassing of possessions, which include cattle and other domestic animals, is cited as a reason for the separation of Lot from Abraham and of Esau from Jacob, since the land could not sustain their possessions (see Gen. 13:5–6; 36:7; cf. Num. 16:32; 35:3).

his life real or simply perceived? Or is his argument to Sarah based on his economic ambition?

Regarding Gen. 12:12, Victor Hamilton sees Abraham as accurately evaluating the situation. He notes that the "law of hospitality" may have been absent from Egypt and that Abraham's request of Sarah to be deceptive about her identity was grounded in the lack of such law.[10] Even so, some portray Abraham as naïve to the possibility that Sarah would be taken as another man's wife—at least Abraham does not introduce that possibility in his attempt to persuade her to participate in the ruse.[11] Yet one must consider that what appears as an effort to persuade Sarah is merely a way to inform her of a decision that he has already made concerning her. What he may be asking is not for a yes or no to his plan, but that she be aware of what he expects of her. Not surprisingly, Abraham does not protest against Sarah being taken as Pharaoh's wife, and neither does Sarah.[12] If Abraham mounted a protest, why would Pharaoh persist in securing Sarah as his wife? We know that Pharaoh would not have taken Sarah, since he later objects to taking another man's wife (Gen. 12:18–20). In light of his response when he found out about Sarah's identity, a protest on Abraham's part would lead to Pharaoh immediately returning her to Abraham. In this case, they may not have killed Abraham as he feared.

Further, after Sarah is taken to Pharaoh's house, Abraham does nothing to correct the situation. Instead, he remains focused on himself and the benefits gained because of Sarah's biological or relational identity. Whatever their biological status toward each other, the narrative is concerned about their functional identity—husband and wife. At times functional status takes precedence over biological status, namely, when stepsiblings are not biological siblings they are functionally defined as siblings because of their parents' relationship. In other cases, functional and biological identity coalesce yet are discounted.[13] What is the case for Abraham and Sarah? It is doubtful that they are biological siblings, namely, that Terah fathered Abraham and Sarah with different mothers (Gen. 20:12).[14] Yet it is common that siblings have different mothers (e.g., Reuben and Joseph, Ishmael and Isaac). If they were biologically related, the identity

---

10. Hamilton, *Genesis 1–17*, 381.

11. E.g., Hamilton, *Genesis 1–17*, 381.

12. Contrast Hamilton, *Genesis 1–17*, 382–83. He compares the separations in Gen. 12 (from Sarah) and 14 (from Lot) and concludes that since Abraham protested in Lot's case, he may have done the same in Sarah's case.

13. Siblings—Amnon and Tamar in 2 Sam. 13.

14. See discussion below for further consideration of Sarah's identity (Gen. 20). Suffice it to say at this point that when she is introduced in Gen. 11:29 her lineage is not mentioned, while those of the other persons are mentioned.

of Abraham and Sarah would be like that of Dinah and Joseph or Dinah and Dan. Nonetheless, whether or not she is biologically or functionally Abraham's sibling, the narrative focuses on her functional identity as his "wife" (*'iššâ*) rather than his "sister" (*'āḥôt*). This basic fact (husband and wife) forms the rationale for the ruse and for the dissolution of Pharaoh's hold on Sarah. While some have seen this as Abraham's use of the Hurrian practice of sister adoption, wherein a husband adopts his wife as a sister and receives compensation, the narrative's portrayal argues against this understanding of what Abraham does.[15] Rather, the story of David and Bathsheba may better illustrate a perceived threat, namely, a husband as a threat when a woman is desirable to other men. David plots and gets rid of Uriah in order to legitimize his access to Bathsheba, Uriah's wife (2 Sam. 11). Nonetheless, Abraham did not confront such a threat as a husband or as a person facing a famine. Instead, he exemplifies power to reshape his domain in his favor.

ABRAHAM'S POWER OVER SARAH

Sarah is Abraham's wife and one who has been taken along with him on his journeys. She is also depicted as silent and relatively passive, having actions done to her or because of her. Yet Abraham's argument presents her as a woman of power, her power inherent in her beauty and gender. While Sarah is at least sixty-five years old,[16] the narrative reports that she is "beautiful" (*yāpâ*). Her beauty is the operative element rather than her age.

Regarding Gen. 12:12, Hamilton observes that perhaps the possibility of Sarah's being taken as someone else's wife does not enter Abraham's mind. Yet regarding 12:14–15 he says: "Abraham's worst suspicions . . . are realized" and that Sarah's silence is her "agreement to cooperate in the ruse."[17] The story does not perceive her being taken by other men and

---

15. The proposal was offered by E. A. Speiser, "The Wife-Sister Motif in the Patriarchal Narratives," in *Biblical and Other Studies*, ed. A. Altmann (Cambridge, MA: Harvard University Press, 1963), 15–28; Speiser, *Genesis*, xl–xli, 91–94. He proposes that in the upper division of Hurrian society a husband had the option of adopting his wife as his sister and receiving compensation. Contrast Thomas L. Thompson, *The Historicity of the Patriarchal Narratives: The Quest for the Historical Abraham*, Beihefte zur Zeitschrift für die alttestamentliche Wissenschaft 133 (Berlin: de Gruyter, 1974), 234–47; S. Greengus, "Sisterhood Adoption at Nuzi and the 'Wife-Sister' in Genesis," *Hebrew Union College Annual* 46 (1975): 5–31; Hamilton, *Genesis 1–17*, 381–82.

16. According to Gen. 12:4, Abraham was seventy-five when he left Haran. In 16:16 Abraham was eighty-six years old when Ishmael was born. In 17:7 Abraham is one hundred while Sarah is ninety; thus he is ten years older. That means that Sarah was seventy-six at the time of Ishmael's birth, some ten years after returning from Egypt. By this calculation Sarah is at least sixty-five when she was with Abraham in Egypt.

17. Hamilton, *Genesis 1–17*, 382.

becoming sexually involved as a risk to her. Rather, Abraham's suggestion depicts a norm that is also seen elsewhere. That norm is that women are sexual objects used to curb men's desires and bargaining chips used to secure men's well-being (Gen. 19:1–11; Judg. 19:22–30).[18] One might even suggest that Abraham's action is that of a powerless man without recourse in the situation. Thus some have argued that "the ruse is the only weapon left for the powerless given over to the mighty."[19] Without a doubt, Abraham is not the most powerful person in this narrative, but he hardly qualifies as powerless. He enters Egypt as a man of means and with enough status to draw attention to someone in his entourage. Here is an instance in which Abraham is using a ruse to provide security for himself, but he does not extend the ruse to protect Sarah. Why does he use the opportunity and his power in this manner?

MITIGATING CIRCUMSTANCES

Abraham's immediate solution does not take into account the long-term implications for Sarah. The Egyptians saw Sarah's beauty and responded to it as Abraham had envisioned. One cannot escape the irony of the Egyptians clamoring after a woman of sixty-five years. Here is an instance where a woman's power is related to her physical appearance. She says and does nothing to draw them in, but simply by virtue of her beauty she has the power to compel them to act to secure her. Irene Nowell argues that there was more to Sarah than her beauty, "since almost no one is described as beautiful in the Bible who is not also holy"—Joseph (Gen. 39:6), David (1 Sam. 16:12), Tamar (2 Sam. 13:1), Abishag (1 Kings 1:3–4).[20] Even if that were the case, the physical appearance of all these persons compelled the response of those around them, and the texts do not assign a negative aspect to their beauty. Their beauty draws attention to them even if that attention may have negative results. It is therefore unnecessary to posit Sarah's holiness as a complement to her beauty. On the other side of this equation is a portrait of men who are so controlled by their perception of beauty that their behavior is predictable. They act without the verification of the woman's identity; they tend to accept things at face value and to trust the word of another. Why would they trust Abraham, a stranger in their midst, to tell them the truth? The

18. In both passages, the men of the city requested that a male be sent to them that they may have sexual intercourse with the male; but a female was offered instead. In Gen. 19 Lot offered his virgin daughter in place of the two men, and in Judg. 19 the Levite offered his concubine. While Lot's daughters were not raped, the concubine was repeatedly raped.

19. C. Westermann, *Genesis 12–36: A Commentary*, trans. John J. Scullion (Minneapolis: Augsburg, 1985), 164.

20. Irene Nowell, *Women in the Old Testament* (Collegeville, MN: Liturgical Press, 1997), 5.

efficacy of the ruse depended on the plausibility of Abraham's claim and the trusting nature of the Egyptians. Fundamentally, it also depended on Sarah's compliance to the ruse.

Regarding the expectations—the second aspect of the circumstances—while all the persons behave as Abraham expects, the Deity also apparently conforms to the expectations and thus facilitates the ruse. Even so, the Deity does not remain silent. A silent Deity in the course of the ruse and an active Deity who enters to dissolve the circumstances of the effective ruse is a poignant depiction. Again one sees a Deity who appears to be absent from the lives of the characters and allows them to do as they see fit. The Deity is thus responsive to rather than generative of what happens.

The third aspect of the circumstances, the power dynamics of the situation, consists of the overlap of several domains as represented by Pharaoh, Abraham, Sarah, and the Deity. Pharaoh and Abraham are two powerful men, but in this instance Abraham is under Pharaoh's control. In contrast, Sarah is under the control of both men—Abraham, who subjects her to the ruse, and Pharaoh, who takes her as his wife and engages her in adultery. To the extent that her beauty compels action on the part of those who perceive it, Sarah's power is that of being desired.[21] Although she does not construct a situation or command persons to act, her presence is the catalyst for other persons' actions and plans. Therefore, she possesses power in her domain as woman and wife. As wife, she has access to Abraham and provides him an opportunity. As woman, she is able to become wife to a powerful ruler and thus affect how Abraham is treated. Nonetheless, these aspects of her power are also her horror. She as woman and wife is in essence prostituted by her own husband for his benefit. The Deity's power in the situation seems restrained in that both Pharaoh and Abraham carry out their actions without interruption from the Deity. The narrator is aware that if the Deity intervenes the Deity can change the whole situation. Yet why does the Deity wait to intervene? One would no more assume the powerlessness of the Deity than the powerlessness of Abraham to remedy a situation gone awry. Thus it is not that the Deity is powerless but rather that the Deity chooses not to intervene at certain times.

These circumstances, however significant, are defined by Abraham's perception of his importance in his domain. If indeed Abraham's effort is to ensure his life and thus his future, it also means that Abraham is willing to sacrifice his wife. While he sees himself as indispensable to the future, he perceives her as dispensable. This portrait of Abraham's view of Sarah as dispensable to his future is again seen in his query

21. Morriss, *Power*, 30–32.

about who may be his heir—Eliezer or Ishmael. In both cases, Sarah is irrelevant. Consequently, Abraham's attitude may be viewed as an option made available by his power. He shows little attachment to and places little value on people in his life, for example, Lot, Sarah, Hagar, Ishmael, even Isaac. He appears ready to part from them for some perceived plan or larger purpose. Thus characterized, Abraham also appears as one who perceives himself to be essential to the Deity's plans, and willing to conform because of his exalted role in those plans apart from how his participation and role affect those closest to him (or anyone for that matter).

Repercussions of the Ruse

SARAH'S PLACE IN ABRAHAM'S PLAN

The danger comes from the one closest to Sarah. The narrator already shows her as connected to in-laws but not necessarily to her family. While the lineages of her husband and her sister-in-law Milcah are cited, nothing is said of Sarah's lineage (Gen. 11:29–30). Along with Abraham and Lot, she is taken away from her homeland (Ur) by Terah, the head of the house, on his journey to Canaan (11:31). They journey as far as Haran and settle there, where Terah dies (11:32). Terah had taken Abraham and Lot, but not Nahor, his other living son (11:28). No reason is cited for this selection, but it is integral to the composition of the family that some of its members are ignored. Terah takes two male heirs and Sarah, the only female mentioned. Terah's wife is not even mentioned as one who was taken on the journey.

Sister, wife, or concubine. First, regarding Sarah as sister, it is usual for the narrator to be reticent about the females in the genealogy. Notably, nothing is said of Abraham's mother or Terah's wives in Gen. 11. In 20:12 Abraham claims that Terah had at least two women with whom he bore children. According to Abraham's claim, Sarah is apparently also Terah's daughter; she was given in marriage to her brother, Abraham. Some have suggested that intermarriage is also evident in the marriage of Nahor to Milcah, his niece (Gen. 11:29).[22] In claiming that Sarah is his sister, Abraham is defining that relational bond as primary when it is not and disregarding his spousal status. In so doing, he omits essential aspects that would change the overall configuration within the social location regarding their relationship, namely, how others perceive and respond to them as distinct persons and as a couple. He sets up a scenario defined by their function as distinct persons who, because of the nature of their relational bond, are also to be treated as two individuals rather

---

22. Cf. Hamilton, *Genesis 1–17*, 362, for the latter perspective.

than two functioning as a relational unit. Since it would be unlikely for an unrelated male and female to travel together, the claim to be brother and sister also facilitates the ruse as an explanation of why they are together.[23] Furthermore, the claim to be her brother thus defines the nature of their sexual relationship in the minds of the Egyptians. They would not expect that Abraham would be sexually involved with Sarah, his sister, and could proceed to relate to her in sexual ways.[24]

As her brother, Abraham would have power of protection and negotiation. Typically an older brother safeguards his sister and looks out for her interest. For example, Laban negotiates Rebekah's marriage (Gen. 24); Simeon and Levi avenge Dinah's rape (Gen. 34); Absalom likewise avenges Tamar's rape (2 Sam. 13). It also appears that older sisters act in a protective manner toward their younger brothers, as Miriam does for Moses (Exod. 2:4, 7). In none of the other instances in the book of Genesis is the sister-wife accepted as the norm. In the case of Isaac and Rebekah, there is clearly no way to argue that she is his sister; therefore, he is deceiving Abimelech. In Abraham's situation, the deceit is that Sarah is functionally his wife and the biological bond (if it is there) had been nullified when they were wed. His argument is then a matter of convenience. In fact, as her brother and guardian he would definitely secure a bride-price. It is just as likely that the basis of the claim, especially during the time of famine, is to ensure the receipt of resources by securing a husband for Sarah. Perhaps, then, it is not that he disbelieved that Sarah would be taken as another's wife, but that he believed and deceived in order to ensure that she is taken as another man's wife.

Second, the promise had been articulated to Abraham at Haran, and he takes Sarah and Lot, just as Terah had taken them (Gen. 12:5). They arrive at Shechem in Canaan, where God promises to give Canaan to Abraham's offspring (12:7). While one may assume that the party journeys on, the narrator who reported that *"they* set out" (masculine plural) in 12:5 now reports that Abraham passed through the land (masculine singular). The narrator continues reporting Abraham's activity, namely, that *he* went from Shechem to the hill country east of Bethel and west of Ai (12:8). *He* built an altar but did not remain there; instead, *he* went toward the Negeb (12:9). Presumably, Sarah and the whole entourage are with him at each stage, including Egypt, where it is finally made explicit that Sarah is with him. He speaks to her when they are about

23. Note Jacob traveling with his wives, Leah and Rachel, (e.g., Gen. 31:17–54) and the Levite traveling with his concubine (Judg. 19).

24. Cf. Lev. 18:9, 11; 20:17; Deut. 17:22. Each text proscribes the sexual relationship between a brother and sister whether or not they are children of the same mother. For this reason some posit that Gen. 20:12 may reflect a time before the legal formulations against brother-sister sexual relationships.

to enter Egypt (12:11); otherwise, it is reported that Abraham acted.[25] Sarah's and Lot's purpose and that of others in the entourage is subsumed under Abraham's. Their importance and significance are measured by their contribution to Abraham's purpose. Therein lies the latent danger to Sarah.

Sarah and Lot are taken along on Abraham's journey, and one quickly realizes that their age is irrelevant to their role. Whether they are adults or children, Abraham's purpose defines their domain. Not surprisingly, Abraham is portrayed as being concerned about his interests at the expense of others. The narrator already shows that Abraham is the focus—his call, his journey—all others are incidental. Abraham's actions therefore simply make more salient what the narrator has already been portraying. When Abraham presents his case to Sarah, he is concerned solely about himself. Sarah's usefulness is that she may deter the Egyptians from killing him and compel their generosity toward him. His plea also sets up a causal relationship that appears to place all the power for his existence in Sarah's hands. She holds the key to his life, safety, and well-being. But with such power to protect Abraham, she does not manifest any power in the situation to protect herself. Apparently, her beauty would solicit responses from those who perceive it. It sounds much like an exaggeration to boost Sarah's ego rather than a statement of a verifiable fact. Yet the officials' response seems to confirm her beauty. The narrative allows for the perception of an excessive beauty but does not explicitly state how such beauty compares to others. Were there no beautiful women in Egypt? Or did they just pale in comparison to Sarah's beauty so that the men focused on Sarah?

As wonderful as that may sound to those who want to embrace Sarah as a powerful figure in the narrative, it elicits horror for others who hear potential blame for anything that may go wrong and adversely affect Abraham. If she is the key to his survival, she is also essential to his demise. His appeal creates a stark contrast between the silent and invisible figure who is simply taken along on the journey and the visible and powerful, yet silent and compliant, Sarah. It will not be the last time that Abraham presents Sarah as the one who has the power to affect another's life. This is seen again when he informs her that Hagar is under her authority and that she (Sarah) may do whatever she pleases to her. Clearly, in that situation, Sarah's positional authority over a subordinate is in full view (Gen. 16:6);[26] but Gen. 12 portrays the subordinate as powerful.

---

25. To avoid the impression that the singular verbs refer to the group as a collective, the narrator uses the plural verb in speaking about the group and tends to identify the members of the groups.

26. See chap. 5.

Because of Sarah, Pharaoh treats Abraham well, giving him various possessions, including animals and servants. Some have argued that Pharaoh gave the gifts to Abraham as a "bride-price" (*mōhar*) for Sarah.[27] Accordingly, Trevor Dennis characterizes Abraham as a simple nomad in somewhat of a rags-to-riches story in which Abraham acquires many possessions from the wealthy pharaoh.[28] Thus he adds property to what he acquired in Haran (Gen. 12:5). Although a nomad, he is not poor and this is not a rags-to-riches story. Even if the gifts given to Abraham are a bride-price, they are given not as a provision to a poor person but as a wedding gift to a male guardian. The term *mōhar* occurs three times in the Old Testament: in the case of a woman who was sexually violated, the man is to "pay a price" to her father and she is to become his wife (Exod. 22:16–19); Saul specifies the "wedding money" that he wants for Michal, his daughter (1 Sam. 18:25); Shechem, after raping Dinah, offers to pay whatever "bride-price" her male guardians set for her (Gen. 34:12).[29] In this last example, some have argued that the willingness to pay the exorbitant price is indicative of Schechem's love for Dinah. However, the fact that he sexually violated her is a more compelling reason for overcompensating her family.[30]

The bride-price does not function in the same way as the price paid to the father when he sells his daughter as a "slave girl" (*'āmâ*, Exod. 21:7–11). It appears that the bride-price is given to the girl's relative, as with Laban, Rebekah's brother (Gen. 24:53), and it may be rendered as services, as in the case of Jacob's years of service for Rachel (29:15–30) or David's efforts to secure Michal (1 Sam. 18:25–27).[31] Notably, Gen. 12:16 does not explicitly mention a "bride-price" (*mōhar*), but the gifts to Abraham may be seen as such. To receive such gifts on Sarah's behalf, Abraham would thus be carrying out the role of the male guardian (brother). The text itself identifies Sarah as Pharaoh's wife (*'iššâ*) rather than concubine (*pîlegeš*). Thus, it is unlikely that Sarah remained a neutral element in Pharaoh's household, and as his wife Sarah may have been intimate with him (see chapter 7).

27. Dennis, *Sarah Laughed*, 39.

28. Dennis, *Sarah Laughed*, 39.

29. Cf. Deut. 22:28–29: fifty shekels is the price to be paid to the father of a sexually violated virgin (*bĕtûlâ*). NRSV translates as "marriage present" in 1 Sam. 18:25 and Gen. 34:12 but as "bride-price" in Exod. 22:15–16 (NRSV 22:16–17).

30. Mignon R. Jacobs, "Love, Honor, and Violence: Socioconceptual Matrix in Genesis 34," in *Pregnant Passion: Gender, Sex, and Violence in the Bible*, ed. Cheryl A. Kirk-Duggan, Semeia Studies 44 (Atlanta: Society of Biblical Literature, 2003), 11–35.

31. Walter C. Kaiser, "מהר," *TWOT* 2:492. The wedding money would "revert to the bride at her father's death or if the death of her husband reduced her to poverty." He sees this as the background of Gen. 31:15, the reason for Rachel and Leah's complaint about their father.

Sarah's compliance. Abraham appears to appeal to Sarah to consent to his plan and thus save his life. However, given her status in relation to Abraham, it hardly seems like a straightforward appeal for Sarah's help. If anything this is a way of informing Sarah of what he is about to do, and she is informed to the extent that she is involved. While Abraham's plea is presented as a way of seeking an opportunity to alleviate the threat on his life, it is also presented as a plan that will be set into motion if it is not already in motion. It is not for Sarah to decline or accept; Abraham already consented for her. Although one may safely assume that Lot is still with Abraham at this stage in their journey, nothing is said of his opinion in the matter. Sarah's power in this situation is her compliance, a choice to survive.[32] Surely Abraham would not have changed his mind if Sarah had declined the ruse. One can hardly miss the irony of the situation and the haunting pleas of her voice as it puzzles about the choice—his life or mine? Yet the narrator avoids her voice through the deafening silence of one whose choice is highly restricted. The narrator does not report her compliance but notes only that she is taken to Pharaoh's house.[33] One could certainly argue that she does not comply but is forcibly taken. Where one has highly restricted options, can one rightly speak of compliance and consent? Consent may be a right of those with the type of power to do so. Indeed, Abraham's appeal seems like a monologue reported only for the sake of disclosing his plan but not for the shared decision between a husband and a wife. Again, one cannot escape the contrast between this Sarah and how she relates to Hagar (Gen. 16). There she speaks out for her cause even to the detriment of Hagar, and Abraham relinquishes any responsibility for Sarah's decisions and actions. Here in Gen. 12 she is silent.

While Abraham cites his motive as protecting his life (Gen. 12:12–13), another motive may be to find acceptance and economic advantage in a foreign city. The narrative portrays other incongruities. For example, the scenario that Abraham uses to present his plan is invalidated by the Egyptians' response. They do not murder Abraham, but discovering that Sarah is his wife, they respect that fact. Whether or not aspects of his fears are legitimate, the extent of the fear seems to be exaggerated. Whatever the nature and extent of the perceived "perversion" (*bĕlîya'al*)[34]

---

32. Fewell and Gunn, *Gender, Power, and Promise*, 43. Accordingly, they state: "Her silence is the silence of a survivor."

33. Contrast Gen. 20:13. Abraham claims that the plan was in motion for the extent of his sojourning, Egypt being one of the places to which he journeyed.

34. Walter C. Kaiser, "בלה," *TWOT* 2:110–11. The term *bĕlîya'al* is used of "worthlessness" but also as a name, i.e., "son(s) of Belial" (*bĕnê-bĕlîya'al*) in KJV (Deut. 13:14 [KJV 13:13]; Judg. 19:22; 1 Sam. 2:12; 2 Chron. 13:7). In Judg. 19:22 the NRSV translates *bĕnê-*

of the men who are seeking sexual intercourse, they do not request a woman who is already another man's (wife, concubine, betrothed) (cf. Judg. 19:22). Nonetheless, Abraham uses Sarah as a bargaining chip and thus persuades others to participate in his ruse and to seek another man's wife. All, including Pharaoh and his officials, become pawns in Abraham's scheme.

Danna Fewell and David Gunn ask whether we can accept Abraham's speech at face value.[35] Apparently, Abraham does not consider the ramifications of the ruse on Sarah's well-being or her desires. By consenting for her and including her in his deception, he acts on behalf of her in a way that denies the existence of her will and choices. So while looking at Abraham's plan to retrieve Sarah, one must also consider that he uses a solution that exceeds its temporal extent and the situation it intends to resolve. There is no inkling of terminating the setup, and in securing wealth, Abraham may not have the urgency to interfere with it and end his benefits. Consequently, Abraham may not have intended to retrieve Sarah, especially if he is concerned about his family line. He could be more inclined to use the situation as an opportunity to replace her with a fertile woman.[36] If this is the case, Abraham manipulates everyone involved to his advantage.

Inadvertent Compliance

In Gen. 12:15 the "officials" (*śārê*) saw and praised Sarah to Pharaoh. Being an official in a ruler's household would denote responsibility to that ruler as well as trustworthiness. Consequently, when they praise Sarah to Pharaoh, these men act in an official manner and represent themselves as reliable sources of information. Their power in the situation is to affect Pharaoh's behavior and decisions. It is therefore not surprising that they report to Pharaoh about Sarah and do so in a positive manner. As in the other instances when a human refers to Sarah, she is not named but is identified as "the woman" or "her" (Gen. 12:14–16). The text does not tell who takes Sarah to Pharaoh's palace but simply reports that she is "taken" (*lāqaḥ*).[37] One could surmise that the officials take her since they have access to the palace and to Pharaoh. The narrator

---

bĕlîya'al as "a perverse lot"; and in the other instances NRSV uses "scoundrels" (ASV "base fellows"). Proverbs 6:12–15 describes the fate of the *'ādām bĕlîya'al* (ASV "worthless man"; KJV "naughty person"; NRSV "scoundrel").

35. Fewell and Gunn, *Gender, Power, and Promise*, 42.

36. Fewell and Gunn, *Gender, Power, and Promise*, 43. Cf. Hamilton (*Genesis 1–17*, 383), who suggests that Abraham was concerned to preserve himself, the one through whom God will actualize a future nation.

37. The passive form of the verb is used, namely, the waw-consecutive Qal passive third feminine singular (*wattuqqaḥ*).

is silent about Sarah's status in the house and appears reticent even to state whether she is taken to Pharaoh. Even when the ruse is uncovered Sarah is described as someone who has been taken as a wife (12:19). From that, one learns that Sarah is not simply taken to live in the palace but that she is assigned the role of a wife to Pharaoh. "To take as wife" usually connotes a sexual union of the man and woman, and that may be the case with Sarah and Pharaoh.[38]

Where is Abraham in all this now that Sarah is polyandrous? Abraham uses her to gain advantage in Egypt—he values his life but expresses no concern for her well-being.[39] Did Abraham plan to retrieve Sarah from Pharaoh? His plan appears to have no provision for Sarah's return, and Sarah's compliance does not address the duration of the situation. Rather it appears that Abraham's decision was to get rid of Sarah permanently to fix a temporary difficulty—survival during a severe famine. By acting in a way that is consistent with the information that he receives, Pharaoh also complies with the ruse, but he is ignorant of the fact that he is being deceived. Nevertheless, he is punished for taking Sarah as his wife (Gen. 12:17), suggesting that in issues of accountability, ignorance is not a basis for exoneration.[40] Ironically, while Pharaoh is ignorant and yet punished for his involvement, Abraham (who deliberately deceives) goes unpunished. Abraham remains alive and is allowed to keep all the gifts that he received through deception (12:20).

GOD'S INVOLVEMENT

One characteristic pattern of the Deity's behavior that is repeatedly portrayed in the narratives of the book of Genesis is initial absence during adversity followed by intervention in the adversity. For example, Adam and Eve eat the fruit, then the Deity enters (Gen. 3); Abraham allows Sarah to be taken as another man's wife, then the Deity punishes the man (Gen. 12 and 20); Leah is handed over to Jacob, then the Deity closes Rachel's womb (Gen. 29); Joseph is sold, then the Deity gives him favor in Egypt (Gen. 37). While these narratives do not use the language of God's remembering and then acting, they reflect the

---

38. In instances when the woman is given as a wife, she engages in sexual intercourse with her husband, as is the case with Hagar (Gen. 16:4), Leah (29:21–23), Rachel (29:28–30), Bilhah (30:4), and Zilpah (30:9–10) (cf. Rebekah in 24:67; 25:21). See chap. 5 for further details regarding sexual unions.

39. The narrative reads like the Levite-concubine story, in which the concubine was sent out to the men of the town while the Levite remained safely in the house. During the night the concubine was repeatedly raped. She eventually collapsed on the door of the house, where she was found in the morning (Judg. 19:1–30). It appears that the Levite's plan was to collect her in the morning and be on his way, but that sordid plan did not work out.

40. See Hamilton, *Genesis 1–17*, 384–85.

absence of the Deity from the situations and raise the question about the Deity's continual involvement (cf. Gen. 8). To impute ignorance to the Deity would be to characterize the situations as being beyond the control or knowledge of the Deity. Yet to attribute to the Deity power, knowledge, and control of the situation is to acknowledge the Deity's participation in various infractions—even when the Deity's presence is not highlighted.

Regarding Gen. 12:17, one observes the Deity's response in breaking the silence and inactivity. This portrayal would coincide with what is seen in Sarah's plan to bear children using Hagar as surrogate. Whether or not the Deity can, the Deity does not control Abraham's actions or prevent Sarah's adultery. Instead, the Deity "strikes" (*nāga'*) Pharaoh and his household with "plagues" (*něgā'îm*). The image is like that of Exodus, where the Egyptian population is subjected to the plagues (Exod. 8:2; 11:1).[41] In Gen. 12 there is no indication of the extent of the plagues or the method of verifying the source, but Pharaoh is astute in discerning the connection between Sarah being Abraham's wife and the plagues.

But where is the punishment on Abraham? He neither confesses his wrong nor appears to have any negative repercussions. In fact, he prospers from Sarah's role as Pharaoh's wife. Dennis, therefore, argues that the plagues on Pharaoh and his household "will foreshadow the events that lie at the heart of the Old Testament's gospel. Sarah will 'play the part' of the trapped Israelites, but if there is a villain of this piece, then it is not the pharaoh, but Abraham, her husband."[42] The Deity appears to side with Abraham by not punishing him and by restoring Sarah to him. Abraham's exoneration is also indicated by the results of his unmitigated self-interest: he gets to keep all the possessions.[43] No indication is given about the duration of Sarah's stay in Pharaoh's household, but it may have exceeded several days. In returning Sarah and condemning Abraham, Pharaoh shows a greater sensitivity than Abraham.[44] Some

---

41. The term *nega'* is used of leprosy in Lev. 13 and 14. In other instances, a plague is sent as punishment on the Israelites for their infraction: the golden calf (Exod. 32:35) and getting too close to the sanctuary (Num. 8:19), or for their complaints (11:33).

42. Dennis, *Sarah Laughed*, 38.

43. Esther Fuchs, " 'For I Have the Way of Women': Deception, Gender, and Ideology in Biblical Narrative," *Semeia* 42 (1988): 70–71. She explains that part of the narrative strategy in depicting male and female deception is to distinguish them by the suppression of an explicit motivation or "authorial judgment" in instances where females deceive (cf. Gen. 31:35) and the explicit inclusion of motivation in instances where males deceive (29:19–30; 30:25–34).

44. Cf. Hamilton, *Genesis 1–17*, 385; Peter D. Miscall, "Literary Unity in Old Testament Narrative," *Semeia* 15 (1979): 32; Robert M. Adams, "Self-Love and the Vices of Self-Preference," *Faith and Philosophy* 15.4 (1998): 500–505.

believe that Pharaoh's awareness of the Deity's power behind Abraham deterred him from retaliating and harming Abraham.[45]

Genesis 20: Strategy for Deception

Having analyzed Gen. 12:10–20, I now focus on a comparison with Gen. 20. I also include various comparative notes to Gen. 26, the third sister-wife narrative (Isaac and Rebekah). As to the relationship between Gen. 12 and 20, they may be simply narratives from two different sources that present a different perspective on the same event. Nonetheless, it appears more likely that there are two events, and that the narrator of Gen. 20 is cognizant of the events depicted in Gen. 12. Accordingly, Gen. 20 provides explanations for some unanswered questions that are raised by Gen. 12, including questions about the reason for travel and for the Deity's intervention.[46]

Circumstances as Opportunity

That all circumstances create opportunity is a basic fact that the narrative confirms. The question therefore is not whether the circumstances created opportunities but rather what opportunities were created and for whom. The difference between circumstances that are consciously reaped for their opportunities and those that are not is a matter of the power of the persons involved to recognize the opportunity and to utilize the circumstances for a particular purpose. Like that into Egypt, the journey into Gerar is explained as part of Abraham's "sojourning" (*gûr*) and not as a response to a famine. He resided in Gerar as a resident alien. While it is a noted theme in the book of Genesis, flight as the solution to a famine in the land is rather troubling. It appears that the journey away from their land is seen as the natural solution to the famine rather than any proactive measure, as seen in the Egyptians' resourcefulness in storing up grain during their times of abundance. It is true that in the Joseph narrative there are prior indications of the impending famine that allow for such preparation; still the question about the frequency of the famines and the lack of resources arises. Even so, one could understand the urgency created by the lack of food and other resources. In the absence of a famine, as a resident alien in Gerar, Abraham was under no duress to locate resources. Nor was there

45. Hamilton, *Genesis 1–17*, 385.

46. John Van Seters, *Abraham in History and Tradition* (New Haven: Yale University Press, 1975), 171–75; T. D. Alexander, "Are the Wife/Sister Incidents of Genesis Literary Compositional Variants?" *Vetus Testamentum* 42 (1992): 145–53.

any immediate threat to his life. The opportunity to deceive was born out of his presence in a foreign land where he was unknown and could reconstruct his identity through deceit. In his interest to protect himself from a perceived threat, Abraham's deception is to claim a relation status of "brother" rather than husband and to reexpose Sarah to harm.[47] Thus the famine provides the opportunity to sojourn, and the deception provides various economic opportunities.

Abraham's ruse also provides an opportunity for Abimelech that is not legitimately open to him apart from the circumstances created by the deception. Since Sarah is Abraham's wife, Abimelech could not knowingly and legally take her as his wife. The right of access to her sexuality belongs to Abraham, her husband. Thus, without Abraham relinquishing access to her through divorce, all extra-marital sexual unions in which she may engage would be unsanctioned and therefore adulterous.[48]

God's Intervention

God's intervention in the situation demonstrates favor toward Abraham and power over the people involved. While the intervention encompasses Abimelech, Sarah, and Abraham, it focuses on Abimelech and his household.[49] In this intervention, the Deity bypasses both Abraham and Sarah and speaks only to Abimelech. First, the dialogue clarifies the relational identity of Abraham and Sarah. Accordingly, the Deity labels Sarah as wife (Gen. 20:3, 7) even though Abraham labels her as sister (20:12). Additionally, in Abimelech's dream the Deity identifies Abraham as a prophet (*nābî'*) and identifies the connection between the adversity and the presence of Sarah in Abimelech's household (20:7–9).

Second, because of the Deity's bond with him, Abraham's presence in the lives of others may be a latent threat if they do not conform to the plans for Abraham.[50] The Deity is not concerned about the intention or

---

47. Adams, "Self-Love," 503–5. He considers the nature of self-love and selfishness in light of good for self and for others.

48. James K. Bruckner, *Implied Law in the Abraham Narrative: A Literary and Theological Analysis*, JSOTSup 335 (Sheffield: Sheffield Academic Press, 2001), 188–89; Elaine A. Goodfriend, "Adultery," *Anchor Bible Dictionary*, ed. D. N. Freedman, 6 vols. (New York: Doubleday, 1992), 1:82–86. Contrast Ze'ev W. Falk, *Hebrew Law in Biblical Times* (Jerusalem: Wahrmann, 1964); Michael L. Satlow, *Tasting the Dish: Rabbinic Rhetorics of Sexuality*, Brown Judaic Studies 303 (Atlanta: Scholars Press, 1995).

49. In Gen. 20 the Deity is identified as *'ĕlōhîm* "God" as compared to *yhwh* "Yahweh" in Gen. 12 (NRSV LORD). For this reason, and because of the use of dreams as the mode of dialogue between the Deity and the human, Gen. 20 is usually attributed to the Elohist (E) and Gen. 12 to the Yahwist (J).

50. God does not conceal his favor toward Abraham even when Abraham is in the wrong. That is detrimental for the Abimelechs, whose encounters with Abraham result in their adversity. One wonders, Where are the blessings that would come through Abraham? En-

motives that result in the compromising situation, only in resolving it. In the resolution, the inadvertent offender is punished while Abraham, the catalyst of the offense, remains unscathed. Everyone in his domain of influence is somehow subjected to adversity because of Abraham's behavior and lack of responsibility. Yet the Deity's purpose for him seems to allow the adversities in order that the purpose may be accomplished.

Third, the Deity is aware of the situation, allows it, and pronounces a judgment of death on Abimelech for taking Sarah, another man's wife (Gen. 20:3). While the pronouncement indicates the Deity's displeasure with Abimelech, unlike Gen. 12:19, where she is referred to as Pharaoh's wife, there is no explicit statement here that Abimelech took Sarah as his wife. Instead, all the references in Gen. 20 concerning Sarah's spousal status are to Sarah as Abraham's wife (vv. 2, 7, 11, 14, 18). The idea that Abimelech took her as his wife comes from the language of the text, namely, that to "take" (*lāqaḥ*) a woman usually refers to the process of making her a man's wife (cf. 4:19; 6:2; 11:29; 16:3; 24:67; 25:1; 28:9; 30:9; 38:6).[51]

The pronouncement of judgment focuses on Abimelech's existence and suggests a contrast between Abraham's fear and God's punishment. On the one hand, Abraham is afraid that he will be killed because of Sarah, his wife. On the other hand, the one protecting him is capable of killing. Ironically, Abraham behaves as if he has no other power to protect himself than his own, while the Deity acts as if Abraham cannot be trusted. Abraham takes matters into his own hands as if the course of his life depended on him. But the narrative shows that the Deity orchestrates his life course. Consequently, even the judgment against Abimelech grows out of the Deity's purpose for Abraham. The force of the judgment in Gen. 20:3, 7 is similar to that of 2:17—"you will die" (*môt tāmût*).[52] The Deity's power to control Abimelech's behavior is expressed in two ways: preventing Abimelech from "touching" (*nāgaʿ*) Sarah (Gen. 20:6),[53] and "restraining" (*ḥāśak*) Abimelech from "sinning" (*ḥāṭāʾ*) against God.[54]

---

counters with him seem to result in trouble for the nations rather than blessings (cf. Egypt and Gerar). Cf. W. Lee Humphreys, *The Character of God in the Book of Genesis: A Narrative Appraisal* (Louisville: Westminster John Knox, 2001), 129.

51. In each of these cases the object of the verb is specified, namely, "wife" (*ʾiššâ*) or "wives" (*nāšîm*) (cf. Judg. 3:6; Ruth 4:13; 1 Kings 16:31; 1 Chron. 7:15; 2 Chron. 11:18). To "take" (*lāqaḥ*) is also used of a concubine (Judg. 19:1; 2 Sam. 5:13).

52. The formulation "you will die" (*môt tāmût*) occurs in Gen. 2:17 and 20:7 to indicate the consequence of a particular behavior. In Judg. 13:22 it is used to express the consequence of seeing God. Other examples of the use of the formulation include 1 Sam. 14:44; 22:16; 2 Kings 1:6 (cf. Ezek. 3:18; 33:8).

53. The construction is a negated finite verb form with object suffix (*nětattîkā*) plus the complementary infinitive form of the verb (*lingōaʿ*) with God as subject.

54. Hebrew *ḥāśak* is used for restraining someone from evil or doing a particular action (1 Sam. 25:39; 2 Sam. 18:16; Ps. 19:14 [NRSV 19:13]; 78:50); it is also used in the sense

The infertility of Abimelech's household is the direct result of God's intervention used to punish Abimelech (Gen. 20:17–18). The Deity's precision in the use of punishment is again seen with regard to "shutting" (*'āṣar*) all the "wombs" (*reḥem*) of women of the household—his wife (*'iššâ*) and slaves (*'āmâ*)—an act that could not be done to a male, but that affects him.[55] In a social structure where much of women's value lies in producing children,[56] this punishment is severe. They are innocent of sin against Abraham and against the Deity, but their innocence is not highlighted. Rather it is only as part of Abimelech's plea for his nation that the women's innocence is disclosed (20:9). Accordingly, the plagues do not affect the whole population, nor does the infertility affect all the women of Gerar. Just as some of the plagues on Egypt are depicted as controlled especially with reference to their target, so the Deity's punishment is specific to Abimelech and those closest to him. Thus the Deity's intervention illustrates a discriminate execution of judgment, showing control over the extent and type of judgment (cf. Exod. 9:6; 12:23).

Fourth, another aspect of the controlled execution of power is that the Deity gives Abraham the key to remove the punishment. The Deity commands Abimelech to "return" (*šûb*) Sarah to Abraham (Gen. 20:7). It would be logical that returning Sarah would lift the punishment from Abimelech. Instead, the restoration introduces a new facet of Abraham's identity and prominence in the Deity's plan, namely, as prophet (*nābî'*). The Deity assigns Abraham the task of interceding for Abimelech and thus gives Abraham, the offender, power over Abimelech, the offended. Here the Deity's purpose is operative and the bias is evident when dealing with those in conflict with the Deity's favorite.[57]

Finally, God's intervention is also seen in the response to Abraham's intercession and the subsequent removal of the punishment from the women of Abimelech's household. Just as the Deity has the ability to close the womb of any woman, so the Deity has the power to open the womb. Perplexingly, the Deity who intervenes to restore Sarah to Abraham as

---

of not withholding something, as in the case of Abraham not withholding his son Isaac from God (Gen. 22:12, 16) and Potiphar giving Joseph authority over his house (not his wife) (39:9; cf. Job 7:11; Prov. 10:19).

55. In speaking about Hannah, 1 Sam. 1:5–6 uses the verb *sāgar* "to close" plus the object "womb" (*reḥem*). Here too God is responsible for closing the womb. The equivalent would be to make the male infertile. See chap. 6 for further discussion of the cause of the Deity's actions, etc.

56. Humphreys, *Character of God*, 131.

57. That God's purpose is more important than the person involved is another dimension of the divine-human relationship. It is not that the Deity wills behavior in the same way in all situations; but the Deity's favorites are given much leeway. Consequently, when they sin against God, their punishment may be deferred or even passed over (see chap. 4).

his wife does not intervene to open her womb; yet, the Deity opens the wombs of the women around her. While remaining infertile, Sarah will observe the fertility of other women. Even more difficult is that Sarah will observe the Deity's act on behalf of others, while she, the wife of his chosen, is ceremoniously overlooked—despite all the promises regarding progeny. The level of tension in the narrative is intensified in relation to the Deity, who is clearly in control of the humans but who acts according to the Deity's own timing and methods.

Meeting of Powers—Abimelech Confronts Abraham

ASPECTS OF ABRAHAM'S ARGUMENT

Abraham's claim that Sarah is his sister appears to explain the reason for his deception;[58] however, he also claims that he has a plan that he sets into motion whenever he journeys to a foreign land (Gen. 20:13). First, Abraham argues that he thought that the people of Gerar do not have the fear of God and thus may kill him for his wife (20:11). In this argument, his predetermined perspective on foreigners appears to be operative rather than the reality of his experience with them, that is, how they receive Abraham and his entourage. Accordingly, Abraham decides that the people of Gerar are immoral or at least disrespectful of the husband-wife relationship of visitors to their city. Abraham assumes that he has the right to misrepresent himself because of his fears and allows his prejudice against foreigners to shape his behavior.[59] In claiming that (the proverbial) "they" would kill him because of his wife (20:11), Abraham does not identify any particular group that would likely kill him; rather, he views the population of Gerar as a collective that would act against him. Unlike Gen. 12, Gen. 20 says nothing about Sarah's beauty as a reason for her being desirable. For the reader, the irony of Abraham's perspective is that the actions of killing a man for his wife are confirmed later in the Old Testament, but not among foreigners. David, the king, desired Bathsheba, Uriah's wife, and took her. When she conceived, he unsuccessfully attempted to cover up what he had done. He then had Uriah killed and took Bathsheba as his wife

58. Cf. Fuchs, "Way of Women," 70.

59. Elisabeth Young-Bruehl, *The Anatomy of Prejudices* (Cambridge, MA: Harvard University Press, 1996), 43–44, 165–67. She considers the various definitions of prejudice, including the degrees and types of prejudice. Of particular interest is her reconstruction of the definition of prejudice that incorporates individual as well as cultural dynamics; therefore, she looks at the group-perpetuating ethnocentrisms and the group-creating ideologies. The former tends to be passed on within the culture by "socializing or acculturating individuals"; the latter is generated by persons of a particular type who form groups "for the satisfaction of their desires and needs."

(2 Sam. 11).[60] Evidently, Abraham's interaction with the foreigners does not confirm his preconceptions, but he perpetuates his preconceptions to accommodate his deception.

The narrator does not offer evaluative comments on Abraham's behavior but betrays Abraham's prejudice, namely, that an entire group of people would not have the "fear of God" (*yir'at 'ĕlōhîm*, Gen. 20:11). Ironically, Abraham relies on that very group to show him kindness during his residence in Gerar. What is his concept of "fear of God"? The text does not say. Even the Deity confirms Abimelech's integrity, thus casting doubt on Abraham's view of Abimelech and his nation (*gôy*). Whether or not it was fear of God, something motivated Abimelech in his benevolence toward Sarah and Abraham.

The second aspect of Abraham's argument—his claim that he is telling the truth, that Sarah is his sister—is connected to the third aspect, namely, that the Deity caused him to "wander" (*tā'â*) in general[61] and to Gerar as a particular place of his journey. Thus the Deity brought him to Gerar just as the Deity caused him to go to all the other points on his journey. In this argument, Abraham's claim is consistent with the behavior of one who is attempting to absolve himself of responsibility in a difficult situation (Gen. 20:11–13). One cannot miss the resemblance to Adam in Gen. 3:12 (see chapter 2). He implicates not only the Deity in his behavior but also Sarah. Whether or not Egypt was the first and Gerar the second place where he had done the same thing, it was not a spontaneous act prompted by an immediate catalyst. Rather, the nature and extent of the deception is planned and implemented when the circumstances allow. Notably, while both Abimelech and the Deity refer to the situation as "sin" (*ḥaṭṭā'â*), Abraham refers to it as a "kindness" (*ḥesed*) that Sarah is to do for him (20:13). Further, the language used of his dialogue with Sarah regarding her involvement is that he "told" (*'āmar*)[62] her what to do as compared to "requesting" (*šā'al*) her compliance.[63] Consequently,

---

60. The narrative represents his action as sending for Bathsheba and taking her as his wife (2 Sam. 11:4, 27).

61. The reference to the Deity presents some challenges in that the term usually translated "God" (*'ĕlōhîm*) here takes the plural verb (*hit'û*). Consequently, some have argued that Abraham was not necessarily referring to the Deity but rather to "gods" in general in order to accommodate Abimelech's polytheism. See Gordon J. Wenham, *Genesis 16–50*, WBC 2 (Waco, TX: Word, 1987), 73, who rightly notes that the majority of interpreters "see the plural verb as an anomaly." Cf. Victor C. Hamilton, *The Book of Genesis: Chapters 18–50*, New International Commentary on the Old Testament (Grand Rapids: Eerdmans, 1995), 65.

62. In both Gen. 12:10 and 20:11 Abraham is represented as speaking to Sarah. Such an important decision is made on the basis of information rather than entreating (*ḥālâ*) her favor (Esther 4:8; usually used of pleading for God's favor—Jer. 26:19; Zech. 7:2; 8:21).

63. In several texts the response to a person's request is noted, as in the case of God doing what Moses asked (Exod. 8:27 [NRSV 8:31]; 33:17). By comparison the people

while Abraham may have lied about Sarah's involvement in the ruse (as a standard operating procedure), she somehow consents to participate. Abimelech claims that when asked Sarah also said that she is Abraham's sister (20:5).

SARAH'S PLACE

While the narrative builds on Sarah's presence, she is identified as the object of concern by Abraham, the Deity, and Abimelech, but she is addressed only by Abimelech. In contrast to the narrator, who identifies Sarah by name and role (Gen. 20:14–15, 18), none of the others speak of her by name; they refer to her only by her gender (the woman, 20:3) or role (wife or sister, 20:7, 11, 12) or pronoun (she/her, 20:4, 5, 6, 13). In Gen. 20:2 she is identified as Abraham's "wife" (*'iššâ*) who is said to be his "sister" (*'āḥôt*). Thus when it is reported that Abraham claims that Sarah is his sister, she is spoken about rather than addressed (cf. 12:11). In addition, the Deity speaks to Abimelech and discloses to him that Sarah, whom he had taken, is another man's wife (20:3). As in the other instances when she is the object of the verb "to take" (*lāqaḥ*), here she is a silent, passive figure. This passivity includes instances when she is taken in the sense of being transported along with another person (11:31; 12:5).

By contrast, when *lāqaḥ* is used in reference to the action that initiates the relational identity between her and a man, it refers to her being taken as wife or potential sexual partner. Thus Abraham took her as wife, as did Pharaoh (Gen. 11:29; 12:15, 19). It is presumably in this manner that Abimelech also took her into his household, where she would live (20:3).[64] Since he took her as a wife, it would have been expected that he consummate the relationship with her; but nothing is said about the length of time that she lived in his household as his wife or whether the relationship was consummated. Rather, the narrator indicates that the Deity spoke directly to Abimelech concerning Sarah and pronounced judgment on Abimelech for taking Sarah.

In Gen. 20:5 Abimelech claims that he acted with integrity and innocence,[65] and the narrator confirms that he did not "approach" (*qārab*) her. Here the claim signifies a range of behavior, including that he did

---

asked (*šā'al*) the Egyptians for jewelry and were given it (12:35). The term *šā'al* is usually used in reference to humans asking something of humans, but it is also used in asking something of God (Isa. 7:11; 58:2). In Gen. 26:7 the people inquire (*šā'al*) of Isaac about Rebekah, and he says that she is his sister (cf. 32:18 [NRSV 32:17]). Cf. R. Laird Harris, "שׁאל," *TWOT* 2:891–92.

64. Cf. Lev. 20:14, 17, which proscribe certain marital partners, including one's sister.

65. Integrity (lit. integrity of my heart [*tom-lĕbābî*]) and innocence (lit. innocence of my hands [*niqyōn kappî*]).

not have a sexual encounter with her. In both Deuteronomy 22:14 and Isaiah 8:3, approaching (*qārab*) a woman results in her conceiving a child.[66] When the Deity speaks of Abimelech's integrity, it is said that the Deity did not allow Abimelech to "touch" (*nāgaʿ*) her (Gen. 20:6).[67] The constraint then is presented as the power of the Deity to control Abimelech and not necessarily his self-control.[68] Clearly, the noted infertility in his household could not be confirmed if he had not been engaged in sexual intercourse with his wives and concubines. Thus, while it may be suggested that his illness hindered him from sexual activity with Sarah and the other women, it is unlikely that he was hindered in this way. His integrity is not that he did not touch Sarah or that he lacked opportunity for sexual conduct with her; instead, his innocence is his ignorance about her relational identity to Abraham.

Sarah's place is also defined by Abimelech's character. His character is revealed when Abimelech speaks to Sarah about her participation in the ruse and when he tells her that he gave Abraham a thousand pieces of silver as "exoneration" or "concealment" (*kĕsût*) of Sarah's role (Gen. 20:16). First, Abimelech spoke to Sarah to confirm her identity; and according to him, she also claimed to be Abraham's sister (20:5). The narrator does not record any conversation between Sarah and Abimelech, nor does he discount Abimelech's claim. Consequently, Sarah is depicted as being informed of Abraham's claim concerning her and as being an active participant in the ruse. Even so, she is not accused of any wrongdoing or asked to account for her involvement. Abimelech blames Abraham and asks him to account for his behavior (20:9–10). Even then, Abraham does not confer with Sarah or even speak of her by name; but he implicates her in his deception, claiming that they have a plan that they implement on their journeys. In this representation, Abraham makes Sarah a partner in his plans to misrepresent the nature of their relational identity. Whether or not she is his sibling, that Abraham took her as wife supersedes her status as his sister. Ironically, the narrator uses two ways of depicting Sarah's active participation, both coming from the men and both without her voiced input concerning her participation (20:5, 9–10). Furthermore, unlike Gen. 3, where the Deity speaks to the woman, Sarah is not addressed; but it is not unique for the relationship between the Deity and Sarah. Apart from the confrontation

---

66. The term *qārab* is also used in lists of proscribed sexual unions; cf. Lev. 18:6, 14, 19; cf. Hamilton, *Genesis 18–50*, 61.

67. Of the range of terms that may be used of sexual intercourse, the narrator chose "touch" (*nāgaʿ*). Another example of a denial about sexual activity occurs in 1 Kings 1:4. There the narrator contends that while David used Abishag, a beautiful woman, to warm him, he did not have sex (*yādaʿ*) with her.

68. Humphreys, *Character of God*, 128, 130.

in 18:15, the Deity and Sarah do not speak to each other. When there are matters that concern her, the Deity speaks with Abraham. In this respect, the Deity remains distant from Sarah in a way that is not seen with Hagar or even Abimelech.

Next, Sarah's place in the narrative as related to Abimelech's character is also shaped by Abimelech's response to her. On the one hand, he claims that she is involved in the deception (Gen. 20:5); on the other hand, he attempts to exonerate her in the eyes of those who are with her (20:16). Here the narrator confirms that Abimelech's gifts to Abraham are not part of a bride-price (20:14–15). What does that mean? Why does Sarah need exoneration (kĕsût)? One wonders if the protest that he did not touch her conceals an unmentioned act that her infertile body would likewise conceal. Yet one is constrained to quell that suspicion since the Deity takes responsibility for stopping a sexual union between Abimelech and Sarah. In any case, Abimelech, the one who was in close proximity to her, demonstrates a need to conceal something. The silver given to Abraham is intended as an exoneration (kĕsût ʿênayim, lit. "covering of the eyes") of all who are with her. Presumably, they would be aware that she, Abraham's wife, was taken as a wife by Abimelech. Furthermore, those in her household would have known that she was in Abimelech's household for an extended period of time, during which a man and a woman would have had ample opportunity to engage in sexual intercourse. In their eyes, then, it is more likely than not that she had been Abimelech's sexual partner. "Most likely kĕsût is used figuratively and is to be connected with the notion of concealing any kind of sexual impropriety."[69] The goal is thus to blind others to any sexual misconduct in which she may have been engaged, since that behavior may be considered ignominious. Accordingly, Abimelech refers to Abraham as her "brother" although the Deity has already clarified to him that Abraham is Sarah's husband. His reference may be a way of saving face for Sarah before the population of Gerar, who were led to believe that Abraham was her brother.[70] Within Abimelech's attempt to exonerate Sarah of any dishonor, he may be continuing the ruse and compromising his integrity by participating in the scheme.[71] Or, he may be seen as a gallant king

69. Hamilton, *Genesis 18–50*, 70. He cites several occurrences of this or a similar expression, including Gen. 32:21 (NRSV 32:20); Exod. 23:8; 1 Sam. 12:3; Job 9:24. Cf. von Rad, *Genesis*, 229.

70. Von Rad (*Genesis*, 229) contends that "the fact that he calls Abraham Sarah's 'brother' is apparently spoken legally and officially. In this way he avoids compromising Abraham."

71. Von Rad (*Genesis*, 229) argues that Abimelech would be discrediting himself in giving gifts to dishonorable people. He reasons that Abimelech's effort is focused on demonstrating that both Abraham and Sarah are honorable. Wenham (*Genesis 16–50*, 74) sees Abimelech's action as evidence of his resentment toward Abraham.

ready to act on behalf of others and not only in his own interest. Such a characterization places him in stark contrast to Abraham, whose behavior is laden with self-interest even to his wife's detriment.

Last, Sarah's place in the narrative is seen in the representation of her identity. According to Abimelech, Sarah also said that she is Abraham's sister (Gen. 20:5). In arguing his innocence to the Deity, the king suggests that he attempted to verify Abraham's claim and that in doing so Sarah also confirmed that she was his sister. Thus while Abimelech then refers to Sarah as Abraham's sister, the Deity does not. Nowhere in the narrative does the Deity acknowledge that Sarah is Abraham's sister. The skill of the narrator is that since the information was also withheld when Sarah was introduced in Gen. 11:29, there is no corroboration of Abraham's claim. Likewise, the narrator's skill opens the suspicion that Abraham is deceiving Abimelech even in this claim. Even so, that deception will not alter the Deity's regard for Abraham. Instead, the Deity puts the power to heal Abimelech in Abraham's hand—namely, that he would "pray" (*pālal*) for Abimelech. While it is not a direct oppression of Abimelech and his household, this is not the only time that the Deity is portrayed as overlooking the faults of the favored and placing the *harmed* under the control of the one who is responsible for the harm (cf. 16:9).[72]

Abimelech and His Nation

Throughout the narrative, Abimelech is portrayed as a man of noble character in his dealings with others. As a ruler his power extends over his immediate household, the people of Gerar, and others who reside in Gerar as resident aliens. However, his taking another man's wife conflicts with other aspects of his behavior. The narrative does not give insight into the process used to take Sarah or the reason that she was taken. Unlike Gen. 12:11, where her "beauty" (*yāpeh*) is cited as the reason for the attraction to her, nothing is mentioned of her beauty in Gen. 20. The narrator makes explicit that Abimelech the king sent for Sarah and took her, whereas in 12:15 she is taken without specification as to who took her to Pharaoh's house.

Abimelech is also identified as "king" (*melek*), and Sarah is identified as Abraham's "wife" (*'iššâ*). In introducing the characters, the narrator signals an inequitable comparison of two persons, the functional identity of the male in contrast to the relational identity of the woman. Abimelech's relational identity is noticeably absent: it is mentioned that he has a wife, but he is not identified as "husband." Rather the woman is labeled as his wife (Gen. 20:17). It is also ironic that Abimelech is portrayed as a man of one wife; Sarah would be the second wife. The

---

72. Notably, Hagar is told to return and to allow herself to be oppressed (see chap. 5).

irony is that men of means are usually noted to be polygynous, having more than one wife at a time—David, Solomon, Abraham, and Jacob.[73] Abraham at this time would have had both Sarah and Hagar as wives (16:3). In taking Sarah as his wife, Abimelech would also become polygynous; and Sarah would be polyandrous—having multiple husbands at the same time. The narrative implies that having only one wife prior to taking Sarah would mean that Sarah would most likely not disappear into a harem. Her visibility and accessibility are the fundamental challenges of Abimelech's claim not to have even approached her in a sexual manner. It is further noteworthy that as a king he has not acquired more wives, and he belies the perception that Abraham may be killed by those who desire to take Sarah.

Whatever the source of Abraham's conception, it clearly does not fit Abimelech. One may find a better fit with Shechem, the prince who rapes Dinah (Gen. 34),[74] or with David, king of Judah, who takes Bathsheba in spite of the fact that she is another man's wife (2 Sam. 11). When seen together, these men demonstrate that there is not a simple portrayal of all men of power in the way that they treat women. Abimelech again stands as a noble example of men, and specifically of rulers, who show regard for a woman.

Abimelech asserts his innocence as one who did not knowingly take another man's wife (Gen. 20:5). Most notably, even before he defends himself against the charge and indictment that the Deity brought against him, he attempts to avert the destruction of his nation. Thus he challenges the Deity to decide whether to destroy an "innocent" (ṣaddîq) nation (20:4). His fundamental argument is permeated by the concept of retribution—that wrongdoing leads to punishment—and specifically that a nation ought not to be punished if it has not merited that punishment. His assertion is not that the nation is free of any committed infractions, but that it is not guilty of deliberately offending the Deity in taking Sarah. Abimelech, in this confrontation, challenges the justice of the Deity. When he confronts Abraham, he also makes the nation his first priority, accusing Abraham of doing something against Gerar (20:9–10). His sense of responsibility is further noted in his challenge to Abraham to be accountable about how he (Abimelech) sinned (ḥāṭā᾿) against Abraham in a way that caused him (Abraham) to bring such a "great sin" (ḥăṭā᾿â gĕdōlâ) on Abimelech and his kingdom. Abimelech again implies that there is a link between sin and punishment. Some speculate that the "great sin" is the adultery.[75] Consequently, if Abraham

---

73. Nahor, Abraham's brother, is also cited as having a wife and a concubine (Gen. 22:20–24).

74. Cf. Jacobs, "Love, Honor, and Violence."

75. See Hamilton, *Genesis 18–50*, 67.

brought the sin of adultery to Gerar, then Abimelech did not initiate the sin and is not guilty of it. Clearly, he is arguing that the actions of one man brought adversity to an entire nation.[76]

When Abimelech becomes aware of the deception and the role that he has inadvertently played in it, he is concerned about how his actions will affect his people—even though he is threatened with death unless he returns Sarah to Abraham.[77] Additionally, he is told that Abraham would intervene for him on that condition. Abimelech vehemently accuses Abraham, claiming that Abraham's actions are unjust, and arguing in essence: *I have done nothing that you should act toward me in this way.* Even with that awareness, Abimelech returns Sarah to Abraham and even gives gifts to Abraham. It is striking that Abimelech had not given such gifts when he took Sarah as Pharaoh had done (Gen. 12:16). He now gives gifts and offers Abraham a place in his country rather than promptly expelling him. One might at first think that this is a measure of consideration for Abraham or even a way of appeasing him; however, Abimelech's action of creating an opportunity for Abraham to stay may be an effort to guarantee his healing and the restoration of the fertility of his wife and slaves. It would most likely be a period of time before the efficacy of Abraham's intercession would be confirmed; so in the meanwhile having him close by would be prudent.

Abraham's Role in the Resolution

The Deity gives Abraham the power to remove adversity by making the removal contingent on Abraham's prayer. Thus the Deity characterizes Abraham as a prophet (*nābî'*) who will pray for Abimelech if he returns Sarah to Abraham (Gen. 20:7). Clearly, the Deity favors Abraham and empowers him as intercessor, one who will "pray" (*pālal*) on Abimelech's behalf. The irony of the narrative is that Abraham is entrusted with a task that would alleviate the suffering of those upon whom his behavior brought suffering; but even more shocking is that Abraham is already prejudiced against the people for whom he is to intercede. Gordon Wenham contends that Abimelech was not as innocent as he claimed and may have had sexual intercourse had not the Deity intervened and made him sick.[78] The sickness is viewed as a deterrent to sexual intercourse;[79] in that context, however, it would be virtually impossible to know if

---

76. Hamilton, *Genesis 18–50*, 67. He compares Gen. 18 and 20: "If a city can be saved by the presence of ten virtuous people, an empire can be dismantled by the actions of one guilty person."

77. See Adams, "Self-Love," 509–12, regarding the concept and development of unselfish self-love.

78. Wenham, *Genesis 16–50*, 71.

79. Wenham, *Genesis 16–50*, 74–75.

one is infertile without sexual intercourse accompanied by the lack of conception.

The efficacy of Abraham's prayer is that it removed the illness from Abimelech and opened the wombs of the women in his household. The nature of Abimelech's illness is not noted; however, the mention of the closed wombs may indicate that the duration of the situation lasted more than a few weeks. After the prayer, the confirmation of its efficacy would be that the women conceived (Gen. 20:18). Undoubtedly, Abraham is able to intercede and secure results on behalf of others. The irony is that in this particular situation the effect of his prayer is the healing of the women's infertility while his own wife remains infertile. Why was the efficacy of his prayer confined to the women of Abimelech's household at the exclusion of Sarah? Was infertility part of the safeguard that the Deity placed on Sarah to ensure that she did not become pregnant, should she have sexual intercourse with someone other than Abraham during the time of the itinerant lifestyle? It is tempting to entertain such a notion unless one remembers that she was in Canaan for a ten-year period without conceiving. In any case, after the Gerar experience, the Deity fulfilled the promise and she conceived and bore Isaac. Since the narrative insists that Abimelech did not touch her (20:6), it rules out any possibility that Abimelech could be Isaac's father. It therefore becomes clear why the narrative is so insistent about nonsexual contact in Gen. 20 but not in Gen. 12, where paternity issues were of no concern. Nonetheless, Gen. 20 raises other questions: If Abraham is an effective intercessor in matters of infertility, why did he not pray for Sarah? If he did, why was his prayer ineffective?[80] Abraham was apparently not authorized to intercede on Sarah's behalf in the matter of her infertility as he was authorized to do on behalf of Abimelech's household. Consequently, Sarah remains infertile while a solution is readily at hand.

Conclusion

These two narratives reinforce several perspectives. First, God selects people to become agents in God's plans. As such, Abraham's actions in his domains (private and public) are not evaluated as reprehensible nor is any punishment directed at him. Rather part of his power is that he is a selected agent, favored as essential to the Deity's plan. One cannot escape the narrative's view of Abraham as one who compels the Deity's favor and protection. Abraham's existence displays the difference between being essential and being dispensable.

80. Cf. Wenham, *Genesis 16–50*, 74–75.

Second, the act of selecting is itself indicative of the Deity's character. The Deity's power is depicted through the orchestrating of events toward a particular outcome. As such, the Deity's domain is formed by a purpose that incorporates both temporal and spatial dimensions. Accordingly, the Deity's plan is defined and the roles of the agents within are prescribed; the Deity is portrayed as one who is biased and who does not regard all persons as equal agents within the domain.

Third, being privileged does not define one's treatment of others. Rather, the person's character and other domain-specific aspects will determine how the privilege is manifested. In both narratives Abraham's character pales in comparison to the rulers he encounters. He bases his behavior on a misconceived notion about others. Even when his misconception is disaffirmed, he sustains his behavior.

Fourth, being privileged does not automatically exclude one from adversity. Rather, adversity may be a by-product of one's privilege, a facet of one's dispensability. In connection with the previous observation, Sarah is noticeably passive in both accounts, seen only through the narrator's and Abimelech's representation. In Abimelech's case, she is implicated in the deception and perhaps for this reason needed to be exonerated in the eyes of those closest to her. For the narrator, as part of Abraham's life and purpose, Sarah is intermittently useful but clearly dispensable.

4

To Persuade and to Deceive

Isaac and Jacob (Genesis 27–28)

Introduction

Though few would dispute that deception has become a normative pattern in human interactions, debates persist about the biblical views of and the ethics of deception. These debates are prevalent in the interpretation of texts that attest the concept of deception.[1] With the goal of examining deception as a model of persuasion, in this chapter I incorporate some of the debated issues to explore the concept of deception in Gen. 27–28. One issue is the blurred boundaries of deception illustrated in the question: Who is deceiving whom in the Isaac-Jacob situation? Specifically, I explore elements of deception within the family domain (e.g., Isaac-Jacob and Rebekah-Isaac) and examine them as factors that define or facilitate deception. I propose that the text illustrates the tension between deception and its efficacy in achieving a desired outcome that may be congruous with a divine plan.

---

1. For example, see Esther Fuchs, "Who Is Hiding the Truth? Deceptive Women and Biblical Androcentrism," in *Feminist Perspectives on Biblical Scholarship*, ed. Adela Yarbro Collins (Chico, CA: Scholars Press, 1985), 137–44; Mieke Bal, "Tricky Thematics," *Semeia* 42 (1988): 148–49.

Perspectives and Concerns

The narrative illustrates a persuasion process where the specific goal is to deceive, "to cause someone to believe something that is not true."[2] Some are inclined to distinguish between lies and deception while conceding that deception is a form of lying. Accordingly, lying is defined as "the intentional prevarication of facts through the manipulation of language. Deception is the intentional production of (a) misleading message(s)—through linguistic or other means—or the intentional concealment of required information."[3] This popular definition points to the fundamental aspects of deception, including the deliberateness, the interpersonal dimension, and the use of persuasion as the decisive component. In light of these aspects, in this investigation I focus on the biblical narratives and propose that there are decisive characteristics that define deception, and that deception is a product of its contexts and the ability to persuade others of the viability of what is presented to them.[4]

With regard to deception within Gen. 27–28, it is essential to understand the family domain as the context in which it occurs. The nature of the biblical text is the first challenge in discerning its representation of deception. While it is not the focus of this chapter to delineate the nature of the biblical text, several points are noteworthy. First, biblical texts in their literary contexts constitute multivalent systems of ideas/concepts and conceptual frameworks that are signaled by conventions of the texts. Second, texts constitute the primary restraint to any interpretation that uses them as the basis of dialogue. Third, texts have limited sets of meanings made up by their generative conceptual frameworks.[5]

The Gen. 27–28 narrative is part of the conceptual framework of the promise-fulfillment pattern in the patriarchal history (Gen. 12–50). This pattern is facilitated by the idea that history is controlled, orchestrated, and executed by the Deity in the lives of the created beings, particularly the "chosen ones." While human beings are not passive entities in the execution of the Deity's plans, human plans, choices, and actions are secondary to the divine plans. Ultimately, the Deity uses the contingencies created by human actions and thus tolerates a wide range of human behavior, particularly the behaviors of the chosen ones around whom the plan is constructed and

---

2. *Oxford American Dictionary*, s.v. "Deceive."

3. Fuchs, "Way of Women," 68. She adds: "The concept of deception is predicated upon the expected correspondence of semiosis and reality, language and fact. To deceive is to signify something to which no real state of things corresponds." See J. L. A. Garcia, "Lies and the Vices of Deception," *Faith and Philosophy* 15.4 (1998): 514–37.

4. Cf. Reardon, *Persuasion and Practice*, 4–20.

5. Jacobs, "Methodological Challenges," 23–25.

executed. Accordingly, the Gen. 27–28 narrative addresses two questions: Who will be heir to the promise made to Abraham? Who decides?

If both Esau and Jacob are legitimate heirs, why choose one over the other? The conceptual framework indicates that the divine plan is formed on mutually exclusive categories. Consequently, some are chosen, some are not, and not everyone is equally important to the divine plan. Yet, while the presence of Esau and Jacob violates the boundaries defined to exclude Ishmael—Abraham's firstborn son—as the legitimate heir to the promise, it affirms that the effective execution of the plan requires the Deity to maintain the domain where people exist in a hierarchical relationship with one another. Gen. 27–28 illustrates a system based on inequity and the power of the system to persuade those involved of their places in it. Those who function well within that domain are aware that some people are central actors, others are supporting actors, while others form the crowd in the background. Inclusion and exclusion are inherent in any plan where only some are selected as essential. Jacob and Esau, sons of Isaac, are born into the plan in which they will exist in a hierarchical relationship. They are twins born to be two nations, separate and unequal in the plan. In this respect, the divine plan uses criteria that equate people's functional worth to their essential worth. In this equation, some are collateral to the effectiveness of the plan. Thus one son will be stronger than the other, and one will serve while the other will be served (Gen. 25:23). Deception and the quest for privilege enter into this divine plan as vehicles and displays of power and persuasion.

To Persuade and to Deceive

Parents in the Family Dynamics

Parents bring a family history to their interaction with spouse and children, and we can see these inherited dynamics in Isaac's family. Isaac is positioned as the head of the family because of the ethos in which he lived rather than his manifestation of power in his family—he is the male head of household.

ISAAC

In Isaac, one sees a man who lives in the shadow of others, especially his father. His life is plagued by the injustices of his parents against his half brother Ishmael and the separation from Ishmael because of that injustice. He would undoubtedly be aware that Ishmael is a firstborn son in name only and is ostracized from the family, though still counted among Abraham's children. Isaac's status is also the product of his father's

concerns and the manifestation of these concerns. Accordingly, in recognition of the Deity's promise to him, Abraham gave his inheritance to
Isaac and gifts to the other sons; he isolated Isaac from his siblings by
sending them away (Gen. 25:6). Consequently, Isaac is in the privileged
position of designated heir and a man of wealth but is isolated because
of that privilege. While this may have been the act of a protective parent
trying to secure Isaac's position and wealth, this is also the action of a
parent infusing his experience of separation into his son's life. In an attempt to resolve the conflict among their herdsmen, Abraham separated
from Lot, his nephew (13:1–12).[6] Abraham's behavior in resolving the
conflict may be an example of his concern to maintain harmony within
the clan. However, the relational costs are a different issue. He is the
older relative, the uncle, who separates from Lot and destroys a family
connection. Thus, as he had done earlier in his life at the prospect of his
death, Abraham solves a difficulty by separating people.

Isaac probably learned lessons from his father that helped to define
his function within his own household. In this respect, his dependence
on his father is noteworthy. His father decided that it was time for Isaac
to marry, made the arrangements, and Isaac simply got married. This
may be seen as Abraham performing his fatherly duty for his son, but
it could also be seen as Abraham's dominance in Isaac's life. Notably,
Abraham took a wife (Gen. 11:29), Esau took wives (26:34), Jacob worked
for his wife (29:18–20), but Isaac was given a wife selected for him and
delivered to him (24:62–67). The dominance of his father made for a
demure son who lived out his father's legacy with little leeway. Isaac
appears to be conditioned to respond rather than be one, like Jacob,
who takes the initiative. He carries the memory of a father who was
willing to kill him to obey the Deity's command (22:1–19); although he
survived the ordeal, his awareness and recollection of it are noticeably
absent from the subsequent narratives. One can only surmise that he
learned from that and other experiences that for Abraham children are
subsidiary to a larger purpose. Within the purpose domain, if there is
a conflict of purposes, Abraham will adhere to the Deity's purpose and
minimize his or any other interest or purpose (cf. 21:9–14).

Clearly, in the biblical text Isaac does not interact with God as much as
his father, Abraham, or his son, Jacob. Quite understandably and in light of
his experience, Isaac may have learned to limit contact with the Deity who
commanded his death. Why would he desire to have sustained interaction
with God? I agree with W. Lee Humphreys: God's savage test of Abraham
may well have had unintended consequences for both God and Isaac.
"God's abuse of Isaac may well trigger an unexpected and unexpressed

6. Cf. Hamilton, *Genesis 1–17*, 391; von Rad, *Genesis,* 171.

guilt that leads him now to leave him largely alone. And this may lead Isaac to rest content with the absence of the sort of engagement with God that marked his father's life."[7] Consequently, it would not be surprising if Isaac is numbed by experiences with his father or is inclined to subject others to what he experienced. Isaac seems to fall somewhere in the middle—not altogether passive but also not proactive in defining and achieving specific goals. He lives his father's legacy and is reminded that God's presence and blessing are because of his father (Gen. 26:2–3, 24; cf. 26:28–29). That the Deity recalls Abraham in the best light sustains Isaac as one link in the actualization of the promise made to Abraham.[8] From this perspective, whether alive or dead, Abraham is a dominant force in Isaac's life as the starting point of a legacy that Isaac is perpetuating.

Isaac's intercession for Rebekah to have children further illustrates another aspect of Isaac's involvement in his family dynamics (Gen. 25:21). His intercession is striking because in all other instances of infertile women, the husbands do not intervene on behalf of their wives. Usually the women voice their complaint to their husbands regarding issues related to their infertility. Sarah complains to Abraham regarding the tension between her and Hagar due to Hagar's pregnancy (16:5); Rachel complains to Jacob demanding that he give her children (30:1–2); Hannah pleads with God (1 Sam. 1:9–18); but none of the men respond by interceding for their wives. Isaac's action is thus different. Perhaps his sensitivity is born out of deference to his mother or to his understanding of the significance of having an heir. In this respect, he embodies the urgency usually observed in the infertile women.[9] The family line and the further progression toward the actualization of the promise articulated to his father hinges on his ability to produce an heir. The urgency is for himself as the bearer of the legacy and for his wife who will produce the heir. It is, therefore, natural that he bonds with the children born because of his prayer. Favoring a person is also a natural part of the relational dynamics into which he was born, and so he favors one son above the other. The narrator illustrates this by indicating that Isaac "loved" ('āhēb) Esau because of Esau's skill in hunting and Isaac's love of meat. Thus the narrator disavows that the favor was due to other behaviors or to Esau's character (Gen. 25:28; cf. 26:34).[10]

7. Humphreys, *Character of God*, 165.

8. Cf. Humphreys, *Character of God*, 162, 168.

9. In Judg. 13 Manoah's inquiry of God is a response to his wife's announcement that an angel visited her and instructed her regarding a child that she would bear—the child being Samson.

10. The narrator does not explain why Rebekah favored Jacob over Esau. In labeling the favor as love ('āhēb) the narrator nonetheless leaves open the possibility that in loving one child the parent does not love the other at all or as much.

Finally, the Deity also blessed Isaac in his endeavors, even when Isaac claimed Rebekah as his sister. As a result, Abimelech cautions the people not to harm Isaac and his wife, designating the death penalty for any who do (Gen. 26:10–11). Isaac is therefore empowered by this protection to live safely in a foreign country with Rebekah as his wife. Additionally, Isaac sows the land, experiences great success, and within the year accumulates further wealth (26:12–14). His success was the result of God's blessing, but the people of Gerar were "jealous" (qānāʾ) of him (26:14). If there was a reason to harm him it would be their jealousy, but Isaac was protected under Abimelech's authority. Even so, the one who protected him was also trying to get rid of him. Speaking as the authority in the land, Abimelech expelled Isaac and had no qualms about admitting that Isaac had become more "powerful" (ʾāṣam) than he and his people (26:16; cf. Exod. 10:28). Isaac seems to compel the same response as the Israelites living in Egypt (Exod. 1:7–9, 20) and the same response that Pharaoh voiced to Moses (10:28).[11]

Although Isaac had wealth as part of his inheritance, it alone does not give him power (cf. Abraham in Egypt, Gen. 12:10–20). His power was also constituted by the protection that he had from the most powerful man in the country and from the Deity. Even so, others tried to run him out of the country and make life difficult for him by claiming possession of the wells he had dug (cf. 21:23–33).[12] Presumably, it did not matter that Isaac and his men had dug the wells, or that he was allowed to do so. The men of Gerar argued that whatever water Isaac (a foreigner) found belonged to them. Isaac responded by digging more wells, and true to form the herdsmen of Gerar also claimed them. In dealing with Isaac in this manner, they demonstrated the semblance of power that they had within the limits of the king's orders. Abimelech commanded that none should "touch" (nāgaʿ) Isaac, and they did not touch him. Rather, they used their nationalistic claims against him—Isaac was a resident alien and they were citizens. In essence, they argued that as a resident alien he had no claim to the natural resources of their land.

Isaac moved around within Gerar to avoid conflict with the men of Gerar, but they persisted until he departed and went to Beer-sheba (Gen. 26:23). There the Deity assured him of the divine presence with him

11. Abimelech compares Isaac not directly to himself but to the others more powerful "than us" (nû, first common plural suffix). Cf. Wenham, Genesis 16–50, 191; Hamilton, Genesis 18–50, 201.

12. Abimelech and Abraham had a treaty that allowed Abraham and his descendants to use the well, so harassing Isaac would violate the earlier treaty. Cf. Wenham, Genesis 16–50, 192.

and reaffirmed the promise made to Abraham.[13] In Abimelech's eyes, Isaac's power came from the Deity, who was with Isaac and blessed him. Whether or not the Deity blessed him because of his father, Isaac experienced blessings and protection (26:24), and his wife Rebekah is key to his experience. Consequently, Abimelech tried to make a covenant with Isaac to guarantee that Isaac would deal peacefully with the Gerarites as they had dealt peacefully with him (26:26–29). The basis of the king's request belied the mistreatment to which Isaac was subjected and his departure from Gerar. The people did not cause him physical harm, but in harassing him they were harming him.

REBEKAH

After traveling a distance to meet her husband for the first time, Rebekah enters the family with the advantage of being a wife chosen for her lineage and suitability (Gen. 24:52–59). Isaac's father had set the criterion for choosing a spouse (24:1–9)—marriage with someone within the tribe (endogamy; 24:3–4, 15).[14] Yet Isaac was exposed to various nations as he journeyed with Abraham, who had fathered Ishmael his firstborn with his wife Hagar, an Egyptian (16:3).[15] Apparently, while a foreign woman is suitable as a surrogate and acceptable as a wife, her acceptability is due more to her status as a maid than her foreign origin.[16] Abraham appears to have had a harmonious relationship with the Hittites, who sold him the field where he buried his wife Sarah (23:17–23). Yet, in spite of the relationship with foreigners, Abraham deemed the women unsuitable marriage partners for his son Isaac.[17] Rebekah enters the family as a suitable spouse—indeed, the ideal woman. Her inherent power is her suitability as spouse vis-à-vis the unsuitability of the women in her surroundings. Later her views regarding the Hittite women would no doubt

13. Isaac is told in Gen. 26:24, "Do not be afraid ['al-tîrā'], I am with you" (kî-'ittĕkā 'ānōkî); cf. Isa. 41:10; Jer. 1:8; 42:11. God also assures Abraham and Hagar with the words, "Do not be afraid" (Gen. 15:1; 21:17).

14. Rebekah is Isaac's second cousin—daughter of Bethuel, Abraham's nephew (Gen. 22:23). In her genealogy, her mother is named, perhaps as a further indication of her suitability. Nahor also had children with a concubine (22:24).

15. See chap. 5 for further discussion of Hagar's status as maid-wife—maid to Sarah and wife to Abraham.

16. The ideology behind the tendency to label Hagar as "concubine" (pîlegeš) rather than "wife" ('iššâ), the label assigned to her in the text, reflects what Young-Bruehl (Anatomy of Prejudices, 428–29) terms "sexist-racism," a form of sexism usually found in polygamous societies. Young-Bruehl further argues that, in this ideological framework, the tendency is to "split [the] object world into madonnas and whores and assign the whore role to a not-mother woman of a darker color or lower class" (428–29). See chap. 5 for further discussion.

17. Esau saw things differently and married two Hittite women (Gen. 26:34).

influence her efforts to present them as unsuitable marital partners for her son Jacob (cf. 27:46).

Rebekah arrives into a privileged status that continues throughout her life. She has a dowry and access to her husband's wealth. She has the protection of her family; and although infertile, she voices no complaint like the other infertile women, namely, Sarah, Rachel, and Hannah. Eventually she becomes pregnant and is told that the older child (Esau) will serve the younger (Jacob), but she loves the younger child (Gen. 25:28). With her sons, she and Isaac journey to Gerar in obedience to the Deity (26:1–5). There Isaac attempts to pass her off as his sister. Like his father, Abraham, Isaac reasons that he might be killed because of Rebekah's beauty (26:7). Unlike his father, who effectively executed the ruse, Isaac betrays himself because he still acts like Rebekah's husband (26:8). She is not subjected to the polyandrous situation that Sarah endured when Abraham allowed her to be taken by the pharaoh and by Abimelech (Gen. 12 and 20). Rebekah's husband becomes rich, presumably adding to the possessions he inherited from Abraham (25:6; 26:12–14). In all, Rebekah epitomizes privilege and security. Even her infertility, the most challenging situation that she faces as a woman, is handled for her.

With this family history, one cannot convincingly argue that Rebekah's ruse is motivated by her powerlessness or lack of options to achieve her goal.[18] If anything, she appears as an insistent woman. She has her way regarding her favorite son, not so much because she acknowledges the Deity's plan, but more because of her privileged position.[19] Unlike her husband, who does not take the initiative regarding his sons' spouses, Rebekah has clearly formulated opinions about whom they should marry. In this way, she is like Abraham in wanting her sons to marry endogomously. Unlike Abraham, Rebekah does not have a harmonious relationship with the Hittites, most plausibly not because of their behavior toward her but because of her bias against them and her privilege as a suitable wife. Like Abraham, Rebekah's use of deception may arise out of an effort to maintain an advantage and to yield one's power to fulfill one's desires.

---

18. Contrast Alice O. Bellis, *Helpmates, Harlots, Heroes: Women's Stories in the Hebrew Bible* (Louisville: Westminster John Knox, 1994), 82. She argues that Rebekah is "the subordinate female who must maneuver around the male structures to achieve her mission."

19. Daniel J. Elazar, "Jacob and Esau and the Emergence of the Jewish People," *Judaism* 43.3 (1994): 296–97; Joseph Rackman, "Was Isaac Deceived?" *Judaism* 43.1 (1994): 39–41. From Rackman's perspective, Rebekah is concerned to ensure that Jacob has material blessings and that he does not have the responsibility of laboring for his wealth. Her concern is a result of her work in her father's household.

Deceiver and Deceived

The situation facilitated by Rebekah exhibits the complexity of deception. Specifically, the line between deceiver and deceived may be blurred if both parties use the same circumstances to execute a deception. Those who are deceived are persuaded to be and consent to be deceived. This is the paradox of deceit and part of the dilemma. One does not consciously consent to be deceived; therefore, if one is conscious that someone is attempting to deceive her/him and knows the matter about which the deceit is attempted, it is unlikely that one can be deceived. Yet one may unknowingly consent to exhibit the behavior that is consistent with the goal of the deception. Fundamentally, deception is a dynamic process that necessitates effective persuasion. The deceiver holds the power in that she/he regulates or controls the portrait of reality and the perceived connections between occurrences and their meaning.

JACOB-ISAAC

Who is deceiving whom? While it is clear that Jacob intends to deceive Isaac, one must also examine whether Isaac is also perpetuating a deception of his own. The brilliance of the narrative is that it is a tool used to persuade. Does it effectively illustrate that Isaac was deceived, or does it create ambiguity to show that Isaac may also be deceiving? The narrative may suggest that there is much more to Isaac than the passive figure he appears to be. As Abraham's heir he receives little attention; but when he is the main figure he repeats his father's behavior (Gen. 26). At first glance, Isaac appears to function under the radar and does not seem to introduce any new challenges into the family line. Nonetheless, another perspective on Isaac may suggest that he facilitates a dilemma in the family.

Jacob as the deceiver. First, Jacob's participation in the situation with Isaac is born out of his motivation as well as Rebekah's. He is not coerced into a behavior that he disdained. Rather, his mother hears Isaac's plan to bless Esau and "commands" (*ṣāwâ*) Jacob to follow her instructions. Noticeably, what she commands him to do is slightly different from what Isaac said.[20] She claims that Isaac intends to bless Esau in YHWH's presence; Isaac does not mention this aspect. Yet upon hearing this,

---

20. Cf. Isaac's formulation "before I die" (*běṭerem 'āmût*, Gen. 27:4), and Rebekah's formulation, "before YHWH before I die" (27:7), signifying in YHWH's presence. The variation has led Sarna (*Genesis*, 190) to posit that "before YHWH" (*lipnê yhwh*) connotes YHWH's approval. Hamilton (*Genesis 18–50*, 214) proposes that the variation does not indicate such approval. Like Eve's variation on the prohibition (2:17 vis-à-vis 3:2–3), Rebekah's variation gives an added dimension to what is said and introduces another aspect that is not part of the formulation that she purports to represent.

Jacob is not deterred at the prospect of committing a deceitful act in the Deity's presence.[21] That his mother commands him to participate would not absolve him of his responsibility in the ruse.[22] He is persuaded to participate and consents to do so. As evident in his objections, Jacob is not deceived into participating. Instead, he understands his mother's plan and that it intends to deceive Isaac. His hesitation to participate derives from his concern that he not be adversely affected by judgment incurred because of the deception—namely, bringing a "curse" (qĕlālâ) on himself rather than a "blessing" (bĕrākâ, Gen. 27:12). Instead, he is willing to allow his mother to shoulder the entire blame and curse rather than to incur any punishment. Ironically, while his mother is willing to risk being cursed for her son, Jacob is unwilling to take responsibility even for his participation. Unlike Moses' objections used to refuse his commission (Exod. 3:11–4:13), Jacob's objections set the stage for his acceptance and participation—namely, making sure that all important matters were covered.[23] His objection is based on Esau's physical characteristics compared to his (hairy versus smooth) and whether his father will discern the difference (Gen. 27:11–12). The concern and envisioned scenario is that Isaac "feels" (māšaš) him, knows that he is Jacob, and concludes that Jacob is mocking (tāʿaʿ) him.[24] Clearly, Jacob is aware of Isaac's mental acuity and does not assume his father's senility.[25] The mockery would be to assume that Isaac, because of his impaired vision, would not know the difference between his sons.

Like Jacob, others have attempted to deceive the visually impaired.[26] They assume that the visual impairment deprives the person of other senses. This is not Jacob's initial assumption, but his mother seems to be a victim of this misconception. On this basis, Rebekah clothes Jacob in Esau's garments and covers his arms with animal skin (Gen. 27:15–16). The hilarity of the manifested plan (a man being disguised by his mother) is offset only by the magnitude of what they hope to gain. At this juncture, the narrator's portrait of Rebekah is detailed, showing a woman with a

---

21. See Hamilton, *Genesis 18–50*, 216; Meir Sternberg, *The Poetics of Biblical Narrative: Ideological Literature and the Drama of Reading* (Bloomington: Indiana University Press, 1985), 390–93.

22. Hamilton, *Genesis 18–50*, 216.

23. Cf. Brevard S. Childs, *The Book of Exodus: A Critical Theological Commentary*, Old Testament Library (Philadelphia: Westminster, 1974), 71, 77–79.

24. Another instance of mockery is mocking the prophet. It is used with its synonyms *lāʿab* "to jest" (2 Chron. 36:16) to characterize what was done to the prophet whom God sent to the people. Other synonyms include *śāḥaq* "mock, laugh, play" (Gen. 21:6; Lam. 1:7), and *lāʿag* "mock, deride" (Isa. 37:22).

25. Hamilton, *Genesis 18–50*, 212; Sternberg, *Poetics of Biblical Narrative*, 350.

26. For example, Jeroboam's wife attempted to deceive Ahijah the prophet (1 Kings 14:1–6); see chap. 7.

strong hold on her sons' lives. Her married son still has his clothes in his mother's house. Bearing in mind that the reason for the clothes is to convey Esau's scent, one should not presume that these are old clothes from his youth. Likewise, the detailed portrait reflects a woman in control enough to change Jacob's mind about Isaac's mental state.

The second aspect of the Jacob-Isaac interchange is Jacob's decisive effort to accomplish the deceit. Isaac attempts to verify the identity of the man in front of him with a simple question, "Which one of my sons are you?"[27] Isaac does not lead by suggesting the desired answer to the question. Yet Jacob responds by declaring that he is Esau. Perhaps he says too much or assumes that disguising his body somehow disguises his voice. Rather than saying as little as necessary, Jacob embellishes his response not only by stating that he is Esau but that he is the first-born, and that he has carried out Isaac's instructions. As if he had not said enough, he also tells Isaac to eat the food he has brought and to bless him (Gen. 27:19). Immediately, the narrative confirms that Isaac is mentally alert enough to recognize Jacob's voice. Isaac's suspicion is heightened; his repeated questions may reveal Isaac's mistrust and attempts to persuade himself to discount his suspicions.[28] With each question, Jacob has the opportunity to end the deception, but he does not. He carries out each step to accomplish his goal of being blessed by his father. Jacob's steps into further deception are punctuated by Isaac's subsequent questions. Regarding time, Isaac is suspicious that his son could execute the instruction in such a timely manner (27:20). Jacob attributes his success to YHWH, Isaac's Deity, and he is not reluctant to implicate the Deity in his ruse. His decisiveness demonstrates a reckless abandon in achieving his goal. The narrative does not specify any divine assistance for Jacob. Nonetheless, while his claim may be outrageous and the narrative is silent about any divine assistance, his success cannot be presumed apart from that assistance. Jacob implies that he hunted, but the narrative tells where Rebekah got the meat, namely, from the flock (27:9).[29]

Being unconvinced by the incongruity between the voice and the answer to his questions, Isaac does what Jacob anticipated that he would

27. Thus Hamilton, *Genesis 18–50*, 217. Cf. NRSV "Who are you, my son?" Hamilton (217n2) compares the question to Naomi's question to Ruth: "Is that you, daughter?" He reasons that in both cases the issue is establishing the identity of someone when vision is obscured—by Isaac's physical condition, and by the darkness of night for Naomi. While agreeing with Hamilton's perspective, Wenham (*Genesis 16–50*, 208) nonetheless follows the NRSV on this point.

28. Von Rad, *Genesis*, 277–78.

29. See chap. 7 for discussion of Judah's similar use of information as a method of deceiving Tamar.

do. Isaac declares his intention to "feel" or "grope" (*māšaš*) Jacob for the specific purpose of verifying whether he is Esau. The image is not of a passing contact but of a thorough search to verify one's suspicion.[30] One wonders that Jacob would subject himself to such scrutiny while wearing the animal skin. Yet even with the magnitude of the matter at hand, the comical display is undeniable. Jacob's audacity alone may have contributed to Isaac's willingness to play along, because who would do something so unthinkable as to parade around in an animal skin and be misguided enough to think that another person could not tell the difference between animal and human skin? One is also perplexed that Isaac feels the hands and confirms that they are Esau's. It must be that Esau is extremely "hairy" (*śā'ir*, Gen. 25:25; 27:11)! Did Isaac not feel Jacob's face or feet where there was no animal skin (27:16)? Further, Isaac appears to be alone with Jacob and does not call for help to confirm his son's identity; he seems certain that it is not Esau before him. Nonetheless, Isaac concludes it is Esau's hand but Jacob's voice.

Given the importance of the event that is to happen, one would think that the scope of his doubt would deter Isaac's original intent, that is, if he intended to bless Esau. On the contrary, Isaac forges ahead with his plan and blesses Jacob.[31] Isaac eats the food prepared by his wife, drinks, and even then he does not confirm his suspicion. Could he not tell the difference between his son's and his wife's cooking? The reticence of the narrator concerning Isaac's reaction to the food is salient since all the other points of suspicion are named and investigated—timing, hearing, touching. Still, the uncertainty leads Isaac to request a kiss from his son and to give him an opportunity to smell his son. In this final attempt at verification of identity, Isaac follows the path laid out for him in the ruse. Rebekah already anticipated that smell would be an important factor and dressed Jacob in Esau's clothes. Isaac smells Jacob and concludes that he is Esau. If one assumes that Isaac is deceived, it seems that he wants to be persuaded that Esau is in front of him. He may not have been entirely persuaded, but he was sufficiently convinced to proceed. If Isaac is deceived, he consents to the deception by making a crucial decision while faced with alarming uncertainty.

30. The term *māšaš* is used to describe futile searches, e.g., in Laban's situation where he rummages through the tent trying to find the household gods (Gen. 31:34, 37). It has the connotation of groping in the dark, either because of the darkness of night (Job 5:14; 12:25), or, as in Laban's case, uncertainty about the location of the object. It is also used of visual impairment (Deut. 28:29).

31. Because there appears to be a duplication of the action in Gen. 27:27, some have argued that 27:23 is a greeting, while 27:27 is a pronouncement of the blessing. Cf. Wenham, *Genesis 16–50*, 209. According to Hamilton (*Genesis 18–50*, 218), Isaac did not bless Jacob but was about to do so.

Isaac as the deceiver. An alternate perspective on the Jacob-Isaac inter-
face is that Isaac may be the deceiver. Part of what persuades us that he is
not a deceiver is his reluctance, but that could be part of his plausibility.
Who would expect Isaac to deceive his son? Who would expect him to defy
tradition especially against his favorite son? But perhaps that is the cover
for the deceit.[32] What does he attempt to accomplish with the apparent
efforts to verify his son's identity? How will Isaac persuade himself of the
identity of the man whom he intends to bless? Isaac uses several means
to persuade himself and thus to verify the connection between the reality
and his perception of that reality. It is the essence of any act of deception to foster such a connection, although that connection may not exist
apart from perception. By assigning an alternate meaning to a perceived
link, the connection may be established. In Isaac's case, the deception
plays on all the senses but primarily on the visual impairment, namely,
his eyes are growing "dim" (*kāhâ*). His physical condition establishes the
mode of the deception. Isaac, like others of reduced vision, is perceived
as vulnerable, and a prejudice against him is manifested.[33] The prejudice
is acting as if the aged and visually impaired person is also mentally impaired. Since it is the nature of prejudices to expect particular behavior,
someone who does not embody the expected traits may pretend to have
them in an effort to deceive. If Isaac is treated like a senile old man, he
acts the role well for those who expect his senility. To one who does not
expect senility, his behavior is perplexingly shrewd, showing a mental
acuity that his son and wife lack or are blinded to by their prejudice
against him. What better cover could Isaac construct?

Continuing with the alternate interpretation of who is deceiving whom,
one uncovers another aspect of the deception. It may be that Isaac is
testing Jacob to see how far he would go to get the blessing. It would be
comical for a man of forty plus years and his mother to underestimate
what impaired vision entails. While some are inclined to see the humor
in this narrative, others deny any such humor by affirming the "moral
seriousness" of Jacob's actions. They usually base their perspective on
the perception that the narrative does not trivialize the crime committed
against a blind man.[34] The seriousness and the humor are not mutually

32. Cf. Rackman, "Was Isaac Deceived?" 37–39. He argues that Isaac intended to bless
Jacob but was being creative in his timing and mode of blessing so as not to offend
Esau.

33. The concept is variously represented, as in 1 Sam. 3:2 (*kāhâ*); Gen. 48:10 (*kābēd*);
cf. 1 Kings 14:4 (*qûm*)—all associated with the aging process. In other instances bad vision
stems from tears and sorrow (Job 17:7; Ps. 88:10 [NRSV 88:9]) and the sheer agony of waiting for God, whose answer and attention have been deferred (Ps. 69:4 [NRSV 69:3]).

34. Von Rad, *Genesis*, 277, 280. He also sees Jacob's actions as blasphemy against
Yhwh.

exclusive in this narrative; rather, the seriousness of the events and their ramifications lead to the humor. As dependent as Jacob is, he is skillful and conscious enough of self-protection to think about who would be punished for the ruse. His concern shows his awareness of the "wrong" he is about to commit and his attempt to avert punishment.[35] Consequently, Jacob objects to being caught, not to the wrongness of his behavior. Isaac persists in showing both mental acuity and gullibility. Or is he simply skilled in successfully performing the role of an old man being deceived for the audience that he is deceiving? This audience would consist of his immediate family and all who had heard the story of how Jacob was designated as the legitimate heir.

The final part of this alternative interpretation is the plausibility of the outcome of the deception. Could he have reversed the blessing and conferred it on Esau? According to Gerhard von Rad, the blessing is independent of the promise,[36] and the promise encompasses Abraham's descendants. On the other hand, the blessing may have been for the firstborn.[37] Joseph Rackman argues that Isaac was deceived but that he already intended to bless both Jacob and Esau. This decision to bless both was an unresolved point of dispute between Isaac and Rebekah. According to Rackman, Rebekah resolved the dispute by using Jacob to deceive Isaac. At stake in the ruse is the double blessing—spiritual (Abraham's heritage) and material (wealth)—and who would receive what. Rebekah wants both for Jacob, while Isaac, seeking to avoid the atrocity of his father's choice between sons (himself and Ishmael), plans to divide the blessings between his sons (Jacob and Esau).[38]

Rackman's perspective has a few compelling aspects. First, Isaac could have given the spiritual blessing to Esau when Esau asked if there were any remaining blessings, but Isaac did not do so (Gen. 27:37–40). Instead, he waited until Jacob's arrival and then knowingly blessed Jacob. Whatever he previously intended—to divide the blessing or to confer it all on Esau—after the apparent deception, he is decisive in blessing Jacob (28:3–4).

35. Jacob is adept at recognizing "wrong" in other people's behavior, e.g., he accuses Laban of deceiving him (Gen. 29:25; 31:7). Clearly, this is not a man bereft of moral sensibilities; but in reference to his own behavior, he appears to be blind to "wrongs" (cf. 31:4–13).

36. Von Rad, *Genesis*, 278. Cf. Gen. 12:1–3; 13:14–16; 22:17; 26:24; 28:3, 13–15.

37. Speiser (*Genesis*, 212–13) argues that the Nuzi texts suggest the irrevocability of a father's blessing and an option to bless a son other than his firstborn. Hamilton (*Genesis 18–50*, 222–23) argues instead that the Nuzi texts indicate transfer of authority and an obligation to designate an heir. This transfer is a legal transaction witnessed by others and not a deathbed occurrence. He cites T. L. Thompson (*Historicity of the Patriarchal Narratives*, 285–93) in support of his argument.

38. Rackman, "Was Isaac Deceived?" 39–41.

Second, given the opportunity, Isaac was holding back on conferring the blessing. If indeed he believed that he was blessing Esau and had intended to confer both blessings on Esau, why did he not do so at the first opportunity—after the meal? In light of the deception, why not reverse the blessing? Isaac was already showing signs of holding back, even before he supposedly discovered the ruse. Perhaps his reluctance to reverse the blessing was due to his satisfaction with the course of events or his inability to do so. Thus Hamilton proposes that "abrogation is not an option for Isaac, for the essence of an oracle is that it is irrevocable" (Gen. 27:34).[39] Perhaps the dynamic of the blessing is similar to Jephthah's vow, namely, that regardless of the consequences, it is binding once pronounced.[40] Another dimension that may have limited Isaac's power to reverse the blessing is that it was made in God's presence and therefore approved by God, including the fact that Jacob was the recipient.

Third, an insightful aspect of Rackman's perspective is Rebekah's motive in securing the blessing for Jacob. Rackman notes that she was motivated by her history, wherein she experienced hardship, and was determined to secure a prosperous existence for her favorite son (Jacob), even at the cost of her other son (Esau). Likewise, Isaac may have been motivated by his family dynamics. Thus he attempted to avoid ostracizing his sons or to prevent animosity between them. Isaac saw that his parents ostracized Ishmael (the firstborn).[41] Isaac may have been sensitized to the effect of parental actions on children's future relationships with each other. Isaac's motivation was to give each of his sons a blessing that would allow for a congenial relationship between them.

As altruistic as Isaac appears in Rackman's portrait, Rebekah appears as a malevolent instigator willing to relegate Esau to hardship in order to ensure Jacob's prosperity. Only to readers who are aware of the larger framework does Rebekah's portrait become refined—she acts in accordance with the Deity's plan (Gen. 25:23). Even so, as with Sarah, the harmfulness of her action is not obliterated because it contributes to the Deity's plan. The narrative does little to explain Rebekah's motives, but it does much to show Isaac's vulnerability and to put Isaac in a more favorable light than Rebekah. Accordingly, if Isaac used Rebekah's ruse to achieve his own ends, he may have spared Esau's feelings and thus avoided negative repercussions to his own relationship with Jacob

39. Hamilton, *Genesis 18–50*, 226.

40. Jephthah keeps his vow even though it was pronounced in haste and could have grisly consequences (Judg. 11:30–35; cf. Num. 30:3 [NRSV 30:2]). Hamilton (*Genesis 18–50*, 226) characterizes it as troubling or disturbing (*'ākar*) that his only child would die because of his oath.

41. Rackman, "Was Isaac Deceived?" 40–41.

and Rebekah.[42] In the larger context, it is also possible that if Isaac was pretending to be deceived in order to conceal his own motive, he was doing so to preserve his own image in the eyes of those around him. More accurately, since it is only through the narrator that we know Isaac, it may be the narrator's attempt to deflect any culpability of Isaac and Jacob. The result is that the narrative makes Rebekah culpable and exonerates Isaac and Jacob; but through Esau it manages to implicate Jacob while exonerating Rebekah.

In looking at the alternatives about who is being deceived, the narrator appears to suggest that there is more to Isaac conferring the blessing to the second-born than first meets the eye. Isaac's attempts to verify the identity of his son suggest that Isaac is doubtful. In the first alternative, his questions are to confirm Esau's identity; and in the second, he is most likely attempting to confirm Jacob's identity. His response to Esau's arrival (Gen. 27:33) is usually taken as an indication that he is surprised. However, given his pervasive doubt, his response is most likely not one of surprise but of anger or even uneasiness that he is now faced with the success of his plan.[43] It is not the only time that a Genesis narrative creates ambiguity, heightens tension, and serves as a caveat against definitive assertions about the actions of one of the patriarchs.[44] Thus it is probable that having executed his ruse, Isaac further perpetuates the deception with Esau.

Isaac-Esau

Fundamental to the understanding of the narrative is the involvement of each of the characters in the deception. While Isaac may have been deceived and involved in the deceit, the nuances of Esau's involvement may have also contributed to the deception. Does Isaac deceive Esau? Esau appears incidental to the various plans that converge to exclude him from his inheritance. Isaac is said to love Esau (Gen. 25:28), but the question is whether Esau's actions influenced his status as heir. Esau sold his birthright (běkōrâ) for a meal (25:29–34) and married foreign women (26:34).

First, that he sold his birthright was probably disclosed to Isaac before Esau attributed the incident to Jacob's action of "taking" (lāqaḥ) it from him (Gen. 27:36). In Esau's representation of the transaction, he reflects Isaac's language that Jacob deceitfully took the "blessing"

---

42. Rackman, "Was Isaac Deceived?" 39–41.

43. Hamilton (*Genesis 18–50*, 224) interprets *ḥārad* as "anger" rather than panic. Isaac was trembling because of anger. Wenham (*Genesis 16–50*, 211) notes that the reaction is seen elsewhere, e.g., Joseph's brothers (Gen. 42:28) and Israel at Mount Sinai (Exod. 19:16).

44. Cf. Abraham's claim that Sarah is his sister (Gen. 20:12). For further details, see chap. 3.

(*běrākâ*, 27:35). Both Isaac and Esau make Jacob responsible for the transference of the object without representing their action in giving it to him.[45] Accordingly, as the ones who possessed the objects that he took, they represent Jacob's power in securing the birthright and blessing and conversely their submission to his power.

Second, Esau married Hittite women knowing that it would be displeasing to his parents (Gen. 26:34). While none of this justifies the ruse that cheated Esau out of the blessing, many consider his conduct when interpreting the narrative.[46] Daniel Elazar posits that Esau did not deserve the blessing because of his behavior and personal traits. He therefore concludes that "the Bible tells us that a bright, calculating person who, at times, is less than honest, is preferable as a founder over a bluff, impulsive one who cannot make discriminating choices."[47] While Elazar's conclusion seems to sanction ethically questionable behavior, it reflects a dimension of the narrative portrayal. It suggests that Isaac had already decided to exclude Esau based on his displeasure with Esau's choice of marital partners. Likewise, it ignores the fact that the birthright is not based on the character of the potential heir, his parents, or his personality traits but solely on his birth order. If Elazar and Rackman's interpretations of the narrative are as viable as they seem, one sees that while the biblical narrative assumes the flawed nature of humans, it indicates that some flaws are preferred over others.[48]

Esau's response to the situation shows that he understood that Isaac was not pleased with the Hittite women that he had married. Therefore, after the blessing is conferred on Jacob, Esau marries his cousin, Mahalath, while remaining married to his previous Hittite wives (Judith and Basemath).[49] This is clearly an attempt to please his father by conforming to his father's perceived expectations for him, namely, an endogamous marriage. The text specifies that Mahalath is Ishmael's daughter, and that Ishmael is Abraham's son (Gen. 28:9). Thus this Ishmael is Isaac's half brother, Esau's uncle. By attempting to please his father, Esau shows self-persuasion and his father's power over him.[50] He may have reasoned that since Jacob is sent to his uncle Laban's house to find a wife, the

---

45. Rather than "in deceit" (*mirmâ*), Targum Onqelos deflects the severity of Isaac's accusation against Jacob by reading: "Your brother came with wisdom (*bḥwkmh*) and received your blessing." Cf. Hamilton, *Genesis 18–50*, 227.

46. Rackman, "Was Isaac Deceived?" 38–39; Elazar, "Jacob and Esau," 295–96; Wenham, *Genesis 16–50*, 204–5; Sarna, *Genesis*, 189.

47. Elazar, "Jacob and Esau," 296; also Wenham, *Genesis 16–50*, 204–5.

48. Cf. Elazar, "Jacob and Esau," 296. According to Rackman ("Was Isaac Deceived?" 38–39) Isaac planned to bless Jacob but attempted to spare Esau's feelings.

49. Wenham (*Genesis 16–50*, 205) indicates that there are also competing traditions that may have been juxtaposed at this point, namely, Gen. 28:9 vs. 36:2–3.

50. Cf. Reardon, *Persuasion in Practice*, 79–90, for a discussion of self-persuasion.

daughter of one's uncle is a suitable marital partner. Thus it would be logical for Esau to assume that marrying the daughter of his paternal uncle would be favorable to his parents. Esau fails to understand that the operative element in the suitability is not solely that one is a relative but that one is the relative from the "right" side of the family. Consequently, he does not please his parents any more by marrying Ishmael's daughter than by marrying the Hittite women. This is Esau's dilemma: for all his actions he is still a marginalized figure within his family and unable to do anything "right."

In his choice to marry an Ishmaelite woman, Esau acts on his own decision without animosity toward his father or regard for his mother's opinion. Interestingly it is Rebekah's dislike for the Hittites that is cited; no comment is made about Isaac's disdain. It appears that Isaac based his actions on Rebekah's opinion rather than his own. In this respect, Isaac is much like Abraham, who acts on Sarah's animosity toward Hagar. Surprisingly, Esau's motivation for choosing to marry an Ishmaelite does not seem to include Rebekah's displeasure toward his Hittite wives. Instead, the narrator reports Rebekah's view as a wife's opinion (to Isaac) compared to a mother's wishes (for Esau). The silence regarding Esau's motive is also noteworthy given two elements: the narrator's observation that Esau and his Hittite wives, Judith and Basemath, made life difficult for Rebekah and Isaac (Gen. 26:34); and Esau's observation about Isaac's displeasure (28:8–9), which suggests his discovery of Isaac's disdain. How could Esau (forty years plus) not know of his father's displeasure when he (Esau) was generating less than harmonious conditions within the household? Clearly, this is another instance where the narrative shows its views about foreign women. This time the bias is represented through female-female animosity, similar to that between Sarah and Hagar.

In comparing Esau and Isaac, one observes that Esau was forty years old when he married the Hittite women; Isaac married Rebekah at age forty (Gen. 25:20). Isaac was sixty years old when Esau and Jacob were born (25:26), meaning that he had to wait twenty years to have children with Rebekah. Isaac, then a man of sixty plus years, passed off Rebekah as his sister (Gen. 26). By comparison, Jacob delayed marriage until he was at least forty-seven years old. Even at that age, he was still under his mother's control. Esau asserted himself as an adult male attempting to establish his own household, but he offended his parents by taking Hittite wives. Isaac did not assume responsibility for finding wives for his sons.

The contrast between father and son is further illustrated by comparing the siblings. Esau and Jacob are quite different in their decision making within the family domain. Jacob is accustomed to using subversive actions as a way of manifesting his power and getting what he wants.

While away from his mother, he behaves like an adult by making his own decisions—whatever the quality of those decisions. Perhaps his apparent assertiveness in dealing with Laban, while a product of experience, is simply a manifestation of domain-specific behavior. When with his mother, he conforms to her expectations—she controls him. It is not surprising, then, that Rebekah is depicted as the instigator of perpetual animosity between her sons. In contrast, Esau makes his own decisions, albeit ones that his parents disfavor. His independence appears to be devalued by the narrative in that all his initiatives are presented as misguided actions—selling his birthright, marrying foreign women, and marrying his cousin.

Finally, although he is disadvantaged by the deception, Esau serves as a point of insight into the deception process. The deceived have some control over the deception but not the type of control that makes them responsible for the deception. Esau's power in the situation is his status as a son who does not allow his father to openly disregard him in the matter of inheritance. In this regard, Esau is the most vulnerable party in his family. He is partially in view both as the deceived and as the motivation for Isaac's involvement. As odd as it may be, the deceived also controls the means of the deception in that the effective deception must meet certain preconditions, including plausibility. If the one being deceived disbelieves and perceives a facade, the deception will be ineffective. Similarly, Esau believes that his father was deceived. Therefore, he pleads with his father and seeks to appease him. Furthermore, Esau's perception allows him to implicate Jacob but to overlook the possibility of his mother's involvement in the ruse.

REBEKAH-ISAAC

Rebekah's power is her function as wife and mother that affords her access to Isaac and her sons. The narrative makes no secret of the fact that Rebekah favors Jacob and attempts to secure the blessing for him. In examining Rebekah, one sees several elements that illustrate her function within the family domain as related to her persuasion and power.

Spousal and parental influence. First, Rebekah's effectiveness lies in her place as wife and mother. As wife, her access to Isaac allows her to hear his instructions to Esau concerning his intent to confer the blessing (Gen. 27:5). Nothing suggests that the conversation between Isaac and Esau was secretive and off-limits to Rebekah.[51] On the contrary, the suggestion is that she hears the conversation as Isaac's wife, who has access to him. The question then is not so much how she acquires her

---

51. Cf. Hamilton, *Genesis 18–50*, 213, who contends that she overheard the conversation.

information but how she intends to use it. Apparently, how she acquires this information is different from the instance when she hears of Esau's intent to kill Jacob. In both instances, she has access to information, but in the latter instance she is not within earshot of the conversation. Rather, an undisclosed informant relays to her Esau's intent, suggesting that Rebekah has allies in her domain (27:42).[52]

Second, as a mother, Rebekah uses information to implement a plan to secure the blessing for Jacob, her favorite son. The narrative depicts her as persuading Jacob to participate in the plan. She does so by taking the responsibility for any negative repercussions that ensue from the ruse (Gen. 27:13). The nature of Rebekah's participation makes clear that she actively intends to deceive and, along with Jacob, deliberately constructs a deception. Nonetheless, while one can argue for her parental influence over Jacob, one must also keep in mind that Jacob is an adult male able to make choices. He is persuaded to participate but not coerced to do so. Yet there is another, subtler dimension of deception in regard to Rebekah. When she reveals her concern to Isaac about Jacob's departure, she bases her argument on the negative presence of Esau's wives.

Third, the convergence of her roles as wife and mother is depicted in her decision to send Jacob away. The narrative at this point presents at least two reasons: the first is articulated to Jacob, her son (Gen. 27:42–45); the second is articulated to Isaac, her husband (27:46–28:2). As a mother, she is told about Esau's plan to kill Jacob and informs Jacob of that plan. Rebekah's power in her domain is evident in her ability to convince both her son and her husband to act as she desires. Yet her ability to persuade Jacob and Isaac highlights a gap in her communication. While she speaks with Jacob and Isaac, she does not speak with Esau, even at this crucial juncture where an opportunity exists to bond with Esau. The silence between Rebekah and Esau highlights the rift in the family. The narrator does not entertain the possibility of Rebekah consoling Esau in his loss, dissuading him from his desire to kill his brother, or counseling him against marrying an Ishmaelite. Rather Rebekah is shown as concerned about two people—Jacob and herself. It appears that everything she did was for Jacob. Not surprisingly, when she uncovers Esau's intent to avenge himself, she is concerned to prevent her loss and therefore seeks to protect Jacob (27:45).

Fourth, one cannot escape the irony of the talk about death in this narrative. Isaac is concerned about preparing for his death by designating an heir (Gen. 27:2–4). Esau is concerned about his father's death as an

---

52. Rashi's perspective is that Rebekah was informed by the "holy Spirit" (*rûaḥ haqqōdeš*) and that Esau did not verbalize his intent but "contemplated in his heart" (Abraham ben Isaiah and Benjamin Sharfman, *The Pentateuch and Rashi's Commentary*, vol. 1, *Genesis* [Brooklyn, NY: S. S. & R. Publishing, 1949], 268).

event that would initiate his period of mourning after which he would kill Jacob. The focal point is not mourning Isaac's death but causing another death in the family. The death of his father would constitute the natural and expected death (cf. 27:1–2), while Jacob's death would be the deliberate termination of life. But why kill Jacob? Did Esau intend to regain the blessing by eliminating Jacob? While this seems a natural conclusion, Esau's rationale is not given. Through Rebekah's voice, one learns that Esau plans to kill, presumably to console himself for losing the blessing and birthright (27:42), but without the prospect of regaining the blessing.

Consequences and motivation. The crude contrast of the activity and its motivation further magnifies the intensity of Esau's anger and sense of loss. Killing one's brother as a way of consoling oneself uncovers the extent of the rift between the brothers and is of course a disproportionate solution—Jacob's death (permanent) vis-à-vis consolation (temporary).[53] It also magnifies the absence of any other form of consolation. Esau's attempts to alter his father's decision were futile, but he does not make an appeal to his mother. By presenting the communication between Rebekah, Jacob, and Isaac, the narrative allows for the question regarding Rebekah's relationship with Esau, "her elder son" (*bĕnāh haggādōl*).[54] Rebekah knows that if Esau kills Jacob she could lose two sons in that Esau may be subjected to the death penalty (Gen. 27:45; cf. Exod. 21:12–14). If she is aware of that penalty, so is Esau. Hence his determination to kill Jacob indicates his willingness to die. Rebekah realizes that the success of the deception would destroy her family—except for her Hittite daughters-in-law, whom she despises. This would be a loss of no small order for an aged woman without a male protector.[55] Consequently, while Rebekah's concern may reflect her regard for the lives of her sons, it is also a matter of personal safety.

Another aspect of Rebekah's persuasive speech to Jacob concerns the extent of Esau's "anger" (*'ap*). She appears to understand that the anger is such that he is willing to kill in order to appease himself. Nonetheless, her muddled understanding also surfaces in her perspective, namely, that time could reduce the extent of the anger and avert the killing (Gen.

53. The Hebrew term *nḥm* "to console, comfort" is used to denote obtaining comfort by avenging one's cause.

54. There are no family meetings, only the distinct dialogues (Rebekah-Jacob; Jacob-Isaac; Rebekah-Isaac; Esau-Isaac). In this way the pattern of conversations conforms to the pattern seen elsewhere in the book of Genesis. See chap. 2 regarding the dialogue in the Garden of Eden.

55. The matter of her age is that she may not have any other children, especially in view of her previous infertility (Gen. 25:21). She would have control of the family possessions and she would become vulnerable without a male protector.

27:43–45).[56] Does she believe that Esau's anger would dissipate and that he would "forget" (*šākaḥ*) what has happened and who was instrumental in bilking him out of his status and possessions? Either Rebekah does not understand Esau's anger or she is overestimating the healing power of time. Curiously, Jacob does not voice any objection to the plan to send him away or to the reasoning behind it. It is also revealing that Rebekah claims that Esau is angry because of what Jacob did to him. In the representation of Esau's anger, Esau, the narrator, and Rebekah all note the anger toward Jacob; but the understandable anger toward Isaac or even toward Rebekah is notably absent. Most likely, Esau is unaware of Rebekah's involvement in the deception.[57] This suggestion, however, does little to affirm Rebekah's apparent virtue in being willing to absorb any blame for the adversity ensuing from the deception. What she voices to Jacob sounds like a mother who is willing to go the distance to deflect any harm resulting from her son's bad behavior (27:13). Yet she does not intervene to take the blame when Esau threatens to kill Jacob (27:43–45). Sending Jacob away is one way of protecting him, but the animosity between the brothers is not alleviated by her action, however expedient it is. In essence, Rebekah allows Jacob to take the full blame for the deception eventuating in what he feared—that he would suffer for his part in the ruse (27:12).[58] The multiple dimensions of Rebekah's participation in her domain thus depict a powerful woman of acute insight and initiative. More so than the males in her domain, she orchestrates the major occurrences in her family and shapes the history of nations—both Israel (Jacob) and Edom (Esau).

The second reason for sending Jacob away is that Rebekah does not want Jacob to follow Esau in marrying Hittite women. When talking to Isaac, Rebekah does not specifically mention Esau.[59] She claims that

56. The connections to the other Genesis narrative are discernible—the older (Cain) seeking to harm the younger brother (Abel). While in Gen. 4 Cain succeeded in killing Abel, in Gen. 27 the mother's intervention defeats that attempt. Regarding 27:45, Rashi contends that it is not that Esau would be punished for killing his brother, but that Jacob might overpower Esau, and Esau's children would retaliate by killing Jacob. Thus Rashi states: "If he will rise against you and you will kill him, then his sons will rise and kill you. And the Holy Spirit was cast into her and she prophesied, that on the same day they would die" (*Genesis Commentary*, 269). Cf. the legal texts about killing in Exod. 20:13; 21:12–14.

57. Cf. Hamilton, *Genesis 18–50*, 211.

58. Specifically, his concern is that because of the deception he would be cursed rather than blessed.

59. According to von Rad (*Genesis*, 279, 281–82), the presence of these two reasons for sending Jacob away is indicative of two sources, namely, the Yahwistic source (J), Gen. 27:1–45, and the Priestly source (P), 27:46–28:2. The juxtaposition of the two is seen as the result of accretion whereby P attempted to reconstruct the portrait of Isaac and his sons to present a more harmonious relationship among the ancestors. The concern about Esau's and Jacob's marriages may reflect the narrator's conceptual framework in which

she "loathes" (*qûṣ*) her life because of the Hittite women and that her life would be worthless if Jacob married a Hittite woman (Gen. 27:46). For undisclosed reasons, Rebekah expresses repulsion toward the Hittite women. It could be that Rebekah is repulsed by their strange practices and has become intolerant.[60] However, it is apparent that her response to the Hittites goes beyond a specific event. She has a sustained abhorrence for the people, much like Moab, Egypt, and Damascus have toward Israel (Exod. 1:12; Num. 22:3; 1 Kings 11:25), and like the Deity has toward the Canaanites (Lev. 20:23). Rebekah's regard for the Hittites reflects the mind-set of her domain in which such prejudice is normative and operative in one's view of the despised group.

Isaac is convinced by Rebekah's argument and responds by calling Jacob, blessing him and charging him to marry not a Canaanite woman but someone from the household of Laban, his maternal uncle (Gen. 28:1–2). Thus while Rebekah is specifically concerned about the Hittites, Isaac extends the concern to the Canaanites. In her role as wife, she taps into an ideological bent as the basis for her argument—namely, marriage to foreign women. As specified above in the discussion of Esau, Rebekah becomes the voice of animosity toward the foreigner, and her husband consents to her perspective. Her argument reflects a bias against the Hittite women that appears to stem from experience with two women—Judith and Basemath, her daughters-in-law (26:34–35).[61] Even so, the reason for the bitterness is unclear and may include Isaac and Rebekah's anguish over the fact that Esau took wives without their consent; Esau's exogamous marriages rather than the endogamous marriage they desired for him; or the behavior of the foreign women toward them. The language used to describe the experienced "adversity" is like that used to describe Hannah's and Job's anguish in their situations (1 Sam. 1:10; Job 7:11; 10:1).[62]

---

marriage to foreign women is as problematic as any issue of faith. This concern and not the matter of deception becomes the focal point of 27:46–28:9. Cf. David Carr, *Reading the Fractures of Genesis* (Louisville: Westminster John Knox, 1996), 85–88, for the various elements that suggest independent sources. With Wenham (*Genesis 16–50*, 204), it may be argued that the narrative is aware of the tension between the brothers and the fact that Isaac did not want Jacob to marry Canaanite women (28:5, 8).

60. Leonard J. Coppes, "קוץ," *TWOT* 2:794.

61. Sarna (*Genesis*, 189) sees Esau's exogamy as an error that he committed. Others see it as a reason that Isaac intended to confer the blessing on Jacob rather than Esau, e.g., Elazar "Jacob and Esau," 296; Wenham, *Genesis 16–50*, 205; cf. Rackman "Was Isaac Deceived?" 38–39.

62. Wenham, *Genesis 16–50*, 205. In Gen. 26:35 the expression is literally "bitterness of spirit" (*mōrat rûaḥ*). In 1 Sam. 1:10; Job 7:11; 10:1, the expression is "bitterness of soul" (*mar nepeš*). Rashi (*Genesis Commentary*, 256) interprets the "bitterness as rebellion": "All their deeds were to vex and to (cause) grief 'to Isaac and Rebekah,' for they were idol worshippers."

As clear as it is that Rebekah masterminded the deception, Isaac's participation is masked by ambiguity. The narrative uses a few elements to clear him of any culpability in Rebekah's plan, that is, his physical impairment (Gen. 27:1) and his apparent shock at discovering he had blessed Jacob rather than Esau (27:33). Even so, distinctive elements indicate his conscious participation: his suspicious questions showing an attempt to verify the person in front of him;[63] his apparent holding back from giving Esau a blessing (27:36–38); and his blessing of Jacob (28:3–5). Together Isaac and Rebekah appear to use the family dynamics to accomplish their purpose.

Conclusion

Having considered the nuances of the narrative, a few concluding observations about the anatomy of deception are in order. These observations build on the assertion that two levels of persuasion are depicted, namely, the narrative and the elements portrayed within the narrative. Regarding the narrative, it is a tool used to persuade. Part of the plausibility of the narrative is that the reader must find the portrayals compelling in order to appreciate the nature and function of the deception. Regarding the narrative portrayals, they are the relational and behavioral dynamics within the narrative that facilitate deception (see chapter 2). Accordingly, the characters show that some people are more easily deceived than others and that the degree of trust between persons influences the nature and probability of deception. To deceive, several conditions must be present, including the following:

First, the plausibility of the situation enhances the chance of deception. To be plausible is to "have an appearance of truth or reason; credible; believable."[64] Within the context of the story, plausibility means conforming to the expected conventions of culturally and religiously defined truth. One alternative is that Isaac believed that Jacob was Esau. In this instance, the plausibility was achieved by altering Jacob's distinctive characteristics. The other alternative is that Isaac believed it was Jacob, not Esau.[65] In this instance, plausibility was achieved by questioning the person whom he was about to bless. Given the ambiguity of the text, it

---

63. Von Rad (*Genesis*, 277) argues that Isaac's questions "show pathetically how the blind man cannot at first master a feeling of uncertainty."

64. *Random House Webster's College Dictionary*, 2nd ed., s.v. "Plausible."

65. Bledstein, "Binder, Trickster, Heel and Hairy-Man," 282. Through a presentation of the various components of Isaac's questions, Bledstein demonstrates the viability of the case that Isaac was in fact deceiving Jacob. Cf. Rackman, "Was Isaac Deceived?" 37–40.

is possible that Isaac intended to bless Jacob in spite of the tradition of the firstborn as family heir.

The second condition of deception is expectation. Expectations and presuppositions about a person's character are the foundation of many successfully executed deceptions. If Isaac was expecting Esau, he was behaving accordingly. Likewise, if he did not expect to encounter Jacob during that moment designated for blessing, his momentary questions were absorbed by his expectation when paired with Jacob's plausibility. Another component of the expectation is the nature of the relationship of Isaac, Esau, Jacob, and Rebekah. Rebekah and Jacob expected Isaac to be vulnerable and he behaved in a vulnerable manner, but they did not expect him to be as shrewd as he may have been in facilitating their ruse and his.

The third condition is trust, which, facilitated by the familial relationship, lays the groundwork for expectations. Isaac disclosed his intention to bless Esau and his desires concerning the moment of the blessing. Apparently, he trusted that Esau would carry out the plans to ensure the receipt of the blessing. Rebekah also trusted Isaac to carry out his promise to bless Esau if Esau brought him the food he requested. It was her trust of Isaac that ensured the execution of her plan to deceive him. Yet the double edge of trust is clearly evident: trust forms the foundation of Isaac—a blind old man—feeling secure enough to depend on his family at a vulnerable time in his life. Trust provides the basic foundation for deception.

Although the text does not advocate deception as a way of persuading someone to act in one's favor, its depiction allows several insights into the persuasion process. First, deception is a manifestation of persuasion. As such, the act of persuasion does not define its goal. Rather the goal regulates the process because the goal qualifies the process as deceitful or otherwise.

Second, skillful persuasion can create a situation in which the line between the deceived and the deceiver is blurred. Within that situation, the deceiver is deceived by virtue of her/his apparent success in deceiving another person. The narrator's skill suggests that the process of persuasion is multidimensional, including the use of vulnerability, predisposition, and sanctioned animosity as preconditions to secure one's wishes.

Third, family relationships do not safeguard against the success of deception. Rather, as seen in Isaac's family, the family domain may facilitate persuasion and deception because family members know one another's vulnerabilities and have access to them. This is seen in Rebekah and Jacob's willingness to fulfill their wishes by taking advantage of Isaac.

5

A Semblance of Power

Sarah and Hagar (Genesis 16 and 21)

Introduction

The women in the narrative exhibit similar power dynamics to that found among men. This suggests that power is a function of socialization rather than inherent to any gender. The female-female dynamics in Gen. 16 and 21, more so than those in Gen. 12, exhibit elements of power as manifested in multiple domains by the same person. My goal in this chapter is to examine the narrative portrayals of Sarah and Hagar in Gen. 16 and 21 as examples of power in female-female behavioral dynamics. I propose that power is domain-specific and that every relationship includes power dynamics in which weakness is a facet of power. As in the preceding chapters, I begin with observations about the narratives. I note that while the two narratives portray a similar relationship dynamic of Sarah and Hagar, they view the power dynamic differently. I therefore look at Gen. 16 and 21 as distinctive narratives and include aspects of the power dynamic in which Abraham is directly involved.[1]

Genesis 16—Domains of Power

The family unit constitutes the main domain in Gen. 16. Even so, the narrative makes clear that other domains exist outside the family house-

---

1. The narratives are often considered the work of two distinct sources. Others view them in a diachronic relationship, wherein Hagar, after returning to Sarah and living with the family, is expelled.

hold but the other domain may present life-threatening challenges. In the family domain the relationships are defined by the identity and status of members. Likewise, the narrative indicates that while the humans are presented as the primary actors, the Deity's presence and purpose define the domain.

Sarah's Identity and Status

One of the ways that the text characterizes the power of individuals is by classifying their roles or other attributes that are essential to the progression of the narrative. While one narrative portrays Sarah as a silent, compliant person (Gen. 12), another portrays her as a woman of few words in charge of the well-being of another person (Gen. 16). One clearly notes the concern about identity as the narrative begins its portrait of Hagar and Sarah. The views of Sarah come from her introduction in Gen. 11:29–30 and her role in 12:1–20. When it is reported that "Abraham and Nahor took wives," Sarah is introduced as a nameless wife (11:29). Following this introduction, Sarah is further introduced as "Abram's wife" ('ēšet-'abrām), and Milcah is introduced as Nahor's wife. The narrator notes Abraham's genealogy, including Terah, Abraham's father, and Nahor and Haran, Abraham's brothers (11:27). It also mentions Haran's son, Lot (11:27). Milcah's lineage is then identified, showing her connections beyond the family into which she has married. She is Haran's daughter and Iscah's sister (11:29).[2]

The information given features all of these persons as connected to others by naming their parents or siblings. In contrast to Milcah, nothing is mentioned of Sarah's parents or siblings. Rather, her fertility status is immediately presented. As it is silent about Sarah's lineage, the narrative is also silent about Milcah's fertility (Gen. 11:30). Perhaps the reticence indicates the insignificance of her lineage, thus signaling that Sarah's definitive attribute within her husband's household is her infertility. As

2. This Haran (Gen. 11:29) is most likely not the Haran who is Abraham's brother and Lot's father (11:26–28). If Haran is listed as having Lot without any reference to other sons and daughters, to argue that Milcah's father is Haran, Lot's father, is to propose that Haran had at least two daughters, Milcah and Iscah, who are excluded from the narrative. Just as one does not assume that the Nahor in 11:22–24 (Terah's father) is the Nahor in 11:26–27 (Abraham's brother), one may allow that there are two different Harans. Contrast Hamilton (*Genesis 18–50*, 118), who asserts that Nahor married his niece (Haran's daughter). He further argues that while the practice is later condemned, when Nahor married Milcah it was acceptable to do so, just as it was to marry one's half sister (see Abraham and Sarah).

According to the genealogy, Isaac's wife Rebekah is one of his first cousins. Nahor and Milcah's son Bethuel is Rebekah's father (Gen. 22:23). That makes Abraham Rebekah's great uncle. Laban was her brother (24:29).

it turns out Milcah's fertility was not an issue. She bore eight sons to Nahor, Abraham's brother (22:23). In addition to these eight, Reumah, Nahor's concubine (*pîlegeš*), also bore him four children (22:24). So while both of his brothers (i.e., Haran and Nahor) effortlessly had children with their partners, Abraham endured years of waiting.

Abraham's wife is infertile, and a note is given regarding what that means. Sarah does not have a "male child" (*wālād*, Gen. 11:30).[3] Elsewhere the term "barren/infertile" (*'ăqārâ*) is used to indicate the infertility of specific women, namely, Rebekah (25:21), Rachel (29:31), Manoah's wife (Judg. 13:2–3), and generally of a set of infertile women (Exod. 23:26; 1 Sam. 2:5; Job 24:21; Ps. 113:9). The masculine form (*'ăqār*) is also used to indicate the sterility of the male (Deut. 7:14).[4] Even in Judges 13:2–3, where an explanatory note is given regarding the woman's infertility, the angel promises the woman that she will bear a "son" (*bēn*).[5]

As a further point of her identity, Sarah's role is referenced in relation to Terah (as "daughter-in-law," *kallâ*) and to Abraham (as "wife," *'iššâ*) (Gen. 11:31). The significance of her infertility is brought into clearer focus when the Deity promises to make Abraham into a great nation (12:1–3). Either the progeny necessary for a great nation will come through another woman or Sarah's condition will be remedied. Since the family line is carried through the male (patrilinear), the solution will be that she has a son.[6] Her identity as wife and mother will define her power in the family.

3. This is the masculine singular noun as compared to *yeled* "male child" or *yaldâ* "female child." The masculine singular noun *yeled* could refer to both male and female. Its plural form refers to children (Gen. 30:26). The feminine singular *yaldâ* is also used of a "maiden," or of a "young woman," as in the case of Dinah (34:4).

4. The infertility of both male and female humans and animals is designated by these terms. The root also occurs as a noun form meaning "offshoot" or "branch," suggesting the opposite of infertility (Lev. 25:47). The verbal form means to "hamstring" or incapacitate animals so that they are unable to function in the capacity to which they had been designated—e.g., the horses are unable to run or move the chariots (Gen. 49:6; Josh. 11:6, 9; 2 Sam. 8:4; 1 Chron. 18:4). It is used in Eccles. 3:2 to speak of uprooting a plant, while in the book of Daniel the term *'iqqar* refers to a stump left in the ground (4:15, 23, 26 [NRSV 4:12, 20, 23]; 7:8).

5. The negated form of the verb is used: "she did not beget/bear" (*lō' yālādâ*), without the use of the specified object "child." Note that the text uses the verb *yālad* "to bear, bring forth" to characterize the state of giving birth to a child. It uses the verb *hārâ* "to become pregnant" to speak of conception. Together these verbs signal the beginning and the end of the process—conception and birth for both fertile and previously infertile women (cf. Gen. 21:2; 29:32, 33, 34, 35; 30:17; 38:4; Exod. 2:2; 1 Sam. 1:20; 2:21). Most often, once it is announced that a woman has conceived, the pregnancy is assumed to be viable—that she will carry the child to term and give birth to the child. In none of these instances of the infertility of a woman is her childlessness due to the nonviability of a prior pregnancy. Ruth 4:13 states that YHWH gave her a pregnancy (*hērāyôn*) and she bore a son.

6. Dennis, *Sarah Laughed*, 36.

IDENTITY AND POWER

In Gen. 16:1, as in 11:29, Sarah is identified as Abraham's wife (*'iššâ*; cf. 11:31; 12:17; 16:3). This identity is well established in the book of Genesis from her first introduction. She is with Abraham as wife when Terah, her father-in-law, takes them from Ur to Haran (11:32). She endures Abraham's journey from one location to another as his wife, even succumbing to his scheme to pass her off as his sister and thus endangering her (12:10–20). Even so, her functional identify as wife is fused with the issue of her infertility. The term "infertile" (*'ăqārâ*) is not used in 16:1. Rather, a negated form designates Sarah's infertility, "she did not bear" (*lō' yālĕdâ*; cf. 30:1). Similarly, Hannah's situation is designated by the absence of children—"without children" (*'ên yĕlādîm*, 1 Sam. 1:2).[7] Sarah then is presented like other childless women, but without any direct specification that the childlessness is caused by the Deity.[8] Because of the importance of having children, in each instance where childlessness is noted there is a complaint and an attempt to remedy the situation. Yet in Sarah's case the search for a solution or a voiced complaint is delayed. Sarah's barrenness may have lasted for a long time if one considers that she was already married to Abraham when they lived in Haran (Gen. 11:33), then in Egypt (12:10–20), and then for ten years in Canaan (16:3). As wife, she had the opportunity to bear Abraham's son and so continue his family line.

The narrative always resolves the issue of an heir in a manner that facilitates the continuation of the family line. Nonetheless, even when the promise concerning a son and her pregnancy is articulated, it is not articulated to her (Gen. 12:7; 13:14–17; 15:1–5; 17:1–8; 18:10–15; cf. 21:12–13; 22:15–17). Interestingly, infertility is always resolved with the birth of sons rather than daughters—Sarah (21:1–2); Rachel (30:22–25; cf. 30:6, 8); Hannah (1 Sam. 1:19–20); Manoah's wife (Judg. 13:2–3)—and the quest for an heir is also resolved in the birth of sons—Tamar (Gen. 38:28–30); Ruth (Ruth 4:13). With the exception of Leah (Gen. 30:21)[9] and Hannah (1 Sam. 2:21), who also had daughters, these heroines reportedly produced only male children, thus solving only part of the equation for continuing the line. These male heirs must therefore find suitable wives outside their immediate context (cf. Gen. 27). The narrator's favor toward male heirs seems to miscalculate the necessity of females, or to pawn it off to "other families," whose primary role is

7. Isaiah 54:1 uses the noun *'ăqārâ* and the expanded note *lō' yālāda to* speak of Israel. Barrenness is also designated by the term *galmûd* in Job 3:7; 15:34; 30:3 (of inanimate objects); and Isa. 49:21.

8. Contrast Rachel, Gen. 29:31.

9. See chap. 6 for further discussion of the birth of a daughter. In Hannah's case, the names of the two daughters are not given.

to supply what the main families need for their continued existence and fulfillment. If endogamous marriages are to occur, then "suitable" females are necessary within the tribe; someone has to produce daughters for the line to continue. It is no wonder that the narrative is aware of the difficulty of finding a suitable wife—the male going to relatives (Isaac and Jacob, Gen. 24; 29–30) or marrying foreign women (Esau, 26:34; Judah, 38:1–3). Even before birth, females are considered less valuable to the family line. Males are the preferred gender and females are considered incidental though necessary to the perpetuation of the family line. Since her necessity is defined by her childbearing capacity, the woman's childlessness impedes the man's progress and jeopardizes his present and future status. Thus both men and women agonize about childlessness.

Abraham was sensitive to the fact that he was "childless" (*'ărîrî*) and complained to the Deity in an attempt to find a solution within his circumstances. Thus he suggested that Eliezer be his heir (Gen. 15:2–4; cf. Jer. 22:30).[10] In several texts, including 1 Samuel 15:33, Jeremiah 18:21, and Jeremiah 22:30, the term "childless" (*'ărîrî*) is used by parents whose children will be exterminated, thus leaving the parents deprived of a future.[11] In addition, the levirate tradition builds on the circumstances of men dying without producing an heir, especially a son (*bēn*) (Gen. 38; Deut. 25:5–10). While in some cases a "daughter" (*bat*) may have been produced, no mention is made of such situations where a daughter carried on the name of her father.[12] The text simply addresses situations where a man dies without an "offspring" (*zera'*) (Gen. 38:6–9) or a son (Deut. 25:5). Even so, the desired "firstborn" (*bĕkôr*) is male;[13] presumably, these are fertile people. Furthermore, without explanation of the cause of their childlessness, some men are

10. Hamilton (*Genesis 1–17*, 420) notes that Nuzi texts attest to an adoption tradition wherein a couple could adopt a servant as a son and designate him as their heir. In the event that a natural son was born to the couple, the natural son would be the main heir and the adopted son the secondary heir.

11. The term *'ărîrî* is used in these two instances to refer to childless males. It is used in Lev. 20:20–21 to indicate punishment on one who commits sexual infractions by having sexual intercourse with one's aunt or sister-in-law.

12. The text specifies that the "firstborn" (*bĕkôr*) resulting from the levirate union will bear the name of the deceased brother. The concern is that the deceased branch of the family may be continued (Deut. 25:6). See John N. Oswalt, "בכר," *TWOT* 1:108–11.

13. It appears that the "firstborn" may be either a male or a female and that the text will specify the gender intended. There are several references to the female firstborn (*bĕkîrâ*), e.g., Laban's firstborn, Leah (Gen. 29:26); Saul's firstborn daughter, Merab (1 Sam. 14:49). Genesis 19:31, 33, 34, and 37 all refer to Lot's firstborn daughter. She persuaded her sister to engage in sexual intercourse with their father. In all of these instances, the firstborn is juxtaposed with the younger daughter (*ṣĕ'îrâ* in Gen. 19:31; 29:26; and *qĕṭannâ* in 1 Sam. 14:49). The plural form "firstlings" (*bĕkōrōt*) occurs in the laws concerning the tithe, namely,

also described as having died "without children" (*lō' bānîm*, 1 Chron. 2:30, 32). It is therefore insightful that Abraham designates himself as childless (*'ărîrî*) rather than sterile (*'āqār*). In this way, the narrative shows Abraham's awareness that the lack of children is not due to him but to his wife, Sarah.

Sarah perceives that the Deity "restrained" (*'āṣar*) her and thus caused her barrenness. Similarly, the Deity restrains the wombs of all the women in Abimelech's house because of Sarah (Gen. 20:18). Genesis 16:2 does not cite the reason that the Deity restrained Sarah from having children; however, the motivation for such action is different from Rachel's case, where it appears that the divine displeasure was due to Jacob's love for Rachel and hatred of Leah (29:31). Hannah's case is similar to Rachel's in that they are both co-wives, both loved by their husbands, and both childless (1 Sam. 1). While Elkanah loves her and shows her favor over his other wife, Peninnah, and their children, the Deity had "closed" (*sāgar*) Hannah's womb (1 Sam. 1:5, 6). Consequently, although Elkanah's love is not explicitly cited as the reason for his wife's infertility, one sees the same conceptual type in Rachel and Hannah. Their favor may be a catalyst for the Deity's disfavor toward them. Sarah's case does not fit into this "type"; neither Gen. 11 nor 16 offers the reason that the Deity would be displeased with Sarah. Sarah, like Rachel, cites the Deity as the cause of her barrenness (Gen. 16:2); however, the narrative does not confirm her observation as it does in Rachel's case (29:31; cf. 30:2). Rachel cites the reason for her barrenness after the narrator reports the Deity's involvement.

The conceptual framework of the texts supports the notions that where there is infertility it is the Deity's doing, and it is the woman who is infertile rather than her husband. Furthermore, the narratives also suggest that the Deity's reasons for causing infertility and subsequently allowing fertility are beyond the control of the women. Thus in such a crucial aspect of their existence within their family, women may perceive themselves to be helpless to fulfill a decisive role—producing an heir. Even if their husbands died before they produce an heir, they are still obligated to do so (Deut. 25:5). Women do not have the power to control their fertility and must rely on the desire of the Deity or resort to the conventions of their society—namely, surrogacy.[14]

---

the flocks, e.g., Deut. 12:6; 14:23 (cf. Neh. 10:38 [NRSV 10:37]). Cf. Oswalt, *TWOT* 1:109. See chap. 4 for discussion of Jacob and Esau.

14. One example of a woman who attempted to resolve her infertility is Rachel. Her solution was the mandrakes that she got from Reuben, her stepson (Gen. 30:14–16; cf. Song 7:14 [NRSV 7:13]). Some believe that the mandrake is an aphrodisiac.

SOCIAL STATUS AND FUNCTION (POWER OF A BARREN MISTRESS)

Sarah is both vulnerable and powerful in a system where her status within her family and the family line hinge on her ability to produce a male heir. Yet in this system she, as a woman of means, is not without options. Her options are a function of her gender and specifically her social status as a wife to a man of means and a mistress over her servants. In her situation, the dual role expedites her plan to raise her status. Therefore, one need not see Sarah's plan to have a surrogate as exclusively for the sake of the Deity's plan for Abraham. Rather, her infertility and her obligation to Abraham would have been a dire concern, a concern that would constitute the expediency of her plan.

Several points are important. First, Sarah made Hagar a wife to Abraham. As argued above, Sarah is identified as Abraham's infertile wife; but having a "maid" (*šipḥâ*)[15] allows her an option that may not have been available to her poor counterpart. That Hagar is a maidservant leaves her at the will of her mistress. Consequently, Sarah gives Hagar to Abraham as his "wife" (*'iššâ*).[16] Nonetheless, some are inclined to designate Hagar as a "concubine" (*pîlegeš*). Like Leah and Rachel, who drafted their maids to perform the role of a surrogate, Sarah gave Hagar to Abraham. In all these instances, the maids are not simply used as surrogates without a specific relational status and identity in the family, namely, maid-wife. Rather, they become co-wives with a specific function and without ignominy to any of the persons involved. Had the situation been reversed, and Hagar was the infertile maid, she could not have called upon Sarah to bear her children. Sarah's privileged status endows her with the power to make Hagar her surrogate.

One sees in Sarah's actions a woman functioning within multiple domains of power. As a wife herself, she complies with her husband's wishes; but as one whose status is diminished by her infertility, she has the power to make demands that would facilitate a family line. Although her options may be restricted to the domains where she functions, Sarah, like all other infertile women in the Genesis narratives, is not powerless. Powerlessness in her situation of infertility would be the inability to procure an outcome that addressed her infertility, and even then she would still have power in other aspects of her life.

Second, Sarah makes Hagar her surrogate with all the expectations of the status of the surrogate. As in other instances where a husband and wife engage in sexual intercourse, here in Gen. 16:4 the text reports that

15. See below for discussion of Hagar's status as "maid" (*šipḥâ*) for further details regarding a maid vis-à-vis a "slave" (*'āmâ*).

16. The same term is used of Sarah in Gen. 16:3; cf. 12:11; 16:1.

Abraham "went in to" (*wayyābō' 'el*) her.[17] Clearly this is not a situation that Sarah offered to her husband as an opportunity for sexual pleasure or emotional attachment. Rather, the primary function of the union is to produce an heir through procreation. There are various formulations used for sexual relationships in the Old Testament whose precise nuances are often obscured in English translations. In some instances, the formulation is "to know" (*yāda'*) a woman, namely, one's wife, used of Adam and Eve (Gen. 4:1, 25), of Cain and his wife (4:17), and of Elkanah and Hannah (1 Sam. 1:19). In the case of Judah and Tamar, they are not married but it is reported that Judah did not "know [*yāda'*] her again" (Gen. 38:26).[18] In these situations, it is the man who is said to "know" the woman; there are no instances where it is reported that a woman "knew" her husband in the sense of sexual intimacy. Thus for Robert Alter, "to know" denotes "sexual possession by a man of his legitimate spouse. Modern solutions such as 'to be intimate with,' 'to cohabit with,' 'to sleep with,' are all egregiously wrong in tone and application."[19] "To lie with" (*šākab* + *'im*) is another formulation used for sexual intimacy. In many instances, it represents a proscribed or dishonorable action, for example, of Lot and his daughters (19:32, 34), of Shechem and Tamar (34:2), of Potiphar's wife's request to Joseph (39:7; cf. 39:12, 14), of Amnon and Tamar (2 Sam. 13:11), and of two men lying with each other (Lev. 18:22). With the exception of Lot and his daughters, none of these sexual relationships resulted in the conception and birth of a child. "To lie with" (*šākab* + *'im*) is used for husbands and wives, including Uriah's refusal to lie with Bathsheba (2 Sam. 11:1; cf. 12:11).[20]

Finally, with regard to the formulation used in Gen. 16:4, "to go in to her," one can make several observations. When this formulation is used for sexual encounters, the object is the woman and the man is the one who enters, for example, of daughters of humans (Gen. 6:4); of wives (29:23, 30; 30:3, 4; 38:2; Deut. 22:13; 1 Chron. 2:21; 7:23), including captive wives (Deut. 21:13);[21] of a prostitute (Judg. 16:1); of concubines (1 Sam. 16:22); and of levirate unions (Gen. 38:2, 8, 9; Deut. 25:5). The union between Judah and Tamar is also portrayed by the use of the formulation "he went in to her" (Gen. 38:18). I agree with Alter that the "term refers not merely

---

17. While the formulation occurs with other prepositions, *bō' 'el* and *bō' 'al* uniformly mean "to go/come in to; to enter."

18. Some modern translations render the text as follows: ASV "he knew her again no more"; KJV "he knew her again no more"; NIV "he did not sleep with her again"; NRSV "he did not lie with her again."

19. Alter, *Genesis*, xxx.

20. Alter (*Genesis*, xxx) contends that the Hebrew does not suggest any obscenity in its use of "to lie with."

21. In 2 Sam. 12:24 both "go in to" (*bō' 'el*) and "lie with" (*šākab* + *'im*) are used in reference to David and Bathsheba.

to sexual penetration but to the whole act of sexual consummation. It is used with great precision . . . to indicate a man's having intercourse with a woman he has not yet had as a sexual partner, whether she is his wife, his concubine, or a whore."[22]

For Hamilton the differentiation in the uses of the formulation "to go in to" (*bō' 'el*) involves the type of sexual encounter being represented, namely, licit sex (Gen. 16:2; 30:3; 38:8, 9; Deut. 22:13; 25:5; 2 Sam. 12:24) and illicit sex (Gen. 39:14; 2 Sam. 16:21). The result of the action is usually cited, indicating that the goal of the sexual union is procreation (cf. Gen. 16:4; 19:31; 30:3; 38:8–9; 2 Sam. 12:24).[23] By contrast, the illicit unions are not shown to produce offspring. The formulations used to portray Abraham's approaching Hagar suggest nothing particularly shameful or secretive in the context. Rather, Abraham is depicted as following a normative course of action that men follow with their socially sanctioned female partners. Like the norm of the action, so is its outcome—Hagar "conceived" (*hārâ*). Yet the very mention of her conception resulting from the sexual union raises a question about the relationship between Abraham and Sarah. Was their childlessness due to their unconsummated relationship? The narrator does not report that Abraham consummated his relationship with Sarah. However, that event is implied in the simple report that she conceived (Gen. 21:2), in much the same way that the narrator reports Rebekah's conception without reporting the consummation (25:21). Thus with both Sarah and Rebekah one must infer the consummation and subsequent sexual unions. Presumably, it is the nonconception of these women that leads to the observation that they are infertile (*'ăqārâ*). In other instances of childless women, the consummation is noted (e.g., Rachel, 29:30). Nonetheless, the sexual encounter that resulted in the conception of an heir is sometimes omitted (e.g., Rachel, 30:23; Hannah, 1 Sam. 1:19). In Manoah and his wife's case, the conception of Samson is not noted but his birth is announced (Judg. 13:24).

Sarah is then sanctioning Abraham to have sexual intercourse with Hagar and approving the union. She is cognizant of the union, though her feeling about it is not an issue for the narrative. When one employed a surrogate, the concern was procreation rather than pleasure. The surrogate would bear a child that would become the child of the wife. The child would be counted as the child of the wife and the husband and as such the husband's heir.[24] In the ancient Near East, Sarah's power to give

22. Alter, *Genesis*, xxx.

23. Cf. Hamilton, *Genesis 1–17*, 442n3.

24. Some deny that Sarah's intention was to employ a surrogate. E.g., Hamilton (*Genesis 1–17*, 444n17) asserts that she may have been attempting to boost her fertility by having a pregnant woman in her household.

her husband a surrogate comes from her status as wife and mistress; so it was entirely possible for a fertile woman to employ a surrogate to further advance her status, as is the case of Leah (Gen. 30). Specifically the servant becomes a surrogate but society determines the terms of the surrogacy. Should the surrogate exceed her role, there are prescribed negative consequences.

Sarah has limited options and in analyzing her situation may have deemed herself to be permanently infertile. While one may view her option to have a surrogate as Sarah's obligation to ensure the future of Abraham's line rather than as a privilege,[25] it is undeniably a privilege afforded her by her status. Hence, in meeting the obligation, she has the privilege of options, whereas another childless woman may not have had access to a surrogate.[26] Her access is in part her power within her social domain. As such, her actions in employing Hagar as surrogate are neither reprehensible nor dishonorable. Likewise, Abraham and Hagar's sexual relationship is not considered an ignominious matter.[27] If anything, Sarah would perceive childlessness as more disgraceful than giving Hagar to Abraham. Sarah is thus at the mercy of her circumstances. Nonetheless, within her ethos she has the power to secure a surrogate and owes nothing to Hagar for being her surrogate.

POWER AS A MATTER OF TIME AND LOCATION (GETTING HER WAY)

What happens when someone of limited power (or the presumed powerless) has the opportunity to wield power? Sarah's actions are depicted in much the same way as Terah's (Gen. 11) and Abraham's (Gen. 12). Sarah is repeatedly "taken" (*lāqaḥ*)—from Ur to Haran (11:31), from Haran to Canaan (12:5), into Pharaoh's house (12:15, 19), and from Egypt (12:19–20). In Gen. 16 Sarah manifests her power over Hagar when she "takes" (*lāqaḥ*) Hagar and "gives" (*nātan*) her to Abraham. The language of the text echoes that of 3:6, where Eve "takes" (*lāqaḥ*) the fruit and "gives" (*nātan*) it to Adam. In both cases the man takes and follows through with the expected action in his particular situation. Thus Adam "eats" (*'ākal*) the fruit and Abraham has sexual intercourse (*wayyābō' 'el*) with Hagar.

Abraham becomes the receiver and Sarah, the pawn, becomes the initiator, the giver. Hagar is the object that is given and as such has little choice in the matter.[28] Both Sarah in Egypt and Hagar in Canaan are

25. Hamilton, *Genesis 1–17*, 445.

26. Dennis (*Sarah Laughed*, 41–42) envisions Sarah as one who is powerless and thus employs a ruse to help her resolve a problem.

27. Hamilton, *Genesis 1–17*, 445.

28. Cf. Hamilton, *Genesis 1–17*, 446; also Phyllis Trible, *Texts of Terror: Literary-Feminist Readings of the Biblical Narratives*, Overtures to Biblical Theology (Philadelphia: Fortress, 1984), 11.

vulnerable because they are on foreign soil, and they acquiesce to the choices made for them. They are both pawns in another person's plan. Nonetheless, Sarah exhibits her situational power over Hagar to her advantage much like Abraham manifested his power to his advantage. The muted Hagar is comparable to the muted Sarah of Gen. 12:10–20. One clear difference is that Abraham spoke to Sarah about his plan and fears. In contrast, he does not consult with Hagar about the plan that Sarah has for her. It is also noteworthy that Sarah does not ask Abraham to consent to the plan but simply tells him to go to Hagar (Gen. 16:2). His task is not to consider the viability of the plan but to execute it (as is).

Beyond Sarah's power to give Hagar to Abraham, there are several aspects of this manifestation. In the situation of the surrogacy, the wife makes the decision to provide a surrogate, and the man complies and produces offspring through the surrogate mother and the maid given as "wife" ('iššâ) (cf. Gen. 29:31; 30:3–5, 7–8, 9–13). Hamilton sees this as a deterioration of marriage, thus stating that Gen. 16 "reflects the replacing of marriage's primary purpose of companionship (Gen. 2:18) by that of reproduction with all the resulting negative effects."[29] By contrast, his perspective minimizes the place of reproduction within the marriage and overestimates the place of companionship, which may not have been so central.

Sarah's power is also manifested over Abraham, who seems to give in to Sarah's desires. Sarah had her way in giving Hagar to Abraham and in having the union between them result in a pregnancy. Yet Sarah's power is also limited. She cannot control the dynamics between her and Hagar or her feelings toward Hagar. She perceives that Hagar does not respect her and complains to Abraham (Gen. 16:5–6). In telling Sarah to do whatever is good in her eyes, Abraham in essence washes his hands of the matter and disregards the fact that Hagar is pregnant with his child (16:6). Regarding Abraham's compliance with Sarah's wishes, Gustav Dreifuss and Judith Riemer argue: "Perhaps the memory of his having asked Sarah to go to Pharaoh's house to save his own life is what guides him here. He does, in fact, owe her his life. Abraham appears powerless to deal with his memory, on the one hand, and with Sarah's anger and jealousy, on the other."[30] Abraham therefore abandons Hagar to Sarah's skewed judgment and in so doing facilitates Sarah's rage and misplaced frustration. In agreement with Dreifuss and Riemer, one "may assume that Sarah does everything she can to encumber Hagar

29. Hamilton, *Genesis 1–17*, 446.

30. Gustav Dreifuss and Judith Riemer, *Abraham, the Man and the Symbol: A Jungian Interpretation of the Biblical Story*, trans. Naphtali Greenwood (Wilmette, IL: Chiron, 1995), 41–42.

and embitter her life. Sarah takes revenge on Hagar for her own out-
raged femininity."[31]

The other side of Sarah's power over Hagar is Sarah's apparent powerlessness to control her own rage. On the one hand, who can blame
her for being angry and frustrated after years of infertility? On the other
hand, who can she blame for her situation? Unlike Rachel, who perceives and articulates the source of her infertility as the Deity, Sarah
shows no such insights in her voiced complaint about and treatment
of Hagar. She hurls her blame at Abraham, who deflects it back to her.
Even so, in attempting to assign blame she takes ownership of her role
by acknowledging that she gave Hagar to Abraham. Sarah is much like
Adam, who takes no ownership for what has gone awry between him
and his spouse.

Dreifuss and Riemer ask some probing questions that shed light on the
dynamics between Sarah and Hagar. For example: How could Sarah be
unaware of Hagar's personality? They propose that Hagar was arrogant
and had already shown signs of arrogance even as a slave.[32] They clearly
have a conceptualized "place" for persons within a domain.[33] Furthermore,
they propose that Sarah is arrogant and does not recognize or acknowledge
Hagar's attributes because it was expedient for her not to do so. Sarah's
arrogance inhibits her from seeing that Hagar, although a servant, possesses her own will and desire.[34] Accordingly, one could readily agree with
the evaluation of Sarah as "unaware, immature, and controlled by her
impulses to anticipate and analyze the consequences of her actions."[35]

While Dreifuss and Riemer raise important questions, one may also
consider that Sarah is functioning within her family as a product of
that domain. Whatever her arrogance, it is endemic to her status as wife
and mistress. Her power to address her needs through employment of
another person's body is built on various assumptions about her rights
and those of the surrogate. Underlying all of these is her perception of
the necessity to act as she does and the sheer convenience of access to
Hagar afforded her by her status over Hagar. Inherent in the practice of
servant as surrogate is the implicit assumption that the surrogate's will
does not exist. The surrogate is treated as useful but nonessential within

31. Dreifuss and Riemer, *Abraham*, 42.

32. Dreifuss and Riemer, *Abraham*, 42. They point to the rabbinic speculation that
Hagar was an Egyptian princess. In accordance with her presence with Sarah, they assert
that she was a part of the bride-price given to Abraham for Sarah. More specifically, the
speculation is that Hagar is Pharaoh's daughter. Hamilton (*Genesis 1–17*, 447) asserts that
Hagar and Sarah experienced the tension between them because Hagar was not part of
the household, as Bilhah and Zilpah were part of Leah's and Rachel's household.

33. Cf. Bernard, *Female World*, 20–21.

34. Dreifuss and Riemer, *Abraham*, 42.

35. Dreifuss and Riemer, *Abraham*, 42.

her domain. The same may apply to the male surrogate. While vocal about the female surrogate, the Old Testament glosses over the practice of the male surrogate, as represented in Exodus 21:4, or even the levirate tradition (Deut. 25:5–10). A male slave, who is given a wife and bears children, is to leave his children and their mother at the end of his six-year term of servitude. He is first a slave and all other attributes are regulated by that functional identity. Accordingly, the slave must choose between his freedom and his family. The convenience of this tradition, to the extent that it was practiced as indicated, was that the master got the children, who being born into slavery were counted as slaves. These perpetual slaves were the products of using the male slave to breed.[36]

Although she is acting out of vulnerability, Sarah functions from a position of power over Hagar. Within that domain, she is like the master who regulates the breeding of his slaves; but her barrenness fuels the execution of her power rather than the direct economic benefits of multiplying one's work force.[37] Some ancient Near Eastern texts represent a tradition similar to the one reflected in Gen. 16, 21, 29, and 30. The Code of Hammurabi is aware that the slave employed as a surrogate has a will. Thus the code addresses situations where the surrogate may assert herself over her mistress and prescribes a course of action.

> When a seignor [i.e., a free man] married a hierodule [priestess] and she gave a female slave to her husband and she has then borne children, if later that female slave has claimed equality with her mistress because she bore children, her mistress may not sell her; she may mark her with the slave-mark and count her among the slaves. (Code of Hammurabi §146)[38]

Whatever Sarah's treatment of Hagar, she is an oppressive force. The very thought that a woman—of any social status—would bear a child for another person acting only as a vessel, and give the child to another woman to be counted as the other woman's child is not in and of itself farfetched. What makes it unique in the Old Testament and the ancient

36. Mignon R. Jacobs, "Family or Freedom: Conceptual Tensions in the Law of Release in Exod. 21:2–6" (paper presented in Biblical Law Group, AAR/SBL Annual Meeting, Nashville, November 2000).

37. Mardy S. Ireland, *Reconceiving Women: Separating Motherhood from Female Identity* (New York: Guilford, 1993).

38. *ANET*, 172, trans. T. J. Meek. Cf. A. K. Grayson and J. van Seters's reading of the Neo-Assyrian text: "If Subetu does not conceive (and) does not give birth, she may take a maidservant (and) as a substitute in her position she may place (her). She [Subetu] will (thereby) bring sons into being (and) the sons will be her [Subetu's] sons. If she loves (the maidservant) she may keep (her). If she hates her she may sell her" ("The Childless Wife in Assyria and the Stories of Genesis," *Orientalia* 44 [1975]: 485–86).

Near East is that the surrogate had no say in being the surrogate. The lack of consent on the part of the surrogate epitomizes the objectification of women by women who are given a semblance of power over those less powerful than themselves. The surrogate had no voice and was used to fulfill another's aspirations.[39] The surrogacy depicted in the book of Genesis shows the power dynamics of a mistress over her muted servant. Yet the particularity of the Sarah and Hagar situation is that it is a scenario of two persons of relatively limited power in their respective domains in which one uses the other. Additionally, the scenario envisions the assertive surrogate as manifested in Sarah's perception.

As harsh as Sarah was toward Hagar, her display was a manifestation of a woman enveloped in her own jealousy, displaced anger, and injured ego. This Egyptian, her functional subordinate, did what Sarah herself was unable to do after years of marriage. Here, unlike Leah's and Rachel's situation where it is made explicit that the Deity is involved, Sarah is simply seen as being unable to conceive. When she conceives she recognizes the Deity's involvement; yet she mistreats Hagar, overlooking the Deity's involvement and the fact that Hagar is her employed surrogate carrying Abraham's heir. Sarah is concerned about the heir, not the biological mother of that heir (cf. Gen. 21).

Consequently, Sarah oppresses Hagar to such an extent that Hagar runs away (Gen. 16:6). Her treatment of Hagar reflects the language of various texts: Abraham's descendant will "serve" (*'ābad*), be "oppressed" (*'ānâ*, 15:13), and endure oppression in Egypt (Exod. 1:11–12; 3:7; Deut. 26:6). Oppression is usually depicted as the act of those who have the power to oppress. Therefore, the Egyptians oppress the enslaved Hebrews (Exod. 1:11–12), the Deity afflicts Israel in the wilderness (Deut. 8:3), and one afflicts one's enemies.[40] Accordingly, Sarah is characterized as an oppressor, thus illustrating that the power to oppress is not monopolized by a particular gender. Furthermore, that she oppresses Hagar also shows that even though her power is restricted in some domains, whatever semblance of power she has she uses to further subordinate another.

Hagar's Identity and Status

As different as they may seem, both Sarah's and Hagar's identities and statuses are defined by their ability to produce children. Both ex-

---

39. Cf. Cynthia Gordon, "Hagar: A Throw-Away Character among the Matriarchs?" in *Society of Biblical Literature Seminar Papers* 24, ed. Kent Harold Richards (Atlanta: Scholars Press, 1985), 271–77, esp. 273; Trible, *Texts of Terror*, 11.

40. Cf. Leonard J. Coppes, "עָנָה," *TWOT* 2:682–84. Notably, *'onî* is used to describe the poor and afflicted, referring to those who are distressed or disabled by pain or economic oppression.

perience complying with another person's plan; however, Hagar resists while Sarah consents.

HAGAR'S IDENTITY

Hagar's identity and status are presented in relation to Sarah. First, Hagar is identified as a "maid" (*šipḥâ*) in Gen. 16:1 as compared to a "slave" (*'āmâ*) in 21:10, 12, 13. Whatever the precise nuance of these terms, they signal Hagar's functionally subordinate status in relation to Sarah. While Sarah is the wife, Hagar is identified as Sarah's maid (*šipḥâ*) and an Egyptian.

Maid. As a *šipḥâ* she may have been a gift to Sarah and may have served as a personal attendant to her mistress. Thus Leah and Rachel are each given a maid (*šipḥâ*) when they marry Jacob (cf. Gen. 29:24, 29). One may also note that "maids" (*šĕpāḥōt*) were among the gifts that Pharaoh gave to Abraham. For this reason some have presumed that Hagar was among the maids that Abraham acquired in Egypt as a bride-price for Sarah.[41] Nonetheless, the matter of Hagar's status is not resolved by this observation, since in Gen. 12:16 "maids" (*šĕpāḥōt*) and "male servants" (*'ăbādîm*) are indicated. Sometimes the term *šipḥâ* seems to refer to a female slave, but where the maid is named, she appears to be closely connected to a married woman, perhaps as a lady-in-waiting.[42]

One may therefore ask whether Hagar's identity is similar to that of the slaves identified in Exodus 21. In particular, in 21:1–6 the Hebrew male slave is designated *'ebed 'ibrî* and subject to a six-year term of service, after which he is free. The female Hebrew slave is designated as *'āmâ*, being sold by her father (Exod. 21:7) and subject to different rules than the male slave. Once purchased from her father, she is not to be resold (21:7). In a similar way Hagar is subject to the desires and control of Sarah, while Sarah is subject to the desires and control of her husband. Given that the issue is control over another, for some interpreters the terms are synonyms used to represent servitude. Thus Alter notes that the "only evident difference is that *'amah*, the more international of the two terms, is often used in administrative lists whereas *shifḥah* occurs in contexts that are more narrative and

---

41. Dennis, *Sarah Laughed*, 62. He notes that the rabbis saw Gen. 12 as an explanation of how Hagar came to be in Sarah's service, identifying Hagar as Pharaoh's daughter, whom Pharaoh gave as part of an excessive price. She is a princess serving a wife of a barren nomad, which would account for Hagar's perception of Sarah and of Hagar's humiliation.

42. Hermann Austel ("שׁפחה," *TWOT* 2:946–47) notes that the term *šipḥâ* is often used interchangeably with *'āmâ* (cf. Gen. 30:3–4; 1 Sam 1:16, 18). The NRSV varies little in its translation of the terms *'āmâ* ("slave," Exod. 21:7; "slave woman," Gen. 21:12–13) and *šipḥâ* ("slave girl," 16:1; "female slave," 12:16).

popular in character."[43] He is concerned that rendering it "maid" will impose on the term a gentility that the sociology of the text does not portray. Alter prefers to translate both terms as "slave" to represent the owners' rights to their property, as in the cases of Sarah, Leah, and Rachel (Gen. 16:2; 29:55, 29).[44] In addition, it is noteworthy that Hagar's nationality is identified along with her functional identity—she is Egyptian (*miṣrît*). In the other cases where a maid (*šipḥâ*) is named, her nationality is not given (Bilhah and Zilpah, 29:24, 29; 30:3, 4, 9). Hamilton therefore suggests that the text shows a pattern in which the matriarch oppresses an Egyptian who flees, while in the book of Exodus, the Egyptians oppress the Hebrews and cause them to flee (Exod. 1:11–12; 14:5).[45]

Maid-wife. The second aspect of Hagar's vulnerability is her status as maid to an infertile mistress. As pointed out above, it was the right of the wife to give her maid to her husband as a surrogate; therefore, Sarah gives Hagar, her surrogate, to Abraham as his wife. Hamilton labels her a concubine, noting that the term *'iššâ* may have both meanings—wife and concubine. However, as he himself notes, the typical term for concubine (*pîlegeš*) is not used for Hagar. In the case of Nahor, Abraham's brother, his concubine Reumah is designated as such, namely, *pîlegeš*.[46] The narrative refers to the fact that Abraham had sons with concubines. To those sons he gave gifts (Gen. 25:6) while reserving all his inheritance for Isaac (25:5). Other concubines include Rizpah, Saul's concubine (2 Sam. 3:7; 21:8–14), and the Levite of Gilead's concubine (Judg. 19–20), whose rape and murder led to the death of thousands. David (2 Sam. 5:13) and Solomon (1 Kings 11:3) had concubines and wives. While each term usually signals a different status, the book of Genesis names other concubines who are also labeled as wives. Thus Bilhah is named Jacob's wife (Gen. 30:4; 37:2) and his concubine, notably in the situation where Reuben, his firstborn, had sexual relations with her (35:22). Zilpah, her counterpart, is identified only as Jacob's wife (37:2). Keturah is a different case in that she is identified as Abraham's wife (25:1) and possibly as a concubine. Since she is not named in Gen. 25:6 it is not clear whether she is included in the general reference to Abraham's concubines. Out-

---

43. Alter, *Genesis*, 67.

44. Alter, *Genesis*, 67.

45. Hamilton, *Genesis 1–17*, 448.

46. Hamilton, *Genesis 1–17*, 442n6. He follows Speiser's (*Genesis*, 117) argument in equating the two terms. While he cites Gen. 22:24 as an example of a concubine, the text refers to Nahor's offspring by his concubine Reumah. Cf. V. P. Hamilton, "פֶּלֶגֶשׁ," *TWOT* 2:724. Based on Judg. 19:3–5, he argues that the concubine was married to the man, and she did not cohabit with him unless she was married to him. In that text the man is referred to as her husband along with references to her father-in-law and son-in-law.

side Genesis, however, she is labeled as Abraham's concubine (*pîlegeš*) (1 Chron. 1:32).[47] It appears that a concubine was given some protection and status in the society, though not that of a primary wife.

In addition, to be a concubine one had to be attached to a man and was obligated to that man. The concubine was of a different status than a "prostitute" or "whore" (*zônâ*). A whore could be male (Exod. 34:16; Num. 25:1) or female (Gen. 38:15; Lev. 19:29; 21:7). The term connotes ignominy or shame (cf. Josh. 2:1; 16:17, 25; Judg. 11:1). The whore is known for having sexual relationships (for compensation) with multiple partners other than those to whom she/he is married (Jer. 2:20; 3:1, 3; Ezek. 16:31, 34; cf. Gen. 38:24).[48] The female prostitute was viewed as an unsuitable marriage partner for a priest (Lev. 21:7, 14). A cultic prostitute (*qādēš*) was either male or female (Deut. 23:18 [NRSV 23:17]) and also viewed negatively. Hagar is neither a whore (*zônâ*) nor a cultic prostitute (*qādēš*) nor subject to the negative portrayal often accorded those identities. The tendency to classify Hagar as a concubine may arise from assigning a negative and illicit status to the role of concubine that the text does not assign to that status. Likewise, the bias of many interpreters against a foreign woman as the wife of one of the patriarchs is also responsible for the tendency to label Hagar as a concubine rather than a wife.

Hagar's status is an amalgamation of roles that includes functioning with a degree of equity alongside Sarah and as Sarah's subordinate. As the surrogate and subordinate, Hagar has little say in the use of her body or about the offspring she would produce. She is to be a vessel to bear her mistress's child, but her vulnerability also facilitates her status change. Hagar is given to her mistress's husband as his wife and thus was made co-wife with Sarah. The ramifications of this are missed if one disregards the designation of both women as "wife" (*'iššâ*). It is the tendency of many to refer to Hagar as a concubine, thus interpreting *'iššâ* as a wife when it refers to Sarah and as a concubine when it refers to Hagar.[49] Yet none would argue that Sarah became a concubine to Pharaoh or Abimelech (Gen. 12 and 20). The tendency to see Hagar as a concubine is clearly fueled by the desire to maintain Hagar in a status that is subordinate to

47. Hamilton (*Genesis 1–17*, 446) assumes that Keturah is included in the reference and that she is labeled as both wife and concubine. He also notes Judg. 19:3 and 20:4, where the Levite is labeled the concubine's "husband." Hamilton therefore concludes that in the book of Genesis women are classified as "concubine-wife." This status would be distinct from both the wife and the concubine in that it may combine facets of both statuses.

48. In many instances Israel is characterized as a whore for turning to idols (e.g., Deut. 31:16; Jer. 3:6; Ezek. 16:26; Hos. 4:12; 9:1). Cf. Leon J. Wood, "זנה," *TWOT* 1:246–47. See chap. 7.

49. Speiser, *Genesis*.

Sarah's.[50] However, without such an interpretation, the narrative already depicts the muddled situation in which Hagar is both co-wife and still Sarah's servant. Their equitable status fuels the tension between them and makes Sarah's treatment of Hagar poignant.[51] Here is a situation that results in staggering complications that would be tantamount to employing an ex-spouse as a maid to the current spouse and expecting no conflict of interest in the performance of the roles.

HAGAR'S FUNCTION AND POWER

Whatever her functional identity, Hagar has power within her domain and manifests that power in her existence and actions. First, Hagar's power is latent in her role as servant (*šipḥâ*) and co-wife ('*iššâ*). She has access to both Sarah and Abraham. Sarah regulates the situation by giving Hagar to Abraham as a wife; however, she cannot regulate Hagar's response to that situation. Apparently, Sarah could not control her own response to the dynamics of the situation that she created.

Second, Hagar is a subversive presence in that she allowed for an alternative that would otherwise not be an option—she provides the opportunity for surrogacy.[52] Nonetheless, her presence is not that of a uniquely qualified person, indispensable to the service that she renders. If Sarah had another maid of childbearing age, she would be just as eligible for the surrogate role. The ethos facilitated the interchangeability of women in the quest for motherhood. The narrative, however, recognizes Hagar by name as well as by her functional status, in contrast to Gen. 21, where she is often nameless when Sarah speaks of her. The irony of the subversive presence is that it often forces an alternative. On the one hand, Hagar represents an alternative to Sarah's infertility, an alternative Sarah chose. On the other hand, she may have been the catalyst of Sarah's oppressive behavior, not because she deliberately provoked it, but because Hagar was what Sarah was not. "Sarah is now a non-child-producing '*iššâ*; and Hagar is a child-producing '*iššâ*. And that is what annoys Sarah and not any barbs that Hagar is throwing at her."[53] The narrator appears willing to assign some blame to Hagar for being oppressed, but one must consider that Sarah's jealousy or other feelings may have been the catalyst that made Hagar the most likely scapegoat for her frustration.

Third, once Hagar conceived, Sarah lost status in her eyes. Hagar perceived change in the power dynamics in that she was carrying a child

---

50. Cf. Dennis, *Sarah Laughed*, 44. He sees Hagar as a "secondary wife."

51. Cf. Alter, *Genesis*, 68. He states, "The terminological equation of the two women is surely intended, and sets up an ironic backdrop for Sarai's abuse of Hagar."

52. Cf. Morriss, *Power*, 50–53.

53. Hamilton, *Genesis 1–17*, 447; cf. Westermann, *Genesis 12–36*, 240.

and Sarah was still infertile. In the other instances of surrogacy (Leah and Rachel) the maids' attitudes are not reported. Instead, it is reported that Rachel rejoiced that Bilhah her maid bore a son, whom she named Dan, and considered herself vindicated (Gen. 30:6). The narrator cleverly indicates Hagar's perception of a rise in her status. Sarah's response is to blame Abraham for the tension between her and Hagar (16:5), although she represents Hagar as the one in whose eyes she (Sarah) has lost status. Sarah assigns to Abraham the power to control the tension and thus blames him. Hagar is conspicuously silent, being represented only through the narrator and Sarah's voice. Nonetheless, it could be that Hagar was simply proud of being pregnant rather than arrogant. Whether it accurately represents Hagar's belief and attitude, the double representation is a way of validating the claim that she disrespected Sarah. Whatever the tension, Hagar is depicted as the instigator. Sarah represents herself as the one who initiated the situation by giving Hagar to Abraham and who now suffers for her effort (16:5). Sarah perceives the need for a power higher than Abraham, so she invokes the Deity to adjudicate the situation. Furthermore, Abraham authorizes her to deal with Hagar as she sees fit, thus empowering her by pointing to the functional status that constitutes the relationship between Sarah (mistress) and Hagar (maid).

Suppressing Hagar

Power has a neutral quality in that it is a generative force. How it is used is often mistaken for the essence of power, but power may be used to bring about both good and evil and every shade in between. Even so, one's motive for using power does not control the extent and type of the effects. Herein one observes another aspect of Hagar's power in that she flees the oppressive situation in order to put an end to her affliction. Demonstrating the power of self-preservation and the belief that she should not be oppressed, Hagar's instinct is to remove herself from the oppressive situation. To return therefore goes against her judgment and natural inclination. Yet she surrenders her judgment to the Deity, not with a promise to resolve the oppression, but with the prospect of a future in which she may be the mother of a nation—a progenitrix. Accordingly, the Deity tells Hagar to participate in her oppression by allowing her oppressor access to her. Clearly, the Deity is not concerned about Hagar's immediate well-being. The Deity mirrors Sarah's offense, or Sarah manifests the Deity's perspective. When Hagar is identified by her functional identity—maid—the Deity also refers to her as such in Gen. 16:8 (cf. Gen. 21).

Undoubtedly the narrator's perspective on the Deity persists in the story. However, one cannot invalidate this portrait of the Deity because it is less than favorable. The Deity is partial toward the Deity's favorites, even when they commit oppressive acts against others. So Hagar's horror could have been that the Deity, the authority in the domain, approves of Sarah's oppressive practices. Having escaped the oppression, Hagar is in the desert at a spring. After ascertaining why she is there, the angel, who turns out to be the Deity,[54] tells her to return to her "mistress" (*gĕberet*) and be oppressed (*'ānâ*) under her hand or authority (Gen. 16:9).[55] In most other instances where the formulation "under the hand of" (*taḥat yad*) is used it denotes authority or power, for example, as "in the hand of" (*bĕyad*) usually denotes "power" (16:6).[56]

It would have been understandable if Hagar declined to return; instead, Hagar conforms to the Deity's wish. Her solace is not that the Deity is on her side to somehow reprimand or punish her oppressor, but that there is an existence beyond the oppressive situation. Hagar is grateful that she has seen the Deity and can "remain alive," and she loses sight of her distress (Gen. 16:13). Like Hagar, some are sidetracked by the encounter and by her naming the Deity (*'ēl rŏ'î*), which no other human does[57]—the Deity usually confers the name (cf. Exod. 6:3; 34:14). For Trevor Dennis, the promise in Gen. 16:10 of multiple descendants gives the Deity a more favorable image than the Deity's command to Hagar to subject herself to oppression. He points out that Hagar is one of only four persons in the book of Genesis to whom a promise was directly communicated by the Deity, "and she a woman, a slave, an Egyptian."[58] Again, as with her status as wife, this interpretation assumes that she is out of place if she

54. While Gen. 16:9–11 uses *mal'ak yhwh* "angel of Yʜᴡʜ," the being is also designated as *yhwh* in 16:13—*wattiqrā' šēm-yhwh haddōbēr 'ēlêhā* "she called the name of Yʜᴡʜ who spoke to her."

55. The verb "to afflict" (*'ānâ*) is the same term used to describe Sarah's treatment of Hagar in Gen. 16:6. Here in 16:9 the reflexive form of the verb is used to connote "let yourself be oppressed."

56. Hamilton, *Genesis 1–17*, 452. In regard to Gen. 41:35 Joseph advises that responsibility for the grain gathered during prosperous times be placed under Pharaoh's authority to anticipate the famine. A similar formulation is used of the Moabites, who are depicted as being under Israel's control (Judg. 3:30; cf. Ps. 106:42; Isa. 3:6). The JSB is one of the few modern translations that reflect the oppression to which Hagar is to return: "Go back to your mistress, and submit to her harsh treatment." At this point, many modern translations diminish the impact of the command to return by softening the language of the text, for example, the NRSV and the ESV: "Return to your mistress, and submit to her."

57. Hamilton, *Genesis 1–17*, 455. Cf. other names for the Deity, including "God Almighty" (*'ēl šadday*, Gen. 17:1; Exod. 6:3); "Jealous God" (*'ēl qannā'*), used to describe Yʜᴡʜ (Exod. 34:14).

58. Dennis, *Sarah Laughed*, 67. Dennis's pointing to Hagar as a woman, slave, and Egyptian is typical. He is surprised that the Deity would dialogue with such a person and in that perspective on Hagar's identity participates in her portrayal as "other" and unworthy of such a dialogue. After all, the Deity also spoke to Eve, Sarah, and Rebekah, and this is not seen as unusual.

is with a being of a "higher" status, in this case the Deity. If the Deity addresses animals, why would it be surprising for the Deity to address a woman and a servant? Clearly, the Deity does not select a dialogue partner on the basis of functional identity or status.

Likewise, one may be dazzled by the declaration encoded in Ishmael's name, namely, that the Deity attended to (šāma') Hagar's "affliction" ('ŏnî). There is no doubt that both Hagar's and the Hebrews' experiences are characterized as "affliction" ('ŏnî; Exod. 3:7, 17).[59] Nonetheless, Hagar's affliction did not compel the Deity to rescue her from the affliction. When the Deity observed the affliction of the Israelites in Egypt, the response was to rescue them from that oppressive situation, although they endured much of it before the Deity opted to respond. In commanding her return, the Deity demonstrates awareness of Hagar's affliction; thus it is all the more horrific that Hagar is told to go back.[60] Dennis's comment captures the horror of the incident: "God's commands to Hagar represent one of the darkest, most unnerving moments in all Scripture. It seems he has revealed his true colours. Here, at least, he seems to be in favor of the *status quo* and on the side of the oppressor, a defender of the interests of the Sarais of the world against its all too vulnerable Hagars."[61]

In manifesting her power, Hagar stands alone against the desires of other agents in her domain. Abraham, her husband, sanctioned Sarah to mistreat Hagar, the younger, pregnant woman. As much as he may have wanted an heir, that desire does not seem to play a role in his attitude toward her and his child. He falls silent while Sarah wreaks havoc on the pregnant Hagar. The wisdom tradition may offer a perspective on the dynamics between Hagar and Sarah: "Under three things the earth trembles; under four it cannot bear up: a slave when he becomes king, and a fool when glutted with food; an unloved woman when she gets a husband, and a maid when she succeeds her mistress" (Prov. 30:21–23).[62] In this tradition, the elevation of the maid (šipḥâ) over the mistress (gĕberet) is deemed unfavorable. As in the case of the other three things, the exaltation of the maid over her mistress is perceived as a profound change in circumstances. Clearly, these texts are designed to maintain a status quo where status elevation was suppressed. Ever so briefly, Hagar exercised her power by choosing to resist the oppression. Apparently, Hagar's struggle was futile because of the divinely approved oppression.

59. Hamilton (*Genesis 1–17*, 449) translates 'ŏnî as "humiliation"; contrast Westermann (*Genesis 12–36*, 234), who translates the term as "cry."

60. Cf. Trible, *Texts of Terror*, 16, who sees the command as a "divine word of terror."

61. Dennis, *Sarah Laughed*, 66.

62. Hamilton, *Genesis 1–17*, 448.

Genesis 21—Uncalculated Outcomes

Sarah's View of Her Circumstances

After all that she endured, Sarah conceived and gave birth to a son whom Abraham named Isaac (*yiṣḥāq*; Gen. 21:2–3).[63] Was it a joyous occasion for all? The name builds on the verb "to laugh" (*ṣāḥaq*); they had laughed upon hearing that Sarah would conceive (17:17; 18:12–13). One may observe that the term "laughter" (*ṣĕḥōq*) occurs in parallel with "to scorn, mock" (*lāʿag*) where it connotes a laughingstock (cf. Jer. 20:7; 48:26, 39; Ezek. 23:32; Job 12:4; Lam. 3:14).[64] In these instances, it is used of a person or nation who would be mocked. Alter thus concludes: "All who hear of it may laugh, rejoice, with Sarah, but the hint that they might also laugh at her is evident in her language."[65] The usage and interpretation of *ṣāḥaq* yield a noteworthy observation, namely, that it means "to mock, joke" (Gen. 19:14; 39:14) and "to play."[66] From Sarah's perspective it could be that she perceived that some laughed at her because she conceived (21:6).[67]

For the Child's Sake—Motive and the Abuse of Power

While having a child of her own should have proven a happy occasion for Sarah, she finds herself battling the situation she created. In Gen. 16 Sarah claims that her motivation against Hagar is that Hagar dishonored her. The narrative supports Sarah's claim and in this way legitimates the negative treatment; but in Gen. 21 nothing is said of Hagar's behavior. Rather, Sarah's motivation is Ishmael, namely, his presence and his behavior. Because of the high infant mortality rate, children were apparently weaned during their third year, and a feast celebrated their survival.[68] Perhaps at the festival that celebrates Isaac, Sarah observes Ishmael in an act that is variously interpreted (Gen. 21:9). That act is the catalyst for Sarah's desire and action to get rid of Hagar and Ishmael. Apparently, Gen. 21 and 16 may be two distinct traditions about the dynamics between Sarah and Hagar. It is because

---

63. Along with the instances where the father names the child, there are other instances where the mother names the child: Eve of Seth (Gen. 4:25); Lot's daughters of Moab and Ben-ammi (19:37–38); Leah of Reuben and her other children (29:32, 33, 34, 35); Rachel of her children—including the sons born to her maid (30:6); and where both parents name the child: Isaac and Rebekah of Esau and Jacob (25:25).

64. The alternate form (*ṣĕḥōq*) occurs in Jer. 20:7; cf. Payne, "צחק," *TWOT* 2:763–64.

65. Alter, *Genesis*, 97.

66. Alter, *Genesis*, 98.

67. The NRSV reads: "God has brought laughter for me; everyone who hears will laugh with me." Cf. Dennis, *Sarah Laughed*, 58.

68. Meyers, *Discovering Eve*, 112; cf. Dennis, *Sarah Laughed*, 58.

of this that I included both here as distinctive perspectives on female manifestations of power.

SARAH'S MOTIVE

The text terms Ishmael's behavior as "playing" (*měṣaḥēq*; Gen. 21:9). What Ishmael is doing to enrage Sarah is a debated issue that centers on the translation of *měṣaḥēq* and whether the different forms of the term represent different actions.[69] Alter asserts that Sarah may have seen Ishmael as "presuming to play the role of Isaac, child of laughter, presuming to be the legitimate heir."[70] He discounts medieval exegetes' explanation that Sarah's response was because of Ishmael's sexual behavior toward Isaac.[71] Even so, Sarah's perception of Ishmael's presence is indicated in her concern about the inheritance. Whatever Ishmael's behavior, Sarah's motivation for getting rid of him is attached to her desire and may have very little to do with the immediate connection to his behavior. She may have already decided to get rid of Ishmael and simply uses the opportunity to bolster her decision. Evidently, in the power dynamics of those involved, Sarah has power over Hagar and Ishmael. Whether or not she is acting to protect Isaac from molestation, her motive is clear—she does not want Abraham's two sons to share in the inheritance. Rather, Sarah wants her son, Isaac, to be the sole heir.[72] The narrative later aligns Sarah's desire with the Deity's, thus depicting the results of Sarah's actions, however harsh, as fitting into the Deity's plans for Isaac as Abraham's heir.

By the sheer number of references to Hagar as a subordinate—the slave (Gen. 21:10, 12, 13)—and not a wife, Sarah highlights Hagar's subordination rather than the possible relational equity of Hagar as her co-wife and their sons as coheirs. She does not refer to Ishmael by his name or as Abraham's son but as Hagar's son, or the "son of the slave" (21:10). Her language shows disdain for Hagar. Abraham is thus asked to respond to Hagar the slave, not Hagar his wife. The complexity of the dynamics is that Hagar's status is constituted of both subordination and a semblance of equality as woman and mother. As a subordinate, she is not perceived as an equal, but her subordination leads her to her relational

---

69. In Gen. 21:9 the Piel form occurs (*měṣaḥēq*), while in 21:6 the Qal form occurs (*yiṣḥāq*). Alter (*Genesis*, 98) discusses some of the perspectives but maintains that Ishmael may have been mocking Isaac. The different forms have led to attempts to differentiate the usage. Alter, however, denies that one can use the semantic difference to assert conceptual differences here. In both 21:6 and 9 the root is usually rendered "laugh" or "mock."

70. Alter, *Genesis*, 98; cf. Meyers, *Discovering Eve*, 193; Dennis, *Sarah Laughed*, 59.

71. Alter, *Genesis*, 98.

72. See chap. 4 for Rackman's view that Isaac was unwilling to bless only one son and so repeat his father's struggle and legacy of alienation between his sons.

status as co-wife and mother. She functions as both maid and wife, but as mother she is equal to Sarah. Sarah's treatment of her depicts the idea of mutually exclusive categories in the actualization of the Deity's plan. Thus to function effectively the plan cannot tolerate Ishmael as heir and must therefore exclude him from that role. Abraham's sons are not seen as equals in the fulfillment of the Deity's plans for Abraham. Consequently, Ishmael and his mother are treated as incidental, and the principals do not refer to them by name. The narrative itself dehumanizes and nullifies them by making them dispensable and nameless entities to be discarded after their usefulness has expired.

Sarah's use for Hagar expires once Sarah's son survives, and Hagar becomes a liability to Sarah's status. Interestingly, the female-female context of Sarah's behavior is shaped by her role as wife and mother. Hagar has been essential to Sarah's status as an infertile wife, to assist in securing Abraham's future. Yet Sarah's achievement of producing an heir through Hagar constitutes the problem for the relationship. While Abraham is not the instigator, his presence as husband fosters a situation of competition between the women, where one mother ostracizes the other and one wife alienates the other. Sarah the stepmother is ready to separate Abraham from his son and the sons from each other. All of a sudden, the son of a servant (Ishmael) is not deemed worthy of the status of heir alongside her own son (Isaac). Clearly, being female does not deter Sarah from oppressing another woman. Her behavior illustrates that her gender does not guarantee solidarity with another woman. Rather, the quality of her behavior is a product not solely of her gender but also of her status and sense of self. Likewise, her limited status in relation to Abraham does not deter her from attempting to limit someone else's power. From this perspective, Abraham is not to be vilified as the "male" antagonist nor Hagar as the foreign servant. Both Sarah and Abraham are sanctioned in their oppression of others, and their power as manifested in their domain is executed against others. Hagar's power is focused on self-preservation, and she maintains dignity while suffering and dying.

Abuse of Power

In her position as wife, Sarah uses Abraham to banish Hagar. Because of this, Dennis sees Sarah's response as the effect of prolonged infertility that results in bitterness.[73] Sarah's interest is to protect her son from his elder half brother. There are several notable instances where the well-being of the younger brother is threatened by the elder brother(s), including Cain killing Abel (Gen. 4:8), Esau threatening to kill Jacob

---

73. Dennis, *Sarah Laughed*, 59.

(27:42), and Joseph's elder brothers plotting to kill him (37:20–21). The motivation for the threat is characteristically different in these situations. Thus while Sarah's motive may be to protect Isaac from the threat posed by his older brother, Ishmael, the threat is not to Isaac's survival as in the other noted instances.[74] The threat would certainly affect his lifestyle depending on whether he is the sole heir to Abraham's blessing and possessions. As evident by the existence and thriving of Ishmael and Esau, who are not the designated heirs, it is possible for Isaac to thrive without being the sole heir.

The command to "banish" (*gāraš*) Hagar and Ishmael echoes the events of banishment from the Garden of Eden and the Cain and Abel story (Gen. 3:24; 4:14). Regarding the banishment, Dreifuss and Riemer counter Rashi's interpretation that they were expelled for "worshiping the pagan deities." Rather, they question, if idolatry existed in Abraham's household, why is it that only Ishmael and his mother are singled out for punishment? They conclude that Sarah capitalizes on Abraham's willingness to replace Ishmael, his firstborn, with Isaac, his second-born.[75] Clearly, the theme of the rejected firstborn looms large in this story, but how does one get rid of a perceived problem that one created?

If one uses the ancient Near Eastern laws to illuminate the situation, Ishmael is apparently the legitimate heir. The surrogacy was effective and Ishmael is the firstborn of Abraham. Now that Sarah has her child, Isaac, Sarah no longer wants the surrogate mother or the child. It is possible that Ishmael may have understood his status as the firstborn poised to inherit Abraham's possessions,[76] but the narrative does not refer to him as the firstborn. Its reluctance to designate Ishmael as the firstborn may already signal the unfavorable view of Ishmael, since the narrative identifies the firstborn as such even though they are not depicted as their father's favorite.[77] Since Ishmael has a legitimate claim to Abraham's property, Sarah may be asking Abraham to do something illegal. In view of the fact that *gāraš* is also used to describe divorced women (cf. Lev. 21:7, 14; 22:13; Num. 30:10 [NRSV 30:9]; Ezek. 44:22), one may propose that Sarah was asking Abraham to divorce (*gāraš*) Hagar by sending her away.[78] Certainly, the command to Abraham leaves no allowance for a resolution of the situation by alternate means—namely, that Hagar and Ishmael remain in the household and Abraham ignore them in his designation of an heir.

74. Dennis, *Sarah Laughed*, 59. He credits Sarah with wanting to protect Isaac's life.
75. Dreifuss and Riemer, *Abraham the Man*, 76.
76. Meyers, *Discovering Eve*, 193.
77. See Esau (Gen. 27:32), Reuben (35:23; 46:8), and Manasseh (41:51; 48:14).
78. Hamilton, *Genesis 18–50*, 79–80; cf. Code of Hammurabi §§170–71.

Sanctioned Abuse of Power

Both Abraham and the Deity participate in Sarah's abuse of her power over Hagar and Ishmael to the extent that they have the power to stop it and do not. Beyond their consenting to her abusive actions, their active participation perpetuates the course of behavior that Sarah implemented. Abraham assists in getting Hagar and her son ready for their departure, thus responding to both Sarah's and the Deity's request. The Deity tells Abraham to do what Sarah tells him to do (Gen. 21:12). The rationale given to Abraham to convince him not to be distressed is that the Deity has a plan for Hagar and her son (21:13). Nonetheless, the Deity confirms Sarah's desire that Isaac will be Abraham's designated heir (21:12). Once again, a person is shown to acquiesce to the desires of the Deity even when that acquiescence entails relinquishing one's judgment and care for oneself or another. Abraham concedes to sustain Hagar's oppression.

The Deity's response is to replicate Sarah's wish for Isaac to be the heir instead of Ishmael. Whether or not this is part of the divine plan, the effect on Hagar and her son is decisively negative. Although the immediate oppression is held up against the backdrop of a future, future progeny and wealth do not nullify the oppression suffered. Clearly, the Deity is on the side of the oppressors, just as in Gen. 16.[79] Even with the nuances of Sarah and Hagar's power dynamics, the operative force in the domain depicted in Gen. 16 and 21 is the Deity's plan for Abraham.

Conclusion

In light of the above discussion several observations about power are noteworthy. First, power is domain specific in its manifestation and influence. It is not abstract from interactions, behaviors, and thoughts, but is manifested in a domain and by particular agents. Power therefore is defined here as the ability to effect change and exercise choice. It is manifested in different ways and because of this may be understood as different types of power.

Second, the manifestation of power may also entail persuasion of others and oneself. Sarah persuaded Abraham to participate in her mistreatment of Hagar, but before she does, she persuaded herself to use Hagar as a surrogate and then to get rid of Hagar.

Third, the abuse of power is not unique to any gender. The abuse is likely to come from anyone who has power, whatever the measure of the

---

79. Cf. Hamilton, *Genesis 18–50*, 81: "Here is an instance of God using the wrath of a human being to accomplish his purposes."

power. The magnitude of the power does not determine whether it may be abused. Rather the existence of power itself and the person who uses it foster its abuse. Thus, for anyone who possesses power the possibility exists that she/he may abuse it.

Fourth, the ultimate use of power to determine the future does not belong to humans. While that is good news for some, it is bad news for the disfavored and for those who are oppressed by those who are the Deity's favorites. In the narrative, this is bad news for Hagar and her descendants. She is asked to accept her marginalization and oppression in light of a promised future still plagued by the residual effect of her present oppression.

Finally, power also resides in weakness. The presence of a subordinate influences the dynamics of a domain and thus alters the perception of all within the domain. Even those marginalized by their experience have power, however limited. In this respect, choice is as much a power as the effective use of choice. Accordingly, there is no such thing as powerlessness, only the perception of it.

6

Quest for Power in the Family Domain

Rachel and Leah (Genesis 29–30)

Introduction

The concern about progeny is fundamental to the relational and behavioral dynamics of Rachel and Leah because Rachel, the primary wife,
is barren (*'ăqārâ*).[1] The Rachel and Leah narrative is embedded in the
Jacob-Laban story in several ways, including a conceptual dependence.
In this chapter I focus on the relational and functional identity of Rachel
and Leah in relation to each other and to their father, husband, maids,
and children. I propose that even in these female-female relational configurations, females operate within the larger framework of a female-male
dynamic as wives, daughters, and sisters; the presence or influence of
males defines the nature of the females' relationship.[2] Consequently, I
discuss the relational and behavioral aspects between Jacob and Laban
because of the influence on Rachel and Leah's existence and well-being
as sisters, co-wives, and mothers. The maid-wives also factor into the

1. The term "primary" here is used to express the favor shown to this wife. Sarah is
considered primary in that she is the first wife. Rachel is primary because of Jacob's love
for her as compared to his disregard for Leah.
2. Cf. Bernard, *Female World*, 20–21, for her idea of "place" conceptualization of the
female role in society where neither male nor female defines the norm but constitute it
together.

relational configuration as those who are used to secure progeny and to facilitate the status of their mistress in the domain.

Becoming Co-wives

Basis of Suitability

What happens when a man meets his future spouse? In the Genesis narratives the predictability is presented in "type-scenes," namely, a man meets a woman at a well and takes her as his wife (Gen. 29:9–14).[3] The pattern is shared with Abraham's servant meeting Rebekah (24:10–33) and Moses meeting Jethro's daughters (Exod. 2:15–21). The components of the scene usually include the following: a hero or his representative who goes to a distant land and stops at a well; a girl (sometimes more than one) who arrives at the well to draw water; the hero or his representative drawing water for the girl or she for him; the girl returning home and reporting the encounter to her male guardian (father or brother); the hero or his representative being brought to the girl's home; marriage between the hero and the girl being arranged and then taking place.[4] For the Gen. 24 and 29 narratives, the land where the hero sojourns is the land of his ancestors and the girl is a relative. The underlying concern is that the hero marry a suitable woman—the first criterion of suitability being that she is of his ancestral house, not a foreigner. That Rachel is suitable for Jacob is an important aspect of the narrative portrayal of Jacob vis-à-vis Esau, who married foreign women (Gen. 26:34). It is Rebekah's concern that Jacob should go to her brother's house. The narrative offers at least two reasons—escape from his brother Esau, and finding a wife—and expands on what happens when Jacob seeks to marry. The familial tie between Rachel and Jacob is identified through the relationship between her father, Laban, and Jacob. Thus the narrative twice indicates that Laban is Jacob's uncle—brother of his mother (29:10). Other instances also point to the relational connection between Jacob and Laban, namely, brother ('āḥ, 29:4); Jacob introduces himself to Rachel as Laban's relative (literally, "brother of her father," 29:12); and Laban refers to Jacob as a relative (literally, "you are my brother," 29:15).[5] In 29:14 it is reported that Laban says, "you are my bone and my flesh" (cf. 2:23; Judg. 9:2; 2 Sam. 5:1 parallels 1 Chron. 11:1), a formula that may suggest "that a reciprocal covenant oath is involved as well as

3. Robert Alter, *The Art of Biblical Narrative* (New York: Basic Books, 1981), 52–56.
4. Hamilton, *Genesis 18–50*, 254–55.
5. Hamilton, *Genesis 18–50*, 255.

a possibility of blood ties."[6] Jacob is therefore suitable for Rachel, but that alone does not establish the terms of the marriage.

Negotiating Marriage

The negotiation for a marriage enters into the dynamic as part of settling the terms of employment. In Gen. 29:15 Laban claims Jacob as a relative but is willing to compensate him for his help, thus making the uncle-nephew relationship secondary to the employer-employee relationship. The layering of these relationships confounds the power dynamics because multiple functional identities define the relational configuration. The layering of relationships usually signals a conflict of domains, especially when the relationships include functional equity and subordination (e.g., maid-wife) or obligation to persons for whom one has opposing or competing regard (e.g., one's child vis-à-vis her/his spouse).[7] In the Abraham-Sarah case, Abraham claims that Sarah is his sister and thus masks the operative spousal relationship. Hagar relates to Sarah as maid and co-wife, being both a functional equal and a subordinate. Rachel and Leah are sisters who become co-wives but without the functional equality of co-wives. Rather, Rachel, the younger sister and second wife, is favored over Leah, the older sister and first wife. With Laban and Jacob the multiple layers of the relationship consist of three configurations: uncle-nephew, employer-employee, and father-in-law–son-in-law. Whether or not there are specific behavioral expectations for each of these, it is clear that many other aspects of the Jacob-Laban relationship may be explored. In this discussion, the negotiations that resulted from Jacob's marriage to two sisters and the ensuing dynamics between the sisters are the particular aspects in view.

In the marriage negotiation, it is unusual that there is an intervening marriage between the male and someone other than the woman for whom he negotiates. In Isaac's case, Abraham's representative meets Rebekah and brokers the marriage with her brother Laban. In Rachel's case, she meets her future husband at the well, and Laban, her father, brokers the marriage between her and Jacob.[8] It is the right of the father or male guardian to negotiate the marriage of the females in his protectorate. More important, however, is the control of her sexuality. As a single woman, the right to consent to her sexual behavior lies with her male guardian, and as a married woman, the right of access lies with her husband. In no circumstances does a woman have the right of consent

6. Hamilton, *Genesis 18–50*, 256.
7. See chap. 7 regarding Judah and Tamar.
8. Cf. James Baker, *Women's Rights in Old Testament Times* (Salt Lake City: Signature, 1992), 41.

to her sexuality unless she has relinquished the authorized channels of sexual expression. In the latter case, she may function as a prostitute, consenting to sexual interaction with the males she encounters. Ruth and Naomi's case also stands out in that a female acts as the protector over another female. Even so, the female's consent over sexuality is usually over the sexuality of one of her subordinates, namely, when she enlists the service of a maid as her surrogate. Ruth and Naomi are different from this model of a female controlling her maid, but their relationship is founded on a hierarchy with Ruth's status being subordinate to Naomi, her mother-in-law.

In brokering Rachel's marriage, Laban has the opportunity to secure a husband for both of his daughters, and to gain economic advantage as part of the bride-price. He negotiates a seven-year term of service toward the bride-price, notably, one year more than the term of servitude for a Hebrew slave (Exod. 21:1–6). As seen in Jacob's offer and Laban's acceptance, the price does not have to be the presentation of property or a person. For example, David's valor is a demonstration of his desire to marry Michal (1 Sam. 18:25–27). The narrator gives the reason for Jacob's preference for Rachel over Leah, but the interpretation of the narrative is ambiguous on this point. In Gen. 29:1–15 there is no mention of Leah nor is there any report that Jacob encounters her during the month he lives in Laban's household. After that month, Laban attempts to make a settlement regarding Jacob's compensation. Almost as an afterthought, the narrator then tells that Laban has two daughters and briefly describes both. Only after the description does the narrator mention Jacob's love for Rachel as if to justify Jacob's request and to set the stage for the selection (Gen. 29:16–18). The narrator contrasts the two sisters by their birth order and appearance but does not compare them in regard to Jacob's disposition toward them. First, regarding their birth order, Leah is "the older" (*haggĕdōlâ*) of the two sisters, but she is not termed the firstborn. Rachel is identified as "the younger" (*haqqĕṭannâ*, 29:16), much like Lot's younger daughter is labeled "the younger" (*haṣṣeʿîrâ*, 19:31, 35, 38).

Second, the adjective "tender, delicate" (*rak*) is used to describe Leah's eyes, while Rachel's "form" (*tōʾar*) is described as "beautiful" (*yĕpat*). The adjective *rak* also means weak, for example, frail children (Gen. 33:13), or timid or soft-hearted (Deut. 20:8).[9] It may also describe something tender (such as flocks, Gen. 18:7), delicate (of women, Deut. 28:56; Isa. 47:1), young and inexperienced (1 Chron. 22:5; 29:1; 2 Chron. 13:7),[10] or soft

---

9. The adjective derives from the verb *rākak* "to be tender, weak, soft." The NRSV and the JSB only rarely translate *rak* as "weak" or "frail."

10. Hamilton, *Genesis 18–50*, 258–59. The adjective "tender" (*rak*) in parallel with *naʿar* "lad" expresses the idea of youthful inexperience. Nowell (*Women in the Old Testament*,

speech (Prov. 15:1). Thus the varying understandings of the description: NRSV, "Leah's eyes were lovely"; JSB, "Leah had weak eyes." Hamilton concludes: "Leah may be older, but her eyes are the beautiful eyes of a person who looks much younger."[11] In this interpretation, Jacob prefers a more womanly appearance rather than youthful innocence.[12] While entire traditions are based on Leah's unattractiveness, it could be that she was being described not in regard to her beauty or lack thereof. Rather, the comment about her eyes may signal a distinctive feature that was not appealing to Jacob. The rationale, then, for choosing Rachel is her physical appearance, just as Leah's rejection is due to her appearance.[13] This dynamic is thus introduced as one not of their behavior, which they could control, but of physical features that they did not create nor could they control. The women do not control why Jacob chooses one over the other, yet the relationship between them will be defined by choices made regarding them.

Consequently, Jacob's wishes define the marriage negotiation, but he does not involve the women as participants in the terms of the agreement. Neither Rachel nor Leah has input in the matter. Rather, the power to determine their future and relationships lies in the hands of their father. In response to Jacob's offer regarding Rachel, Laban observes that it is better to give "her" to Jacob than to give her to another man (Gen. 29:19). Laban does not specify why it is better and does not name the daughter to whom he refers. There is no indication that another was vying for Rachel or that she was otherwise designated for another man. It is therefore striking that the options that Laban considers are not the terms offered, but rather the possibility of offering his daughter to another. His represented concern is to secure a marriage for his daughter, and his words seem to confirm a man of options rather than a man without.

---

31) suggests that *rak* refers to Leah's "blue eyes, a rare occurrence in the Middle East. Her eyes were her distinctive feature and mostly sensitive to light." Cf. Wenham, *Genesis 16–50*, 235, who argues that her eyes did not sparkle and thus she was not as distinctive.

11. Hamilton, *Genesis 18–50*, 259.

12. "Genesis Rabbah 70:16 chose to translate *rak* as 'lovely' (*y'yn*). It adds, further, that Leah's eyes were 'weak' on account of her weeping over the possibility that, as the elder sister, she would have to marry Esau the older brother" (Hamilton, *Genesis 18–50*, 258n6). According to Hamilton, the reason for this interpretation is to avoid disparagement of a matriarch and patriarch of Israel. The concern was that a patriarch rejected a matriarch because of her appearance, which suggests that Leah was not beautiful. Rather the reluctance to say that she was beautiful already suggests that she was not. The narrator may have been silent about that and focused on one particular feature, since her overall form (figure) was not as beautiful as her sister's.

13. Cf. Alter, *Art of Biblical Narrative*, 56. Hamilton (*Genesis 18–50*, 259) identifies this as evidence of love at first sight; however, the text does not indicate an instant love. After a month, Jacob declares that he loves her. Whether he loved her when he first saw her is open to question.

The idea that other men may have wanted to marry one of Laban's daughters alerts Jacob to Rachel's desirability. Given that the narrator has disclosed Rachel's beauty and Jacob's love for her, one may presume that Laban is speaking about Rachel. The connection between a woman's beauty and her desirability is thus a matter of consideration, as it was in Abraham's anxiety about Sarah (Gen. 12:10–20). Nonetheless, the ambiguity attributed to Laban is the narrator's way of suggesting that Laban has an ulterior motive in accepting Jacob's proposed bride-price.[14] Clearly, Laban has the power of consent regarding his daughters' marriage. As he did with Rebekah's marriage to Isaac (Gen. 24), Laban appears to negotiate Rachel's marriage to Jacob.

Power of Privilege

Choices and Power

The manifestation of privilege is seen in the availability of choices for both men and women. First, with regard to the men, Laban has the option of giving his daughters to the men he sees fit (Gen. 29:19). As a father, he may consent to their marriages to a particular man or decline such consent.[15] Because of his status as Jacob's employer and uncle, Laban also has the option to regulate the terms of the marriage. That he selects an option that appears to violate the terms of the agreement is itself an exercise of power. This is clearly different from Abraham's presumed restricted options about whether to consent to Sarah becoming another man's wife. Laban was under no duress to give Jacob either of his daughters, but he opted to deceive Jacob, his nephew and employee. According to Laban, the basis of his action is not to violate the practices of the region by giving the younger daughter before the older. Given that he represents his reasoning as a practice, it hardly seems logical that he would agree to give the younger daughter first. Some therefore propose that his ambiguity in agreeing to give "his daughter" was deliberate, namely, he does not specify that he would give Rachel. Perhaps he hoped to find Leah a husband before the end of the seven years, when he would have to give Rachel to Jacob.[16] If this is the plan underlying his ambiguity, the ruse may have been one of his choices used to secure husbands. Whatever Laban's motives, the narrator does

14. Hamilton, *Genesis 18–50*, 259. He argues that Laban "may be intentionally ambiguous" as he "lays the groundwork for his forthcoming act of deception."

15. Even in cases where the woman is sexually exploited, the father still has options, even if they are more restricted (Exod. 22:15–16 [NRSV 22:16–17]; cf. Deut. 22:28–29).

16. Wenham, *Genesis 16–50*, 235.

not comment on them or evaluate them, thus leaving the reader in the dark until Jacob uncovers the deception.

Like Laban's, Jacob's options are variously manifested. First is his option to choose between the sisters. He opts for the younger and more beautiful of the two. Second is his option for negotiating a bride-price. He names a seven-year term of service as an economic equivalent for a bride-price. The latter option means that he would work during that period without access to Rachel as his wife. Whether he specifies that term of service because of her age when he encounters her the narrative does not say.[17] Jacob also has the option of abandoning his original agreement with Laban given the extensive period that he labors; but his love for Rachel sustains him (Gen. 29:20). Once he finds that he is married to Leah rather than Rachel, he has another opportunity to bypass the option of marrying Rachel; but he opts to be polygynous by marrying the sisters (25:28).[18] His power as Leah's husband allows him sanctioned and repeated contact with her, but he also has the option of no sexual contact with her. Additionally, he is then privileged to be the father of several sons who would continue his line (Reuben, Simeon, Levi, 29:32–35). Therefore, he does not have to take the maids as wives (30:4–5, 9–10).

The power of privilege is also manifested in Rachel's and Leah's choices. Leah's power is seen in her choice to persist in having children with Jacob even as she realizes that he does not love her. This does not suggest that sexual union is legitimized by the love of those involved; love has been used as a reason to sexually violate another (cf. Amnon and Tamar, 1 Sam. 13:1–13). What is distinctive about Leah's choice is that she sees a correlation between having children for her husband and garnering his love for her. She somehow misses a vital point: bearing children for a man does not secure his love for her or for the children. If simply having children for one's husband would secure his love, then the maid-wives would have secured Jacob's love by bearing his children. The fallacy of Leah's misconception is that she believes she is different from the other women who bear children for Jacob. Why would her fertility produce a result that the fertility of his other wives does not produce? Leah's privilege and the choice to use it toward her goal is a manifestation of her power to persuade herself into a particular course of action and her power to dictate the role of her maid in her plan.

Similarly, Rachel's choices reflect her privilege. She has the privilege of having a maid whom she gives to Jacob as wife and surrogate. This

17. Whatever her age, it was within the realm of acceptable behavior for him to express his intention to take her as his wife.
18. Polygyny may be permissible, but being married to two sisters at the same time is not (Lev. 18:18).

is not a case where Jacob is without an heir, so there is no urgency to provide one to continue his line. The issue then is Rachel's ability to produce offspring who would be counted as her contribution to Jacob's lineage. In this regard, Rachel's desire for a child is multifaceted. First, a motivating factor is that her sister has children and she does not. While Jacob loves her, still Rachel is "jealous" (*qānāʾ*) of Leah and competes with her to produce children for Jacob (Gen. 30:4–8). One cannot tell whether her displeasure stems from her desire for children quite apart from her sister's fertility or is simply one part of her desire to be a mother. Clearly, Leah's fertility magnifies Rachel's infertility; so while Rachel remains childless, Leah already has three sons (Reuben, Simeon, and Levi, 29:32–35). Yet there is no suggestion that Leah "provokes" (*kāʿas*) Rachel, as Peninnah is noted to have done to Hannah (1 Sam. 1:6–7).[19] In this regard Leah shows great control in not retaliating against Rachel by provoking her to anger. In all the cases of infertile women, except Rebekah, there is concern about the negativity directed toward them.[20] Leah does not exhibit the competitive tendency to harm the other wife as a matter of retaliation for not being the favorite wife. However, Rachel competes with Leah and rejoices that she has triumphed over her sister (Gen. 30:8). The irony is that in Rachel's moment of rejoicing she is not yet a biological mother. Even so, she counts the children born through the surrogate as her own, namely, Dan and Naphtali (30:3–8).

The second facet of Rachel's desire for children is her perception regarding the cause of her infertility. She confronts Jacob, demanding that he give her children, thus revealing her perception that he is responsible for her childlessness. Her desperation is evidenced by the alternative to her childlessness that she perceives, namely, death (Gen. 30:1). According to Gerhard von Rad, there was a procedure for childless wives to acquire children; but as seen in Jacob's reaction to Rachel's suggestion, the practice may not have been favorably accepted and may have garnered criticism from some.[21] In contrast to von Rad, I would argue that the text does not comment on the acceptability of the practice of using one's maid as a surrogate. Additionally, Jacob's anger is not at the sug-

---

19. Peninnah is labeled as Hannah's rival (*ṣārâ*), but neither Rachel nor Leah is labeled as the other's rival. Even so, Rachel's behavior portrays a rivalry. Cf. John E. Hartley, "צרר," *TWOT* 2:778–79. The verb *ṣārar* "to show hostility toward" refers to an act of harassment, usually from one's enemy (cf. Num. 33:55; Esther 3:10; 8:1; Ps. 42:11 [NRSV 42:10]). It is used in Lev. 18:18 to speak of taking a sister as a co-wife, thus suggesting a rival.

20. This includes Sarah's contention that God mocked (*ṣāḥaq*) her (Gen. 21:6); Hannah's being provoked by Peninnah; and Rachel, though neither Leah nor God mocks or provokes her. See chap. 5 for discussion regarding the interpretation of the verb "to laugh, jest, mock" (*ṣāḥaq*).

21. Von Rad, *Genesis*, 294. Wenham (*Genesis 16–50*, 7) supports this perspective because it took initiative to solve a problem apart from God's plans.

gestion that he should take the maid as a wife and bear children through her. Rather, his response is to Rachel's demand that he impregnate her. Jacob thus insists that he is not in the place of God (*'ĕlōhîm*) to effect such a change in her. In this instance, she does not voice her perception concerning the Deity's involvement in her infertility. Rather, she directs her frustration at Jacob, her husband, demanding that he give (*yāhab*) her children (30:1). Rachel's assertion is as strong as Jacob's command to Laban to give him his wife (29:21; cf. 30:26).[22] There is no ambiguity concerning what either of them wants. The difference is that Jacob is a man speaking to another man who has authority over him, and Rachel is a woman speaking to a man who has authority over her. Yet her tone is like that of Jacob. In this instance, the strength of her demand may be due not to her gender but to the family domain, where she expresses herself. Jacob exonerates himself by challenging her perception that he is responsible for her infertility. Instead, he argues that God has "withheld" (*mānaʿ*) from her "fruit of the womb" (*pĕrî-bāṭen*, 30:2).[23] The Deity's involvement in her infertility is confirmed by the narrative in its report that God remembered her and opened (*pātaḥ*) her womb (*reḥem*) (30:22). Nonetheless, the narrative shies away from attributing infertility to the Deity at the outset and does not explicitly state that God closed her womb as it does in Hannah's case (1 Sam. 1:5, 6).

Thus comparing the fertility status of Leah and Rachel makes several elements prominent. Leah is listed first, as in the other points of comparison—the older is fertile, the younger is not. The older gives birth to Jacob's firstborn, but the older is hated. Another element of comparison regarding their fertility status is that the Deity perceives the circumstances in which fertility may be a point of contention. The Deity observes (*rāʾâ*) and then acts on Leah's behalf (Gen. 29:31). This is a distinctive pattern of the Deity's response to adversity; however, it is

22. In both instances, the verb *yāhab* "to give" is used in the imperative form followed by the objects, specifying what to give and to whom. This is the verb used in several passages to command that one "gives, ascribes" glory to YHWH (e.g., Deut. 32:3; Ps. 29:1–2; 96:7–8; 1 Chron. 16:28–29) and to ascribe righteousness (Job 36:3). Genesis 30:26 uses the imperative form of *nātan* "to give" in reporting Jacob's demand of Laban to give him his wife and children. Cf. Paul R. Gilchrist, "יהב," *TWOT* 1:368.

23. "Fruit of your womb" (*pĕrî-biṭnĕkā*) occurs in Deut. 7:13; 28:4, 11, 53 in speaking of the blessings and curses. Both *beṭen* (belly) and *reḥem* (womb) are used interchangeably to denote the womb. The term *beṭen* is used for Rebekah (Gen. 25:23–24) and Tamar (38:27) and the twins in their wombs. It is also used for Samson's presence in his mother's womb (Judg. 16:17). Typically, *reḥem* is used for God closing the womb, specifically of the women in Abimelech's household (Gen. 20:19) and of Hannah (1 Sam. 1:5, 6). It is used for Leah, "YHWH opened her womb" (Gen. 29:31), and for the firstborn that opens the womb of a human or an animal (Exod. 13:2, 15). In speaking of Naomi's infertility (due to age), Ruth 1:11 uses *mēʿeh* (inward parts, belly).

not the only pattern. The current pattern consists of the following: the Deity's observation and understanding of a situation and acts in response to what is perceived. Accordingly, the Deity perceives that Leah is hated (*śānēʾ*), and the Deity responds to alter the situation by intervening on her behalf. Unlike Hagar's case, where the intervention puts Hagar back into the hands of her oppressor, the Deity's intervention is punitive toward Rachel, although Rachel may not be the direct source of the hatred directed at Leah (compare Jacob). Even so, the behavior of others or their regard for Leah is the catalyst for the Deity's intervention.

The final aspect of the sisters' fertility status is the Deity's involvement. While the narrative has the Deity opening (*pātaḥ*) Leah's womb, the Deity is not similarly represented in Rachel's infertility. Rather, where one may expect the opposite to be stated—that the Deity closed (*sāgar*) Rachel's womb—the adjective "barren" (*ʿăqārâ*) is used to describe her (Gen. 29:31; cf. 1 Sam. 1:5, 6). As in Sarah's case, the Deity's responsibility for the infertility is circumvented (Gen. 11:30; 16:1). Because the Deity's involvement as the cause of infertility is often implied rather than directly attributed, when Rachel voices her frustration to Jacob she does not attribute her infertility to the Deity. Of the instances where the Deity's involvement is identified, it is usually punitive, especially in response to proscribed sexual unions (20:19; cf. Lev. 20:20–21).[24]

In both Rachel's and Hannah's case, infertility is connected to the fact that their husbands favor them. In both cases, the favored co-wife is infertile while the disregarded wife is fertile. The Deity's role appears to be an equalizing force that creates a difficulty for the favored wife that she cannot correct within her body. The underlying challenge (surfacing in Leah's rationale) is that the husband's love for his wife will diminish because of her infertility. This is in contrast to Leah's rationale that having children for her husband would make him love her. Just as Leah's reasoning proves to be a misconception, so the restrictions on Rachel, the beloved wife, prove to be ineffective in making Jacob disfavor her. The Deity's control over fertility is a demonstration of a punitive and oppressive response, especially in an ethos that places much value on having children. It is no wonder then that the narrator is reluctant to identify the Deity's responsibility in Sarah and Rachel's infertility; Abraham and Jacob, however, implicate the Deity (Gen. 15:3; 30:2). Yet unless the Deity is effective in controlling infertility, one cannot embrace the Deity's control over the timing and fact of fertility. Even in the issue of infertility, the Deity is implicated as the power to grant or to withhold

24. The penalty for dying "childless" (*ʿărîrî*) in Lev. 20:20–21 may indicate that the couple who commits the infraction will be without someone to continue their family line. Thus John E. Hartley, *Leviticus*, WBC 4 (Dallas: Word, 1992), 340–41. Cf. Satlow, *Tasting the Dish*, 26–29.

offspring.[25] The Deity ensures the fertility of the unloved while restricting it for the loved so that no woman has the full gamut of joy and fortune. In this way, the narrative at least suggests the Deity's disfavor toward a woman who is otherwise favored by her husband.

The law recognizes the situation of the unloved wife and the potential disadvantage toward her child and seeks to protect the children in matters of inheritance (Deut. 21:15–17). From this perspective, the Deity is involved as the cause of both fertility and infertility whether or not the reasons are stated. Even though the reason remains undisclosed in Sarah's and Rebekah's case, the Deity is involved seemingly to ensure a challenge and thus to secure an unquestionable place in the eventual conception and birth. Meanwhile the women endure the struggle of waiting, seeing other women have children, resigned to their infertility, and eventually taking matters into their own hands to remedy the situation. Undoubtedly, the narrative is aware of the Deity's unmitigated power to control women's bodies for the Deity's purpose. That purpose does not respect the privilege of those involved.

Rachel's Power and Perception

Rachel's infertility is the Deity's way of challenging an otherwise privileged life. Rachel's perception about her situation is accurate but misdirected, leading her to address Jacob, her husband, rather than the Deity. Like Sarah, she does not confront the Deity about her infertility. By contrast, Hannah pleads with the Deity—not because her husband is without an heir, but because she wants to be a mother (1 Sam. 1:9–17). Jacob refocuses Rachel's attention away from himself and in so doing deflects her concerns (Gen. 30:2). He declines involvement and leaves Rachel to resolve the situation on her own (contrast Isaac).[26] One can hardly miss the irony of Jacob's behavior toward her as compared to his love for her. Like Hannah, though loved she is on her own to wrestle with her infertility; but unlike Hannah, who appeals to the Deity, Rachel resorts to her own means. Also in contrast to Hannah's situation, where Elkanah reaffirms his love for her (1 Sam. 1:8), Jacob does not affirm that his love for her is better than having children. Both responses have their challenges: Elkanah's is that he does not comprehend that being loved by one's husband and being a mother are vastly different things that meet vastly different needs in a woman's life. Jacob's response is challenging to Rachel because it tells her that the cause of her infertility is beyond her control. When Rachel confronts Jacob, she exhibits the

25. Fewell and Gunn (*Gender, Power, and Promise*, 80) comment that God both blesses and curses these women.
26. See chap. 4.

tendency to target what one can control in a situation that appears to be beyond one's control. She can interact with Jacob and control the behavior that leads to conceiving; but if, as Jacob claims, the Deity is responsible, then she is not as in control of her fertility as she may have thought. Even so, Rachel's response is to use the resources over which she has control. As a woman of privilege she has access to another woman who may serve as her surrogate. This access constitutes a measure of power in her situation that would not be available to the maid whom she is using to enhance her status.

Rachel uses her maid Bilhah as a surrogate in the manner that Sarah used Hagar (Gen. 16:1–4). Bilhah was part of the dowry that Laban gave to her when Jacob married her (29:29). The advantage of having a surrogate is her availability and the lack of shame attributed to the practice. She gave Bilhah to Jacob as a wife and Jacob "went in to her," as he had done with Rachel and Leah (29:23, 30; 30:4) and as a man does with the women to whom he is married.[27] In contrast to Rachel, who was infertile, Bilhah conceived and bore a son; she did what Rachel was unable to do. Consistent with the practice of surrogacy, Rachel took the child as her own and named him Dan. She also recognized that her circumstances were due to the Deity's involvement—both her infertility and the opportunity to have children via a surrogate (30:6). Thus while producing an heir may be one reason for using a surrogate, there are other reasons, including becoming a mother or being prolific. Bilhah had another son, Naphtali, and Rachel named him in recognition of her struggle and triumph (30:8).

Producing an heir is important as a by-product of a woman's ability to produce children. Consequently, even after having children through her maid, Rachel wants to become a biological mother. She barters access to Jacob for some mandrakes and for the possibility that she would conceive.[28] As compared to the man regulating access to the woman, the reversal of consent is depicted, namely, the woman determines sexual access to the man and he complies. It is like the woman's control over her maid when she gives her maid to her husband and he complies by having children with the maid-wife. In the family domain, and specifically in relation to surrogacy, the woman exercises the control over sexual access to her surrogate. Rachel allowing Leah access to Jacob already suggests an inequity between the wives in their access to Jacob.

27. For further details concerning the use of "he went in to her" (*wayyābō' 'ēlêhā*) as a designation for sexual union, see chap. 5.

28. Wenham, *Genesis 16–50*, 246–47. A mandrake is a plum-like fruit reputed for its medicinal power in helping infertile women to conceive. It is also used as an aphrodisiac. There is some doubt as to whether the plant would have been available in the region near Paddan-Aram and therefore accessible to Reuben.

Yet Leah bearing six sons shows that there was ample opportunity for her to conceive. Even Zilpah's access indicates the availability of Jacob to the women in his life; but Leah's access is also restricted or at least placed under Rachel's control. Rachel, the one who is jealous and actively competing with her sister, has control over access to Jacob's body and hence the possibility of Leah having more children. Notably, Rachel has several conversations with Jacob, including the one at the well and the one about her infertility. In contrast, even with all her children, there is no report of Leah conversing with Jacob until she tells him how she bartered for a night of sexual access to him (Gen. 30:16).

Leah's Power in Relationship

Because of her self-persuasion, Leah overcompensates for being hated by being prolific in all the ways available to her. Though hated, she bears sons in her effort to secure Jacob's love (e.g., Reuben, Simeon, Levi, and Judah). Her attitude may reflect the values assigned to her as one who bears children. However, the concept that love develops because of children and that her husband would respond favorably because of the children ignores one basic fact—Leah became Jacob's wife through deceit. Although he continues to have sexual intercourse with her, as is evident by her fecundity, Jacob does not love Leah. The assistance from the Deity does not help her in the way that may seem apparent at first. Whether or not the intent was favoring her with children, the assistance gives her the opportunity to disconfirm her belief about securing Jacob's love. Conversely, she remains committed to her ideas and actions, having persuaded herself that love is the possible outcome. The aspect of her womanhood that her context has persuaded her is her asset has not yielded her what she really wants—Jacob's love. Unfortunately in Leah's view, her children are incidental to her quest for Jacob's love, a man who objected to her when he discovered she was his wife. Jacob, as a husband, controls Leah's behavior relative to having children by impregnating her and thus sustaining her hope that he could be persuaded to love her. One also sees a woman who has convinced herself of a plan that has failed repeatedly. After four children—sons at that—and Jacob's persistent disdain, Leah clings to her plan to secure Jacob's love by using her maid to further her efforts. In this way, she funnels her power into a virtual dead end by repeating futile behavior. She has two more sons.

In contrast, Rachel, loved by Jacob, envies Leah. Neither woman is fulfilled in her gender role as a wife—Rachel is loved as a wife, but she is not a mother; Leah is a mother, but she is an unloved wife. Jacob loves Rachel with or without children and hates Leah with or without children. Clearly, the narrative suggests in this portrayal that Jacob's love is not contingent on the ability of the women to produce children. As women, they are competing with each other, one for love and the other for children; but Jacob's valuation of them is independent of their proclivity. He had already made his choice before marrying either one. Thus for them to persist in their competition is to be blind to the reality that the contest is nonexistent. They are competing for their satisfaction, not for a greater regard from Jacob. Yet in their sustained competition they empower Jacob to control their behavior toward him, each other, and their children. Jacob voices the perspective that the Deity caused Rachel's infertility, not because of his privileged access to the Deity's motive or decisions, but because of the socioconceptual framework in which bearing children was seen as a gift from the Deity. Leah has a similar perspective when she acknowledges the Deity in naming Reuben, Simeon, and Judah (cf. Gen. 29:32, 33, 35).

The Deity aids Leah's fecundity and effort to win love. In her effort and success at producing children, she perpetuates hatred or at least the indifference toward her children. The Deity's favor toward Leah is also noted in actions taken on her behalf (Gen. 29:31). Even so, Leah's power to alter Jacob's regard for her is ineffective; instead, her power is not in altering his regard but rather in bearing children. The Deity gives her this power in response to the fact that she is hated (*śānē'*, 29:31). The narrator does not specify who hates her; thus the narrative allows for a broader understanding that Jacob and others hate her.[29] It is noted that Rachel is jealous of her perhaps because she has children while Rachel has none (30:1).

The law is aware that men tend to favor the children of women they love and so it makes stipulations about how men are to dispose of their inheritances among their children. Nonetheless, stipulations and societal expectations could hardly regulate a person's love for another. According to Deuteronomy 21:15–17, if a hated wife bears the firstborn (*běkôr*) to her husband and the loved wife subsequently bears children, the husband is to honor the firstborn by giving him the inheritance as prescribed. The law presupposes polygyny and an inclination to subvert the rights of the firstborn of the unloved wife. Thus the law regulated the father's power to designate arbitrarily the inheritance to one other than the firstborn.[30] The law recognizes that the dynamics of the husband-wife relationship carry over to their children, and it sought to protect the rights of the children—particularly the firstborn.

29. The verb *śānē'* (to hate) occurs in the Qal passive feminine singular participle, "she is hated" (*śěnû'â*).

30. Cf. Carolyn Pressler, *The View of Women Found in the Deuteronomic Family Laws*, Beihefte zur Zeitschrift für die alttestamentliche Wissenschaft 216 (Berlin: de Gruyter, 1993), 15–17.

Leah as a wife is entitled to fair treatment, but compelling or securing love by favorable behavior is beyond the jurisdiction of the law. While she does not retaliate against Rachel, the Deity essentially retaliates for her. In the end, she does not acquire the goal of all her behavior, namely, Jacob's love for her. Jacob continues to play favorites with the children, thus favoring Rachel's firstborn over the sons of Leah, Zilpah, and Bilhah. Likewise, Leah's sons continue the family dynamics by hating their brother Joseph, Rachel's firstborn (Gen. 37:4, 5, 7).

Leah's power in the relationship is also seen in her control over her maid, Zilpah, who is available to Leah because of Leah's privilege. That her husband does not love her is partly a result of her father's actions, namely, tricking Jacob into taking her as his wife. While she may have been unable to consent to or decline the marriage to Jacob, she became the embodiment of the deception by simply being his wife. Nonetheless, even in this difficult situation, Leah's status as a wife is also a privileged position. Like Sarah, Leah lives the anomalous existence of the privileged person who is oppressed. As wife, she is given a personal maid (*šipḥâ*) as part of her dowry (Gen. 29:24). Leah uses her fertility as a way of winning her husband's love. Therefore, as a way of securing love, she continues to have children with a man who does not love her. Her self-persuasion is evident in her response to the birth of her sons and in her naming of them. With Reuben's birth she reasons that "YHWH looked at my affliction" (*'onyî*), referring to her being hated (29:32).[31] She also reasons that Jacob will love her because of the Deity's response to her. She gives Jacob his firstborn son, who would by his presence carry on the family line. Perhaps as mother of the firstborn she raises her expectation regarding how Jacob will regard her. With that failed attempt, however, she is aware that she is hated and that the Deity is involved in her fertility as a response to her being hated (29:33). She has no doubt that she is unloved, but she continues to have sex with Jacob and to bear his children. She persuades herself that having three sons would be more effective than having one in securing her husband's love (29:34). Likewise, Leah's struggles with her thoughts and perceptions are reflected in her reasoning as she names her sons. Having gone through the futile experience of trying to win Jacob's love, she resolves simply to thank the Deity for her fourth son, Judah (29:35).

Even with the multiple children that she bears to Jacob and his incessant hatred toward her, Leah does not alter her misconception. Leah employs her maid, Zilpah, as a surrogate to bear her more children, partly

---

31. This is a distinctive element in the narratives where oppression is depicted. God saw the affliction of Hagar (Gen. 16:11) and of the Israelites while they were in Egypt (Exod. 3:7).

in response to Rachel using Bilhah to bear her children (Gen. 30:5–9). The children born to Leah by her maid will be counted as hers, namely, Gad and Asher (30:11–13). To bear more children she also hires Jacob from Rachel and as a result bears Issachar (30:18). Even after her sixth son (Zebulun), and the two through Zilpah, Leah still persuades herself that Jacob will change his regard for her (30:20).[32] Leah's persistent behavior speaks to the power of her persuasion and effort to secure love. This is a person whose access to power has further entrenched her in a debilitating perception wherein all her efforts are channeled into one goal—to secure love.

Leah's negotiation skills with her sister also attest to her preoccupation with winning love. When the opportunity presents itself, Leah uses her power to secure time with Jacob, specifically to have sexual intercourse with him so that she might conceive. So when her sister Rachel requests some mandrakes from her, she barters for access to Jacob. Thus Rachel apparently controls sexual access to Jacob. Leah, as the older sister and the fertile wife, is still devalued within the marriage. Like Esau, who bartered away his birthright, Rachel hires out Jacob to Leah for mandrakes. Both women want the plant for fertility purposes—Leah to reinvigorate herself and Rachel to conceive for the first time. Still, Jacob does not object to sexual activity with the women provided to him.

Nonetheless, Leah's perspective is that Rachel took Jacob from her (Gen. 30:14). In the course of the negotiation some of Leah's residual resentment toward Rachel surfaces. She is reluctant simply to give mandrakes to her sister. Rather she equates Rachel's request for mandrakes with Rachel stealing Jacob from her (30:15), possibly by becoming his wife and regulating her sexual contact with him and thereby also regulating the prospect of more children. The connection of the two elements portrays Rachel as one who wants *everything*, at least everything that is important to Leah. As is typical of resentment, it seems to misconstrue the events upon which it is sustained. When did Rachel take Jacob from Leah? And how does Leah understand the role of her father in her situation? Leah is persuaded that the cause of her trouble is her sister. Leah's muddled perception is a gnawing reminder of her place in her family. Although the narrator does not make any evaluative comments about her regard for Rachel, the narrator reports Rachel's jealousy (30:1). Nonetheless, the males in Leah's life disregard her, and her closest female relative, her only potential ally, resents her. When she takes the opportunity to overpower Rachel, Leah succeeds. Consequently, Rachel offers to hire out Jacob for the

32. Humphreys, *Character of God*, 177–78. Rachel and Leah recognize that the Deity is involved in granting them children.

night in exchange for the mandrakes; she grants consent to Leah to lie (*šākab*) with Jacob—to have a conjugal visit.[33]

Leah's communication with Jacob about spending the night with him is her first noted conversation with him, but it is more like a briefing since he does not respond to her in words. She represents the encounter as a business transaction; she has hired (*šākar*) him and deals with him as a hired person. She relates to him just as Laban, her father, relates to him, namely, as his employer who hires him to perform a service (Gen. 31:7, 8, 41).[34] The haunting image emerges of a woman wrestling with her unrequited desires and prolonged pain. She appears to distance herself from the intimate moment and introduces an air of condescension by specifying the price at which he has been hired—a fruit rather than an abundance of goods or possessions. Perhaps to further devalue his significance to her, she indicates that Jacob's hiring price is her son's mandrakes, but does not name her son or cite his relational status to Jacob (30:16). Likewise, Leah does not mention Rachel or the specifics about the hiring process. Even so, it may have been understood that Rachel would be the only person who could have granted her access to Jacob, Rachel being the primary wife. Certainly neither of the maid-wives (Bilhah or Zilpah) could have made such arrangements. Perhaps because of these dynamics, in Leah's moment with Jacob, she plays the part of a woman in charge.

Leah voices no complaints to him about being hated by him or about her status as a wife who is usurped by her sister. With no mention of her quest for his love, she keeps to the purpose of being there. In this regard, Leah is in control of herself by withholding the main concerns that have occupied her existence throughout her marriage. Jacob responds and performs the task for which he was hired, and Leah conceives again. With all her sons and those of the maid-wives, an etiology of their names is given that connects the name and the incidents surrounding the birth (however remote the connection); but for one who has been disregarded, Leah's behavior toward her seventh child is startling.

Leah has six sons and her seventh child is a daughter, Dinah (Gen. 30:21). Nothing is said about Dinah other than that she is born and is a daughter.[35] The narrative thus already signals that Dinah is not valued in the same way as her brothers. Regarding Dinah, Leah's refrain about

---

33. The specific intent is that Leah will have Jacob for sexual contact for the night. As discussed above, the expression "lie with" (*šākab ʿim*) is used to denote sexual intercourse.

34. Jacob's complaint is that Laban continues to change his wages (*śeker*), making clear that while he is a son-in-law the definitive relationship is employer-employee. Cf. Wenham, *Genesis 16–50*, 247.

35. Accordingly, von Rad (*Genesis*, 295) notes that Dinah is included as an afterthought rather than an integral part of the narrative. Cf. Hamilton, *Genesis, 18–50*, 276.

winning Jacob's love is absent, as is any thanks to the Deity. Dinah is disregarded not because of her behavior or her appearance but because she is female. Ironically, the hated wife bears the daughter, and the children of the hated wife usually inherit the negative behavior directed at their mother. By including Dinah, the narrative interrupts Leah's long record of producing sons. The relative silence regarding Dinah's reception into the family may also hint that the negative cycle has been passed on to the next generation of women. In a system where sons are highly valued, if sons were not enough to win Jacob's love then Dinah, a daughter, most likely would not have been. If Leah's preoccupation with winning love was still crucial to her existence, Dinah's birth would be insignificant even to Leah, and it would not be perceived as strengthening her hold on Jacob. Even the tradition seems to buy into the devaluation of Dinah by omitting her from her father's genealogy (35:22–26; Exod. 1:2–5).[36] This is particularly striking since a daughter is also included in the Nahor genealogy (Rebekah, Gen. 22:23) and in the notices of the children born to specific persons (Gen. 11).

Conclusion

When viewed in the context of the Old Testament (i.e., intertextually), the narrative reflects the disparity between the value placed on Rachel and Leah in their nation's history and the reality of the behavior and motivations that propelled their lives. The difference is between an *outside* as compared to an *inside* view. Consequently, within the narrative (i.e., intratextually), some dimensions of these persons are portrayed as glossed. In the book of Ruth the people voiced a wish for Ruth to be like Rachel and Leah, who are extolled as the women who built up Israel together (Ruth 4:11). In that commendation of their contribution to Israel, the focus is on their unified contribution, not their competition to be other than they were—Rachel, a mother, and Leah, the beloved wife.

Several noteworthy observations arise from the discussion: First, the ideal life is simply a construction of an external perspective about a person's place in a particular domain. The irony of Rachel's and Leah's lives is that, despite their hardships, the outside perspective idealizes them. Like many people of privilege, how they are perceived often does not cohere with the reality of their lives. The disparity between perception and reality that is basic to human existence, however, is usually facilitated by some types of privilege. People from the outside may equate persons of privilege with a particular attribute of their privilege and sometimes

36. She is included in Gen. 46:15.

ignore the other essential dimensions. Even in their relationship to each other, Rachel's and Leah's perspectives were skewed. Each saw the desirable aspect of the other's existence and sought that aspect. Like them, people tend to desire a perceived privilege as an addition to their own privileges. So Rachel wanted children to add to her status as the primary wife, and Leah wanted to be loved in addition to having children. Each had the outside perspective to the other's experiences.

Second, especially in situations of apparent disparity, humans tend to prefer and to desire to be the "privileged other." The example of Rachel and Leah may also be instructive in understanding the reality of their lives. As with Sarah, they are extolled in the history of Israel's development and in their existence as matriarchs. Their contribution, however, came at a great cost to them. They struggled within their families to be fulfilled in their role as wives and mothers. Rachel suffered as the beloved wife who had to share her husband with her sister, a highly prolific mother. The fallacy of preferring the "privileged other" is that being privileged is not always preferable to being underprivileged. Some situations that offer material privileges may also include aspects that are detrimental to one's well-being, for example, the woman who has economic and social advantages through marriage but is wife to a man who does not love her.

Third, the dynamics of women's relationships are often the by-product of systems implemented by men. Out of their sense of control, Laban and Jacob fostered circumstances in which Rachel and Leah were placed in competition with each other, or at least placed at odds with each other. For Rachel the quandary may be represented by a question about whom to love: her husband (who declared his love for her), her sister (who became a co-wife through deceit), or her father (who orchestrated the deception)?

Fourth, self-persuasion is usually the mechanism for maintaining and changing behavior. Leah's perception that she could win love through favorable behavior set her in opposition to the reality of her existence. She courted that dissonance as a way of dealing with being unloved, and she remained stagnant in a way that further entrenched her in her own self-delusion.

7

Unleashed Power
through Disguised Identity

Judah and Tamar (Genesis 38)

Introduction

Genesis 38 depicts persuasion within interpersonal, familial, and community domains. Defined by these relational contexts, the persuasion process takes on various forms, including deception through disguising one's identity. Several texts portray disguised identity and thus illustrate the varied uses of disguise in the relational contexts. These narratives concomitantly challenge the ethical appropriateness of using a disguised identity for attaining goals.

Within this chapter I define identity as the set of characteristics that distinguishes a person, event, or entity among others sharing similar or different characteristics. There are several types of identity, depending on the set of characteristics. Consequently, one may classify natural characteristics (e.g., age, gender, ethnicity)[1] and functional (or nurtured) characteristics (e.g., culture, status, role, belief/ideology, behavior), and the many configurations resulting from the coexistence of these in one person. Relationships are also part of identity and may be both natural and functional depending on the nature of the relationship.[2] While no

1. This classification takes into account the challenges of understanding ethnicity and gender, namely, their place and function in human relationship and the inherent dangers imbued in ideologies and historical atrocities.

2. For example, parent-child and sibling relationships are natural to the extent that there are biological dimensions, and functional because of the role-specific behaviors,

one exists without an identity, and identity is perceived in relation to other persons or entities, functional identity is a product of context and convenience. Consequently, a change of context may redefine a behavior and a person and thus alter functional identity, namely, the distinctive characteristics connected with one's role, status, behaviors, and so on. Likewise, this type of identity is convenient because it is used to facilitate sociopolitical, economic, religious, and other forms of organization within a given domain.

In each domain and because of the nature of identity, some modes of concealment are better suited to some types of identity. For example, natural identity may not be as easily concealed as functional identity. There are also various modes of disguising identity, including altering physical appearance and adapting normative behavior to conceal one's belief, status, or role. The Gen. 38 narrative illustrates functional (especially relational) identity as the vehicle for deception. In this narrative as elsewhere, the effectiveness of deception indicates a successful persuasion. In deception, however, the alternatives may be distorted to hinder awareness of an attempt to persuade. The use of disguise obscures the existence of a deliberate process; but even within an overt process, it masks the goals and motives of the persuasion (see chapter 2).

Fundamentally, deception and persuasion are intertwined. First, deception utilizes persuasion. Hence, the use of disguise itself exemplifies a form of persuasion wherein the one who employs the persuasion is convinced of its potential effectiveness. Second, deception and persuasion are goal oriented. Using deception includes the basic goal of convincing someone to accept the perceived as being consistent with reality. The goal of deception is to influence a person/group to adjust their behavior and attitude toward a particular and predetermined way or belief. Because they perceive a causal relationship between the deception and a particular outcome, the deceivers accept deception as a way of accomplishing a goal. The biblical narratives illustrate these two aspects of the relationship of deception and persuasion.

Using the conceptual framework of various narratives, in this chapter I focus on Gen. 38 and examine two dimensions: the disguise as a mode of deception used to exert one's power and the internal tensions within a domain that facilitate deception, including its ethical anomalies.[3]

---

expectations, and interactions. In contrast, husband-wife and blended families may be first defined by functional characteristics rather than close blood ties (e.g., prohibitions against marriage between siblings; cf. Lev. 18).

3. By labeling Tamar's behavior as more righteous than Judah's (Gen. 38:26), the narrative itself raises the issue of ethical appropriateness. In other ways, the narrative alludes

Intertextual Parameters as the Basis for Inquiry

In this section I delineate aspects of disguised identity and the sociocultural factors that contribute to the effectiveness of this form of deception. Disguising one's identity is an attempt to persuade other people that appearance equals reality. Furthermore, as a method of persuasion, disguise is multifaceted, including changes to one's external appearance (e.g., Jacob, Tamar), concealment of relational identity (e.g., Abraham, Joseph), and concealment of motive (e.g., Judah, Onan). Part of the challenge in this discussion is to present the ethical nuances of the various modes and uses of disguises.

In addition, this section illustrates how the narratives designate deception. One way that the text indicates the action is by using the term *ḥāpaś* "to disguise" (e.g., 1 Sam. 28:8; 1 Kings 20:38; 22:30//2 Chron. 18:29; 2 Chron. 35:22).[4] In other instances, where the term is not used, changing one's clothes is identified as a way of concealing identity (e.g., Gen. 38:14). The 1 Kings 14 narrative uses the term *šānâ* "to change" to report Jeroboam's request that his wife disguise herself so that Ahijah, the prophet, would not recognize her (1 Kings 14:2). In Jacob's case, Rebekah disguises him in Esau's clothes and covers his hands with animal skin (Gen. 27). In both instances, the particular mode of disguise targets the visual impairment of the intended person and illustrates the adaptability of deception to its goal. The following examples illustrate the various modes of disguised identity.

External Disguise

SAUL (1 SAMUEL 28)

Having exhausted the sanctioned means of discerning the Deity's will, Saul is afraid. The Deity has already rejected him as king, but he persists in maintaining a semblance of power. Saul disguises himself and visits the medium of Endor. The mode of his disguise is replacing garments typical of his role with garments that would signal a role other than that of a king. Hence the effect of his disguise is to conceal his physical and role identity, and he acts differently from what is expected of him as a king or as a compliant citizen of Israel. Since he "had expelled the mediums and the wizards from the land" (1 Sam. 28:3), who would expect him to

---

to the conflict of interest where the rights of one person curtail other people's interests or vice versa.

4. Note that the term *ḥāpaś* "to search" is used in some instances for an attempt to find hidden objects or persons (Gen. 31:35; 44:12; 1 Sam. 23:23; 1 Kings 20:6; 2 Kings 10:23; Amos 9:3; Zeph. 1:12). In some instances the situations in which the search is undertaken include deception (e.g., Gen. 31:35; 44:12).

counter his own action by seeking a medium?[5] Aware that the king had expelled mediums and wizards and that she could be put to death for practicing her craft within that domain, the medium hesitates to consult on behalf of Saul. Consequently, Saul swears by YHWH and convinces her that she will not be punished for consulting the dead on his behalf. The medium summons Samuel, but when he appears he immediately knows that Saul is the disguised person for whom she summoned the dead (28:12).[6] The external disguise conceals his identity from the medium but not from the Deity, who still refuses to respond (28:15).[7]

JEROBOAM'S WIFE (1 KINGS 14)

Although the Deity had given him the kingdom, Jeroboam was characterized as an evil king. He offended the Deity and sold the office of the high priest. When his son fell sick, Jeroboam believed that the prophet Ahijah would refuse to see him. Yet he wanted the prophet's insights into what would happen to his son. Consequently, Jeroboam requested that his wife disguise herself and go to the prophet. Without the prophet knowing that she was Jeroboam's wife, she was to find out about the fate of her son. Jeroboam and his wife believed that Ahijah's age-related vision impairment would result in the successful use of her disguise (1 Kings 14:4; cf. Gen. 27:1); accordingly, they attempted to deceive the prophet and the Deity into predicting the future. Even so, the disguise was faulty because the Deity revealed to Ahijah that the woman was Jeroboam's wife. While the deception failed, Jeroboam succeeded in getting the information that he sought, though it was not good news. As in Saul's case, the king's negative relationship with the Deity led to the attempted deception. Nonetheless, the use of deception is not the act of a powerless person.[8] The kings are not powerless, though they may perceive themselves to have limited options.

A PROPHET OF ISRAEL (1 KINGS 20)

King Ahab of Israel is in conflict with Ben-hadad, the king of Damascus, who manages to escape after a defeat (1 Kings 20:1–21). Given another opportunity to capture Ben-hadad, Ahab is persuaded by Ben-hadad to let him go and to enter into an agreement (20:26–34). The narrator portrays Ahab's actions as being in tension with what the Deity wants him to do. To communicate the Deity's message to Ahab, an unnamed

---

5. This is an observation about the narrative's internal representation of Saul. However, Saul's tendency to flout expectation and thus challenge the responsibilities of his role is evident in his attempts to kill David.

6. Cf. Richard J. Coggins, "On Kings and Disguises," *JSOT* 50 (1991): 56–57.

7. Coggins, "On Kings and Disguises," 57–58.

8. See chap. 8 regarding the concept of an action as a "last-resort" effort.

prophet persuades someone to wound him, after which he bandages his eye and waits for Ahab.[9] When the king comes by, the prophet fabricates a story. He claims that he lost a hostage who was entrusted to him and that there was a penalty of death or a fine for failing to keep the hostage (20:35–40). The king condemns the prophet for the loss, saying that a penalty should be exacted for the failure. Removing his disguise, the prophet discloses his identity and tells the king that the king is guilty and would be punished for releasing his hostage, Ben-hadad (20:41–42). Apparently, the narrator views the use of the disguise as an acceptable way of situating the prophet and of communicating the Deity's message to the king. Much like the story of Nathan and David (2 Sam. 12), the prophet's intent in telling his story is to engage the king. In both cases, when the king evaluates the situation presented, he condemns himself for instigating the situation.[10]

Jacob (Genesis 27)

Jacob disguises himself as Esau and secures the birthright and blessing (Gen. 27; see chapter 4). Jacob's external disguise and Isaac's impaired vision contribute to the effectiveness of the ruse (27:1). Anticipating that Isaac may use his other senses, Rebekah and Jacob incorporate all the senses in the disguise. Jacob wears Esau's clothes, places animal skins on his hands and neck to resemble the hairiness of Esau, performs the task that was requested of Esau, and claims to be Esau (27:1–19). Isaac may have been aware that he was blessing Jacob rather than Esau. Hence his awareness would signal that he was using Jacob's disguise to fulfill his own goal to bless Jacob and to deviate from his verbal intention. There are then several levels of disguise in the narrative, including (a) using another person's actions to deflect attention from one's motive; (b) concealing one's motive in the perception that one has been deceived; and (c) using one's physical vulnerabilities to conceal one's other acuities and strengths.[11] The multiple layering in this instance exhibits the aspect of

9. The text says a prophet and may refer to a court prophet (1 Kings 20:22, 35). Cf. Coggins, "On Kings and Disguises," 57.

10. I designate the method of convincing a person of his wrong as the Nathan Principle. Cf. Coggins, "On Kings and Disguises," 60. He notes other stories similar to this in which the king is the "victim."

11. Cf. Coggins, "On Kings and Disguises," 61n1, regarding Gen. 27. He perceives that Jacob tricked Isaac and that the disguise is acceptable to God because it carries forward God's plans. He builds his discussion on the Deuteronomistic History, specifically 1 Sam. 28; 1 Kings 20; 22; and 2 Chron. 35 (cf. 1 Kings 14). Regarding the theme of disguises, he concludes, "What is really going on in any given set of events may in fact be disguised; there may be a deeper level of significance than that which appears on the surface; and the way in which frequent use is made of this disguise theme helps to reinforce that perception" (62).

deception as a mode of persuasion—that while the presence or goal of the deception may not be apparent, its covert nature may be key to its effectiveness.

Concealed Motive (Genesis 37)

Joseph's brothers disguised their action from their father, Jacob, whom they convinced that Joseph was dead. They sold Joseph to merchants (Gen. 37:26–28), stained his coat with animal blood (37:31), and took his coat to Jacob that he might identify it (37:32). Through their presentation of the coat, they disguised what happened to Joseph and allowed Jacob to use the circumstantial evidence to draw his own conclusions. By not contradicting Jacob's assumptions, they concealed the truth from him and supported these assumptions by seeking to comfort him while he mourned. They disguised their role as participants in separating Jacob and Joseph. This example can also be considered a clear indication of deception achieved by omitting decisive information.

As seen in the other instances presented here, typically an individual disguises himself/herself as part of a ruse. In Gen. 37 a group uses a disguise to deceive a person. With the exception of Reuben, the brothers act collectively in their behavior toward Joseph. Reuben disguises his motive in his intervention on Joseph's behalf (Gen. 37:21–22, 29–30).[12] He behaves as if he wants to find an alternative to killing Joseph, while in fact his motive is to rescue Joseph. Reuben's proposal is plausible as an alternative; thus the brothers accept Reuben's participation with them in their plot. Even so, the success of Reuben's plan hinges on the trustworthiness of his brothers to adhere to an alternate plan—leaving Joseph in the pit.

Relational Identity (Genesis 42)

Joseph hides himself in full view of his brothers by acting like a stranger, someone who does not know them (Gen. 42). Since his identity was not necessary for them to secure the grain, it would seem harmless to reveal his identity and to treat them as any other group of persons who came to purchase food. Instead, his identity as their brother leads him to treat them differently. Part of Joseph's effectiveness is the brothers' expectation that he is dead. Likewise, the reality of Joseph's status as compared to the status into which the brothers sold him seems implausible. His role therefore conceals his relational identity and motive.[13] In part, their vision is clouded by their lack of

---

12. Jacobs, "Conceptual Dynamics," 319.
13. Jacobs, "Conceptual Dynamics," 319.

imagination, by the time gap between their last encounter, and by Joseph's physical maturation. Other instances in the Joseph narrative exemplify the use of disguise as a strategy to persuade others into a course of action, for example, placing the brothers' silver in their sacks, accusing them of stealing, and requesting proof that they have a younger brother (Gen. 44).

Finally, if we keep in mind that the larger framework illuminates rather than prescribes model behavior, the following discussion of Gen. 38 illustrates that the use of disguises is not unique to women or to a particular status or group within a domain. Disguise is an attempt to secure an outcome that is perceived to be beyond the grasp of conventional means.

Power Dynamics and Disguise

Rights and Privileges

A brief overview of the Genesis narrative establishes the conceptual framework for understanding Tamar's actions. Likewise it shows that Judah's choice of a wife is not impeded by the noted animosity toward foreigners exemplified elsewhere (Gen. 24; 27). Judah chooses Shua's daughter as a wife for himself from among the Canaanite women (38:2). She has none of the fertility problems that Sarah and Rachel experienced, but rather she bears three sons to Judah: Er, Onan, and Shelah. In this respect, Judah's wife is like the maid-wife (i.e., Hagar, Zilpah, and Bilhah) and marginalized wives (i.e., Leah and Peninnah) whose fertility stands in stark contrast to their co-wives (i.e., Sarah, Rachel, Hannah).[14] The narrative thus illustrates that infertility was not necessarily as problematic as may first appear in looking at Israel's matriarchs.[15] The observation is fundamental to understanding the lack of offspring in Tamar's union with Er and Onan, and the rapidity of her conception resulting from her sexual encounter with Judah.

The narrator is not as concerned about the nationality of Judah's wife as Abraham was about Isaac, or Rebekah was about Jacob. As an Israelite, Judah is involved in an exogamous marriage and arranges an exogamous

14. With respect to the fertility of Judah's wife, the narrator reports three times that she conceived (*hārâ*) and bore (*yālad*) a son without any intervening challenges to the births. Wenham (*Genesis 16–50*, 366) thinks that Judah's lust for his wife may be reflected in the rapid succession of the pregnancies.

15. This awareness of the fertility of foreign women is also seen in the representation of the Deity closing the wombs of the women of Abimelech's household and then reopening them in response to Abraham's intercession. The cause of their infertility was as much the working of the Deity as was the cause of the matriarch's infertility.

marriage for his son Er to Tamar.[16] In contrast to Abraham's concern about Isaac, there is no report of Judah's concern, the process, or the criteria for selecting a wife for his son (cf. Gen. 24:2–9). Instead, the narrative is concerned about Er's character—a man deemed evil (*ra'*) in God's sight (38:7). While the text does not delineate the particular nature of his evil, it reports a consequence—that God puts him to death (*mût*, 38:7). The timing of his death seems to disadvantage Tamar, who has no children, and Er, who has none to carry on his name. When juxtaposed to Judah's relative ease of producing children, Er's situation seems to conceal another dynamic of his childlessness, most likely God's intervention. Nonetheless, the narrative does not attribute his childlessness to God.[17]

Judah, who selected Tamar as Er's wife, commands Onan to fulfill his obligation (*yābam*) to her, namely, to raise up an offspring (*zera'*) for his brother.[18] According to Deuteronomy 25:5–7, the brother of the deceased was to take (*lāqaḥ*) his sister-in-law as his wife (*'iššâ*) and "go in to her" (*yābō' 'ālêhā*).[19] Judah's command makes no mention of marriage. Hence the issue of whether Onan's levirate obligation includes marrying Tamar is debated.[20] Based on Judah's command (Gen. 38:8) and his action of refraining from further sexual contact with her after

16. Tamar's nationality is not made explicit but is inferred from her return to her father's house, which is in the same region.

17. Leviticus 20:20–21 and Jer. 22:30 attribute male childlessness to punishment from God whether that is a result of killing their children or male infertility (cf. 1 Chron. 2:30, 32).

18. The verb *yābām* (to do the duty of brother-in-law) occurs also in Deut. 25:5, 7, where the levirate obligation is prescribed. The brother-in-law's (*yābām*) duty is to produce an heir through his sister-in-law (*yĕbāmâ*) (cf. Ruth 1:15). Deuteronomy 25:5–6 speaks of son (*bēn*) and firstborn (*bĕkôr*) rather than daughter (*bat*) and female firstborn (*bĕkîrâ*), implying that a male heir is envisioned in this prescription. Cf. Jeffrey H. Tigay, *Deuteronomy*, Jewish Publication Society Torah Commentary (Philadelphia: Jewish Publication Society, 1996), 231, 482. He also reasons that the text does not mean to include daughters in the formulation of the levirate obligation. On the other hand, Num. 27:1–11 may include the possibility of a daughter carrying on her father's name. See Donald A. Leggett, *The Levirate and Goel Institutions in the Old Testament with Special Attention to the Book of Ruth* (Cherry Hill, NJ: Mack, 1974), 33–41. He argues that the obligation includes the younger brothers of the deceased but does not include marriage.

19. The formulation "to go in to her" (*yābō' 'ālêhā*) is among others that denote sexual encounter. See chap. 5 for further details.

20. Some suggest that the responsibility does not include marriage: cf. George W. Coats, "Widow's Rights: A Crux in the Structure of Gen. 38," *Catholic Biblical Quarterly* 34 (1972): 463; Leggett, *Levirate and Goel Institutions*, 39; Hamilton, *Genesis 18–50*, 435; Esther Marie Menn, *Judah and Tamar (Genesis 38) in Ancient Jewish Exegesis*, Journal for the Study of Judaism Supplement Series 51 (Leiden: Brill, 1997), 57. Others argue that the obligation is to marry; e.g., Wenham (*Genesis 16–50*, 361) translates Gen. 38:8 as follows: "Go into your brother's wife, marry her, and produce descendants for your brother." See also Tigay, *Deuteronomy*, 483.

her conception (38:26), he is not offering her marriage but simply the opportunity to bear a child. Hence the obligation is to produce a child rather than marriage.

In continuing the overview of Gen. 38, one may note that upon perceiving that her rights are being violated, Tamar uses the advantages of her gender to secure what is being denied her. Thus Tamar engages in sexual union with her father-in-law and readily conceives. Clearly, the narrative opens further avenues of suspicion regarding Er's childlessness by showing the potency of Judah, the older male relative. As the narrative had done in the portrayal of Judah and his wife, it again illustrates Judah's virility in contrast to his son's lack thereof. In suggesting this contrast, the narrator also suggests God's involvement in causing Er's infertility. Moreover, the suspicion arises that Er's childlessness was non-congenital and functional, imposed on him because of his evil. Tamar's behavior would also reveal fertility and erase any latent suspicion that she was the reason for her lack of offspring. Finally, the narrative also contrasts the behavior of the female and the male, showing the female to be more righteous than the male, specifically Judah, and implicitly Er and Onan. Nonetheless, rather than an inherent quality of her gender or the methods used to secure her rights, Tamar's righteousness is a product of her conformity to the goal to procreate.

Conflict of Domains—Personal versus Family Concerns

To the extent that they are integrated and function in various domains, people transmit their character traits into each of their domains. While the manifestations of these traits are filtered through the particularities of the domain, one's concerns in a particular domain may obliterate the expectations and requirements in another. This conflict of domains appears in Gen. 38, specifically as it is related to the individual's concerns and rights within the family domain.

ONAN

The conflict of domains is exemplified in several ways. First, Onan's awareness of the levirate obligation would affect him because his offspring would be used to ensure another man's future (Gen. 38:9). Judah commands Onan, specifying the goal of the union but not the nature or duration of the union. Conceivably, the union is a temporary sexual union for the sole purpose of procreation.[21] Through its use of the language

---

21. Tigay (*Deuteronomy*, 483) notes that the levirate obligation is variously conceived in laws, including Hittite, Assyrian, Arab, and Hindu laws. In Hindu law, the union is a temporary one expressly for the duration and purpose of producing an heir. In Hittite and Assyrian laws, the marriage is not solely for producing children but rather to protect

typical of marriage (the verb *lāqaḥ* "to take"), the law specifies marriage, but Judah does not.[22] He commands his son to "go in to his brother's wife" and perform the duty of raising (*qûm*) a seed for his brother. The disguise enters into the dynamics of the events when Onan seems to assume his responsibility as levir. Instead of expediting the process of producing an heir for his brother, he impedes it by spilling his semen to ensure that Tamar would not conceive. Presumably, as part of the facade, he disguises his motive by continuing to have sexual contact with her. Through his disguise, Onan deceitfully converts procreative sex to nonprocreative sex;[23] hence his action would be concealed from others. From the perspective of the law, Onan may have had the right to refuse marriage to Tamar (cf. Deut. 25:5–7). Yet it may be that the escape clause that allows a "refusal" of the obligation (*ḥaliṣah* ceremony) was not among his options.[24] Nonetheless, while presented as obligatory, being a levir involves a willingness to make one's concerns secondary to that of the family. Since she is never identified as Onan's wife but always as his brother's wife, Tamar's situation further indicates that prohibitions against unions between brother-in-law and sister-in-law are outside the purview of the levirate obligation (cf. Lev. 18:6; 20:21), and not a basis for refusal.[25]

Second, Onan's conflict of domains is between the obligation to procreate and his interest to prevent procreation. Because procreation is

---

the father's investment—the bride-price he paid for the widowed woman. See Leggett, *Levirate and Goel Institutions*, 63–81. Cf. *ANET*, 182, 196: Middle Assyrian Laws §§30, 33; Hittite Laws §§193, 195.

22. Several instances in the book of Genesis attest the use of *lāqaḥ* (to take) in reference to taking a woman as wife, including 4:19; 11:29; 24:67; 25:1, 20; 26:34; 28:1, 6, 9; 31:50; 34:4, 21; 38:6. Cf. Menn, *Judah and Tamar*, 57–58.

23. There is some question as to the mode of "spilling his seed" (lit., "spoiled it on the ground"). First, that he masturbated; see E. Ullendorff, "The Bawdy Bible," *Bulletin of the School of Oriental and African Studies* 42 (1979): 434. Second, coitus interruptus (withdrawal) as a method of birth control; see Hamilton, *Genesis 18–50*, 436; Wenham, *Genesis 16–50*, 367. Third, according to Satlow (*Tasting the Dish*, 241), anal sex, which "wastes the woman's unique attribute."

24. Tigay (*Deuteronomy*, 483) argues that the law had evolved and that Onan may not have had the option of refusing to marry Tamar. Calum M. Carmichael explains the *ḥaliṣah* ceremony in Deut. 25:7–10 as a response to Onan's death and the ensuing concern to prevent such deaths. See Carmichael, *Law and Narrative in the Bible: The Evidence of the Deuteronomic Laws and the Decalogue* (Ithaca, NY: Cornell University Press, 1985), 291–99. Michael L. Satlow observes that levirate obligation underwent changes even within Israel, including the presence or absence of the *ḥaliṣah* ceremony and the observed tension with the prohibition against marrying the brother's wife. Satlow also contends that the Lev. 20:21 punishment of childlessness may be a polemic against the procreative levirate union. See Satlow, *Jewish Marriage in Antiquity* (Princeton, NJ: Princeton University Press, 2001), 186, 343n27. Cf. Leggett, *Levirate and Goel Institutions*, 37, 55–56.

25. Cf. Menn, *Judah and Tamar*, 60–61. Also Lev. 18:15 and 20:12 prohibit the sexual union between father-in-law and daughter-in-law.

the primary goal of the union and because he continues to engage in nonprocreative sex, Onan would implicate Tamar as an infertile woman, and perhaps as a woman ineligible for the levirate union.[26] Moreover, he would construe the union as licentious.[27] Since his firstborn would be his brother's heir, it is a conflict between securing his brother's future and risking his own. Onan thus exemplifies the other side of surrogacy. In female surrogacy, the children born to the surrogate are the children of the father and counted toward the offspring of the wife who facilitated the surrogacy. The maid-surrogate did not have the option of practicing a birth control measure to ensure that she did not conceive.[28] On the contrary, the male counterpart and surrogate father had the option of practicing a birth control measure to ensure that conception did not occur. That was Onan's power in a situation where presumably he was not given the option to refuse.[29] Even so, his use of this alternative is myopic because of the challenges resulting from the continued sexual liaison—no expected progeny. The text does not suggest that the Deity would punish those who do not procreate. Rather, because Onan violates his responsibility, his action of nonprocreative sex is identified as an evil deed (rā'a').

JUDAH

As father and father-in-law, Judah exhibits the conflict of loyalties within the family domain. First, he attempts to fulfill the levirate obligation by giving Onan to his widowed daughter-in-law, yet he also generates tension about whether he was obligated to give Shelah, his youngest son, as levir.[30] Consequently, after Onan's death Judah advises

26. Satlow, *Tasting the Dish*, 224, 227, 231. He notes that there are several categories of nonprocreative sex: "Any intercourse with a congenitally infertile, pre-menstrual or post menopausal woman is non-procreative" (224). Likewise, "According to the *Mishnah*, a congenitally infertile levirate widow (*'ilonit*) is exempted from the obligation to the levirate marriage, and releases her co-wives as well, upon whom the obligation should now descend, from this obligation" (224).

27. Satlow, *Tasting the Dish*, 230. The union of a woman with an infertile male (*bi'ilat znut*) also constitutes nonprocreative sex. In this case, the infertility may be congenital or due to old age. In such instances, the man is not obligated to perform the levirate obligation and the widow is released from the obligation.

28. This is not a denial of the availability of birth control methods, but rather the observation that they were not used by the surrogates. Their role disallowed for such methods.

29. Cf. Satlow, *Tasting the Dish*, 236–27. In considering Onan's act, he cites the rabbinic discussion about Er's and Onan's sin including the reason that Tamar did not conceive with them.

30. Menn, *Judah and Tamar*, 59. She discusses the various manifestations of the levirate obligation, including the possibility of the father-in-law's obligation to be levir. Wenham (*Genesis 16–50*, 366) argues that the Gen. 38 manifestation displays an earlier form of the law wherein the widow's father-in-law was obligated to enforce the law, though perhaps he himself was not a levir.

Tamar to remain a widow until Shelah comes of age (Gen. 38:11).[31] Judah's advice is motivated by fear for his son, which results from perceiving a pattern in which Tamar is the common denominator. He does not reflect on what the narrative already disclosed about why his sons died; thus he is convinced that anyone who marries or has sexual encounters with Tamar will die.[32] Consequently, Judah's advice to Tamar to return to her father's house disguises his motive. He has already decided to ignore the levirate obligation, so Judah crafts his language as part of his deception. Notably, he does not promise marriage, though it may be implied in his command to Tamar. If indeed it is implied, it would be so only to one who is already predisposed toward marriage. In Tamar's case, her disposition arises from her awareness of the levirate obligation. Judah's power to persuade her, therefore, lies in his role as father-in-law and his prior action of giving Onan to her as a levir. Through these channels, Judah secures the guise of being trustworthy. Tamar's inadvertent compliance to her father-in-law facilitates the temporary success of his deception. His deception creates a double bind for Tamar because in returning to her father's house she is no longer a vital part of Judah's family. Yet she is a widow tied to Judah's family without the viable prospect of marrying outside that family.[33]

Although the conflict seems dormant, three things propel the story: the death of Judah's wife (Gen. 38:12), Tamar's awareness that Shelah has grown up (38:14), and Tamar's awareness that Judah has not kept his obligation as father-in-law (38:14). These elements also highlight the tension that ensues from Judah's concealed motive and his tendency to act on his perceptions. Judah journeys to Timnah where Tamar has adorned herself and waits at the gate. Seeing her and not knowing who she is, Judah figures (ḥāšab) that she is a prostitute (zônâ, 38:15). Consequently, he negotiates with her to determine the compensation (38:16). After the sexual act, they part company until it is learned that Tamar is pregnant. Judah plays the role of the judge and condemns Tamar for being pregnant by unsanctioned means (38:24). She then reveals the identity of the male with whom she conceived, and Judah concedes that she has acted rightly in her situation (38:26). By becoming the levir, he

31. Leggett, *Levirate and Goel Institutions*, 31. The youngest son was also included in the obligation.

32. Mary E. Shields, "More Righteous Than I? The Comeuppance of the Trickster in Genesis 38," in *Are We Amused? Humour About Women in the Biblical Worlds*, ed. A Brenner, JSOTSup 383 (London: T&T Clark, 2003), 33. She notes Judah's tendency to see only what he wants to see.

33. Fewell and Gunn, *Gender, Power, and Promise*, 88: "He does not want her to remain part of his family, but he won't release her to become part of someone else's. He plays games while her future hangs in the balance."

does not incur the shame that may have been attached to an incestuous relationship between a father-in-law and his daughter-in-law (cf. Lev. 18:15; 20:12).[34] From another perspective, the death of his sons may have eliminated the ignominy of his actions and redefined his functional status. Since Tamar is widowed, Judah would not be her father-in-law.[35] This argument ignores the continuation of the functional status beyond the death of the first spouse. Thus arguing that Judah's role is dissolved also indicates that Onan's role as brother-in-law was dissolved upon Er's death. On the contrary, the existence of the levirate obligation indicates that the in-law roles transcend the death of the spouse. While Judah's conflict of interest results from the continuation of the relationship and obligation, the conflict does not obliterate his power to fulfill his responsibility within the circumstances.

Manifestation of Power

Both Judah and Tamar exemplify how to reassess a situation and adjust behavior to address the perceived circumstances. Their exercise of power is closely tied to their awareness and intention.

Awareness of Her Options

Tamar's awareness is a result of a process that persuades her of her place and function within her domain. Subversive as it may be, Tamar's power is both in her restricted options and in the available avenues for securing her rights. The restrictions are a function of an ethos in which her gender entails particular normative options defined vis-à-vis her relational identity (i.e., wife, sister-in-law, and daughter-in-law). As a widow, Tamar is allowed to have an heir with her brother-in-law, who would otherwise be prohibited from sexual access to her (Lev. 18:16; 20:21). Also, as a widow of a childless man she is entitled to bear a child with her brother-in-law, but not entitled to be his wife.[36] Unless one believes that sexual intercourse constitutes a marriage, one cannot conclude that the levirate obligation necessarily means marriage. Conversely, many instances suggest that sexual intercourse alone does not constitute a marriage (e.g., rape).[37] Quite apart from Tamar's expec-

---

34. Cf. Menn, *Judah and Tamar*, 59; Alice Bach, *Women, Seduction, and Betrayal in Biblical Narrative* (Cambridge: Cambridge University Press, 1997), 62–63.

35. Menn, *Judah and Tamar*, 60–61.

36. Cf. Coats, "Widow's Rights," 463; Hamilton, *Genesis 18–50*, 435; Menn, *Judah and Tamar*, 57; Pressler, *View of Women*, 103, 104n25.

37. Compare the list of proscribed sexual partners as well as instances of proscribed marital partners (Lev. 18, 20). Other instances include 11QTS66 and the case of the seduced or raped maiden (cf. Exod. 22:15–16 [NRSV 22:16–17]; Deut. 22:28–29). In the latter cases,

tations and without the mention of marriage, Onan is asked to father a child with her. Nonetheless, Tamar thinks about marriage to Shelah and waits for Judah to make it happen (Gen. 38:14).[38] The dissonance within the obligation is thus apparent. While the males do not necessarily include marriage as part of the obligation, Tamar does. Thus within the relational scope envisioned by the society, she may engage in nonmarital sex to produce an heir for her deceased and childless husband. If she engages in sex outside the acceptable parameters, she may be deemed a prostitute (zônâ).[39] Even so, it is not simply her status as widow that generates the option of participating in the levirate union. Rather, her cluster of circumstances allows an option that would be unavailable to a single woman (never married) or to a widow with a child. Likewise, these circumstances empower her to secure her rights.[40] Since her rights would potentially be violated by the failure to fulfill the levirate obligation, it may have been her responsibility to ensure their fulfillment.[41] Yet she does not have the power to decide when to secure a levir.

One of Tamar's options is to remain within the system and thus to conform to the expectations of those in authority over her. Initially she conforms to Judah's command by returning to her father's house (bêt-'āb, Gen. 38:11). In this instance, Judah is an authority figure who regulates her life and her potential to bear children, but the Deity overlooks the process. Even so, when he withholds Shelah and impedes the procreative process, Judah's power over Tamar seems to supersede the Deity's. It appears that the Deity had protected her rights when Onan failed to meet his obligation. When Judah appears to be shirking his responsibility toward her, the Deity is conspicuously silent, leaving Tamar to wait.

Accordingly, Tamar could find a suitable man who would fulfill her rights to bear an heir for her deceased husband. Ironically, her waiting obscures this option and highlights the improbability that she could find

---

the marriage ensues from the violated maiden and is seen as an act subsequent to the sexual violation. See Mignon R. Jacobs, "Comparative Analysis of 11QTS66, Lev. 18:6–18, and Related Texts: An Examination of Their Conceptualities" (paper presented in Reading Biblical Law in the Qumran Era, AAR/SBL Annual Meeting, Toronto, November 2002).

38. The nature of levirate obligation in this instance may not include marriage even though that was Tamar's expectation. Cf. Pressler, View of Women, 103–4, esp. n. 25.

39. Cf. Satlow, Tasting the Dish, 121–22. He explains that in biblical texts, zônâ is a female prostitute. "In rabbinic usage activities termed bî'ilat znut usually fall into two categories, non-marital intercourse or non-procreative intercourse" (121).

40. Cf. Tigay (Deuteronomy, 483), who proposes that in Assyrian and Hittite laws the goal of the levirate obligation is not procreation but protection of the father-in-law's economic investment, namely, the bride-price.

41. Cf. Susan Niditch, "The Wronged Woman Righted: An Analysis of Genesis 38," Harvard Theological Review 72 (1979): 143–49.

her own levir.[42] In this respect, she is her own obstacle because she is persuaded that Judah will act in her best interest by giving her the opportunity to marry Shelah (Gen. 38:14). Whatever she may have heard in Judah's command to remain (*yāšab*) a widow, she is convinced that it somehow meant marriage. Like Judah, Tamar observes a set of external events and attributes to them a meaning that is at odds with the perceived reality. Tamar took Judah's words as a promise; however, Judah's intention may have been to get rid of Tamar and her perceived link to death. It is only when faced with her fraught expectation and assumption about Judah's trustworthiness that she becomes aware of the direness of her circumstances. She realizes that the option has been nullified through Judah's exercise of his power to withhold his son. Clearly, it was not the fact of the withholding that constituted the problem for Tamar, but the intended duration. Judah is deliberately ambiguous when he tells her to remain a widow until Shelah comes of age. Yet he never says that he will give Shelah to Tamar as her husband (38:11). Likewise, he mentions nothing about the levirate obligation in reference to Shelah. Judah creates ambiguity by mentioning Shelah's age and suggesting that he is considering Shelah for Tamar (38:14).[43] Thus, by selectively omitting vital information, Judah masks his intention and deceives Tamar.[44]

Tamar's interpretation of Judah's gesture of sending her back to her father's house holds the key to her behavior. It is the same gesture that Naomi employed with her daughters-in-law in telling them to return to their mother's house (Ruth 1:8). Her effort was to deter them from having false hopes that she would provide sons for them (1:8–13). Judah's action is ambiguous because he discloses that he fears for Shelah's life (Gen. 38:11). It thus appears that sending Tamar away is part of his ruse to protect his son.[45] In both cases, the gestures indicate the lack of options for the daughter-in-law with her husband's family. Naomi's action is built on her inability to provide a son, but Judah's is built on his reluctance. Tamar misinterprets Judah's gestures out of her conviction that he is trustworthy and exercises her option to trust him and

42. Menn (*Judah and Tamar*, 59) notes that the scope of possible levirs may have expanded as reflected in the book of Ruth; however, these options may not have been part of the earlier form of the tradition.

43. The question of the age of marriage is raised here. She no doubt would have been aware of Shelah's age during her stay in Judah's household. While the narrative does not indicate how long she had been waiting, that he is now of age indicates that she was waiting a year or longer—most likely longer.

44. Garcia, "Lies," 514–37. The selective communication of information is one way that deception is achieved. In this instance, the deception is achieved by withholding information that is required for a full representation of the circumstances. Cf. Fuchs, "Way of Women."

45. Cf. Hamilton, *Genesis 18–50*, 441; Bal, "Tricky Thematics," 148–49.

to wait. Nonetheless, her conclusion leads her away from the results she sought.

Perhaps another option would be that Tamar discusses with Judah what had happened to cause him to withhold Shelah from her. This option would presume that a discussion would resolve the problem. Yet the narrative presents her as being sure of the injustice committed against her and acting on that certainty. When Tamar realizes that Judah does not intend to keep his word, she sets aside (*sûr*) her widow's clothes, signaling that she has replaced passive waiting with decisive action (cf. Gen. 38:11). Indeed, she constructs the situation and the alternatives, and her waiting is designed around an imminent event rather than a remote and unlikely one. Could it be that she simply intends to remind him of his obligation?[46]

POWER OF PERCEPTION AND INTENTION

The narrative displays several actions that Judah and Tamar adapt to sustain their perceptions and intentions. For both persons, perception is key to the deliberate use of power to secure a particular outcome.

Judah. After his wife's death, Judah sets out for Timnah to attend to his business (Gen. 38:12). This shows that he is a man of both economic and relational resources. First, Judah's stated intention suggests that after the completion of the mourning period Judah proceeds with his business and is not debilitated by the death. Whatever the duration of the mourning period for his wife, it is evident that Judah did not have a mourning period as long as his father had for Joseph (37:34–35; cf. 27:41; 50:10, 11) or Tamar endured for Onan. The death of his spouse is quite different from Tamar's situation. As a function of the domain's construction of male identity, the death of his spouse did not create a vulnerability to his social status or endanger his family line. That endangerment came from the deaths of his childless sons and perhaps his monogamous union (46:12).

Second, while Judah intended to conduct business, his attention was diverted from his business by his desires. He perceived an opportunity for a sexual encounter with a prostitute (*zônâ*) and acted to secure that sexual encounter (Gen. 38:15). Presumably, because Tamar covered (*kāsâ*) her face with a veil and positioned herself in a public setting, Judah propositioned her (38:14, 16).[47] It is unlikely that prostitutes veiled themselves

---

46. Menn, *Judah and Tamar*, 24–25. Through her deception, Tamar gains control over Judah and thus convinces him to give her what she desires. By being compliant, he fulfills the levirate obligation to her. The verification of paternity is also tied to Tamar's positioning and whether this is in fact a normative occurrence or the first and only one. That none had seen her leads Menn to believe that she had not been a prostitute before or since.

47. To cover one's face is also mentioned in several texts to indicate shame or dishonor (2 Sam. 19:6 [NRSV 19:5]; Ps. 44:16 [NRSV 44:15]; 69:8 [NRSV 69:7]; 89:46 [NRSV 89:45]; Jer. 51:51) and to prevent someone from seeing something (e.g., land, Ezek. 12:6, 12). The

as a sign of their functional identity. Instead, it appears that they applied facial makeup to identify themselves as prostitutes. Thus the use of a facial covering was to conceal her identity from her companion.[48]

Judah takes the initiative in asking for a sexual encounter without any verification of his perception that he is approaching a prostitute (Gen. 38:16). He negotiates on the basis of his perception and yields to the stranger's demands. In his negotiation, Judah displays his understanding of a prostitute (zônâ), namely, one who consents to and performs sexual acts in return for compensation.[49] Whether or not she lived as a prostitute, Tamar conforms to this identity by using sex for compensation, namely, Judah's signet ring, cord, and staff (38:18). She deliberately asks for elements of his personal identity, and he agrees to her terms because of the immediate gratification that he seeks. In that situation, desire rather than prudence persuades Judah to leave such identification markers with a perceived stranger.[50]

Third, after the encounter, both Judah and Tamar go on their way, each having achieved a purpose and each leaving loose ends. For Judah, the loose end is the whereabouts of his identification markers, which he intended to retrieve in exchange for the animal he first offered as compensation for the sexual liaison. Having failed in his goal and fearing the prospect of ridicule, he concedes to allow the prostitute to keep his signet ring, cord, and staff (Gen. 38:23).[51] He is clearly more concerned about the public opinion stemming from exposure of his liaison with a prostitute than the actual liaison. His concession shows his confidence that this stranger would not use the liaison or evidence of it to accomplish another purpose; therefore, he considers the matter closed. This assumption that his decision to close the matter terminates risk of public ridicule is another example of Judah's propensity to misperceive what is happening around him.

Fourth, based on his perception of Tamar's unsanctioned sexual behavior, Judah intends to punish her for the subsequent pregnancy (Gen.

---

act of covering is also done to conceal one's nakedness (Gen. 9:23), and to demonstrate sorrow accompanied by weeping (2 Sam. 15:30; 19:5 [NRSV 19:4]; Esther 6:12). Rebekah covered her face in anticipation of Isaac and of sexual activity (Gen. 24:65), but her act was not that of a prostitute.

48. Hamilton, *Genesis 18–50*, 441–42.

49. This is not a question of whether she was a cultic prostitute. In this case, the nature of her role is defined by her action, not the label of her functional identity. Cf. Deut. 23:18–19 (NRSV 23:17–18), which prohibits men and women from being cultic prostitutes (qĕdēšâ/qādēš).

50. Fewell and Gunn (*Gender, Power, and Promise*, 88) comment: "His failure to recognize his own daughter-in-law points to just how far she is from his mind. He sees what he wants to see, defining this woman in a way that is convenient to him."

51. Hamilton (*Genesis 18–50*, 447) argues that there would not be ridicule attached to "sexual congress" with a Canaanite cultic prostitute.

38:24). He orders that she be burned in an attempt to take control of the situation.[52] It is not simply that she is pregnant but that she is pregnant through practicing prostitution, albeit with Judah (38:24). As is typical of Judah, he does not verify the information that was reported to him but simply assumes that it is true. Ironically, Tamar is pregnant via an act of prostitution, and for that she could have been burned.[53] Since instances of illicit sex were thought to defile the community, the burning becomes a means of removing the defilement. In spite of his involvement in prostitution, Judah assumes the authority to pronounce a verdict on Tamar and does not attempt to be lenient toward her.[54] Tamar derails his intention when she produces the evidence of the father of her child. To punish her, Judah would have to condemn his participation in her prostitution. So Judah acknowledges that Tamar is more righteous (ṣādĕqâ) than he in the levirate matter (38:26).[55] Nothing is said of his reaction to the disclosure of his involvement; presumably, the shame was the situation (prostitution) resulting in a pregnancy rather than his sexual encounter with Tamar (as a levir).

Tamar. As a widow, Tamar dresses herself in the garments that signal her particular status within the community. While usually silent about community support for Tamar, the narrative signals two ways that the community may have supported her. First, an unnamed source discloses to her that her father-in-law is journeying to Timnah (Gen. 38:13). There were those who knew that she was widowed and living apart from her husband's family. Upon hearing that Judah is coming to her region, Tamar realizes that Judah does not intend to fulfill his obligation to her. She decides to address the matter, so she changes her clothes and places herself at the gate. Like Rebekah, Tamar promptly acquires information that may have otherwise eluded her (27:42) and uses it to formulate a plan that subsequently alters the family structure. Tamar's receipt of the report illustrates the intent and function of the community to support her (38:24). She has conformed to Judah's expectation by remaining a

---

52. Cf. Tikva Frymer-Kensky, "Gender and Law: An Introduction," in *Gender and Law in the Hebrew Bible and the Ancient Near East*, ed. Victor H. Matthews, Bernard M. Levinson, and Tikva Frymer-Kensky, JSOTSup 262 (Sheffield: Sheffield Academic Press, 1998), 23; Frymer-Kensky, "Virginity in the Bible," in Matthews, et al., *Gender and Law*, 93.

53. Cf. Code of Hammurabi §§110, 157, in *ANET* 170, 172; Hamilton, *Genesis 18–50*, 449; Hartley, *Leviticus*, 339, 349. Burning was a penalty for illicit sexual acts, including instances where a priest's daughter commited an act of prostitution (Lev. 21:9) and for all parties in a union of a man with a woman and her mother (20:14).

54. Frymer-Kensky, "Virginity in the Bible," in *Gender and Law*, 93. She observes that in Deuteronomy (e.g., 22:13–21) the father's authority does not include control over life-and-death verdicts. Rather the community has the authority in those matters.

55. Shields, "More Righteous Than I?" 33. She also cites other instances where a foreign woman is the "vehicle of divine providence," namely, Rahab and Ruth.

widow, awaiting the fulfillment of the levirate obligation toward her. Certainly, the information she receives jars her out of her persuasion and her trustful waiting. The combination of the specific information, the impeded effort to provide her with a levir, and her awareness empowers her to alter her disposition toward her circumstances and to redefine her reality. She is no longer convinced of Judah's positive intention toward her or of the viability of waiting for marriage.

Second, the community support results in the success of her plan. Rosemarie Anderson asks how Tamar, inexperienced in harlotry, manages to change out of her widow's garments, position herself at the gate, and go unnoticed by everyone except Judah and his friend. Anderson reasons that the other women of her community assist Tamar by dressing her for the occasion, getting her to the gate, and having a place for her to take Judah for their sexual encounter.[56] The narrator is silent about any assistance in carrying out the plan but leaves clues. Certainly, the community may have covered for her when Judah later sends Hirah to find her. Thus when Hirah enlists the support of the community by asking them about a temple prostitute (qĕdēšâ), he is told that there are no prostitutes there (Gen. 38:21). Apparently, Hirah's inquiry about a temple prostitute is an effort to deflect any shame associated with having a sexual encounter with a recreational prostitute (zônâ).[57] His choice of terms is best understood as a euphemistic reference rather than an honest attempt to find a temple prostitute where there was no temple. The narrator's observation that none is to be found is evidence of incongruity—either Tamar dressing as a prostitute is an oddity and thus highly conspicuous and surely memorable, or Tamar simply blends in with the others. Perhaps there are no prostitutes in the area, and she is not dressed as a prostitute but is only mistaken as one. This would leave open the question of how she is dressed and what gives the impression of her intention or role. Most likely, her location and posture more than a particular piece or type of apparel suggest that she is a prostitute.

At issue is Tamar's motive in going out to the gate dressed as she is. Does she intend to deceive Judah, or is the plan hatched upon seeing him and noting his response to her? Fewell and Gunn suggest that she does not intend to act as a prostitute but rather to show herself ready to become a wife. Instead, when Judah sees her, assumes she is a prostitute

56. Rosemarie Anderson, "A Tent Full of Bedouin Women: Tamar in Gen. 38," *Daughters of Sarah* 19 (1993): 35. She bases the observation on anthropological arguments about the behavior of bedouin women.

57. His language may simply be an adjustment for public purpose in an attempt to be polite, namely, by saying "temple prostitute" (qĕdēšâ) rather than "whore" (zônâ). While it is reported that Judah mistakes Tamar for a "prostitute" (zônâ, Gen. 38:15), his friend inquires about a "temple prostitute" (qĕdēšā, 38:21).

(*zônâ*), approaches her, and propositions her, she decides to play along in order to "beat him at his own game."[58] Whatever her motive in being veiled in a public setting, once she enters into negotiation with Judah to exchange sex for compensation she is acting like a prostitute.

In Tamar's attention to details, she establishes the basic conditions for the effective execution of her plan—plausibility, focused expectation, and trust defined by the nature of the relationship in which the disguise is used. The disguise indicates the deliberate nature of her deception and the systematic efforts to ensure its effectiveness. She alters her appearance simply by removing her external identifiers—her widow's clothes. Even if she is unveiled, that she no longer dresses as a widow would deceive any who identify her by her widow status. By breaking expectation, she demonstrates that she is deliberate about her course of action and that she does not build her future on the possibility that Judah might live up to his obligation. Tamar transforms herself from the passive woman who waits into the active woman who orchestrates her future.[59] Her disguise also illustrates her awareness of her culture and its norms. As a widow she could be reprimanded for sexual relationships outside the predetermined relationships, but as a prostitute she has a wider range of possible behaviors. Accordingly, the functional identity and the situation constitute the basis of her power. She uses her sexuality to compel someone's response and to secure what is otherwise elusive.[60]

Power and Restricted Options

While restrictions are normative for most people in a community, some have more options than others. Both Tamar and Onan exemplify persons whose domain restricts their options. Tamar's first husband exercised the option of accepting her as his wife, but Onan's options were restricted by the tradition of the levirate obligation. This tradition dictated that the brother-in-law would assume the responsibility of fathering his brother's heir with the childless widow. While the brother-in-law would contribute to the deceased's legacy by having a child with his sister-in-law, marriage

58. Fewell and Gunn, *Gender, Power, and Promise*, 88. They argue that the veil signals not prostitution but readiness for marriage, as in Rebekah's case. While this is a compelling argument, it may not explain why Judah assumes that she is a prostitute. The narrative assumes that either her clothes or where she positioned herself indicates that she is a prostitute.

59. M. E. Andrew, "Moving from Death to Life: Verbs of Motion in the Story of Judah and Tamar in Gen. 38," *ZAW* 105.2 (1993): 266. Contrast Fewell and Gunn (*Gender, Power, and Promise*, 88), who depict her as adopting another form of passivity by waiting to be recognized as ready for marriage.

60. Hamilton (*Genesis 18–50*, 443) sees Tamar's behavior as comparable to Esther and Naomi's use of sexuality to achieve a goal.

was not necessarily envisioned as part of the levirate obligation.[61] Indeed, Tamar is not identified as Onan's wife; the reference to her as wife occurs in the context of her expectations to become Shelah's wife (Gen. 38:14).

Accordingly, Tamar's options are much more restricted than is readily apparent. As Er's widow, within the levirate obligation she has the right to conceive with one of his brothers. While she could aspire to be a wife, perhaps becoming a wife is a remote option.[62] Tamar has an opportunity for sexual intercourse with her brother-in-law and perhaps with any relative who may fulfill the levirate obligation. Whether there would be further cultural pressure on the man to marry the woman with whom he has fathered a child remains a question. Onan's avoidance of conception may signal that the obligation is more extensive either because of the ongoing provision for the child or because of the cultural value attached to his duty.[63] Consequently, Onan's restricted options lead him to disguise his motive by actions that would appear to fulfill his obligation to Tamar. Onan attempts to protect his legacy in a domain where relational obligation impinges on his desires and rights to procreate for his name's sake. His deception also illustrates that disguised identity functions within gender-specific roles, normative behaviors, and obligations. Accordingly, Onan's choice of a disguise was consistent with his gender and would be impossible for a woman. Even so, like Tamar's, his disguise ensues from a perceived lack of viable alternatives.

Implications of Disguised Identity

Conditions for Deception

As demonstrated above, all the central human characters in Genesis 38 employ disguises to persuade others. Their disguises suggest several conditions that are also evident in most persuasion processes.

POSSIBILITY FOR SUCCESS

By spilling his semen rather than overtly opposing the levirate obligation, Onan contributes to the context of Tamar's actions. He perceives

---

61. Coats, "Widow's Rights," 463. He concedes that the obligation is to produce an heir, not to marry Tamar. He also compares Gen. 38 to Deut. 25:5–10. See also Pressler, *View of Women*, 103–4; Leggett, *Levirate and Goel Institutions*, 39; Hamilton, *Genesis 18–50*, 435; Menn, *Judah and Tamar*, 57.

62. Cf. Coats, "Widow's Rights," 463–65.

63. Coats ("Widow's Rights," 465–66) denies that the levirate custom included marriage. On the basis of the narrative ending he argues that the goal is simply conception and that with the achievement of that goal the conditions of the obligations are fulfilled. Tamar, he rightly notes, remains a widow.

the possibility of successfully executing the deception. Therefore, he pretends to attempt to impregnate Tamar when he is simply engaging in sexual intercourse without any effort to conceive a child. Presumably, he would be negatively perceived if he refused his obligation.[64] In disguising his motive and actions, Onan manages to persuade some that he is acting in Tamar's best interest. Certainly, the Deity sees through the deceit. Thus, while it is possible to successfully deceive humans, it is impossible to deceive the Deity.

As with Onan, the effectiveness of Tamar's plan is that it uses non-advocated means to achieve a goal. The possibility of her success becomes clearer to her after exhausting the conventional means of producing an heir for Er, her deceased husband. She waits for the sanctioned opportunity of bearing a child with Shelah, but that possibility is withheld. Consequently, she orchestrates a situation of prostitution where she could become pregnant and bear an heir.

Denial of One's Rights

When one's rights are denied, it may lead to the construction of alternatives to fulfill those rights, or resignation to the denial of the rights. The denial itself may take on various forms, including ignoring the time for executing the rights. Presumably, those within the domain know the appropriate time to execute the rights but opt not to do so. For example, both Onan and Judah are aware of their obligation but carefully construct reasons for denying Tamar her rights. Onan's choice is to disguise his denial by appearing to perform his obligation. His disguise is thus twofold: he appears compliant with the traditions, and he does not violate his legacy. The Deity punishes his choice, thus presenting Tamar's rights to an heir as the overarching concern of the narrative. Even so, punishing Onan raises several questions and places the rights of two persons in tension. The main question is how to determine the priority of exercising one's rights. When securing one's rights violates the rights of another person, whose rights should prevail? Should both persons' rights be surrendered? Through the rationale given for punishing Onan, the text indicates that the rights of some take precedence over the rights of others. Thus, while Onan violates Tamar's rights, his rights appear to be violated by the attempts to secure hers. Consequently, although each has latent power in his or her situation, the domain restricts both Onan and Tamar.

These conflicts of rights may be anomalies in the narrative. Apparently, sometimes the rights of one person are subject to concerns other

---

64. Unlike Deut. 25:7–10, no refusal rite is cited in Onan's case.

than equitable achievement of rights.[65] Furthermore, the narrative demonstrates that the use of disguise is not entirely reprehensible. After all, Tamar is commended by Judah for securing her rights (Gen. 38:26). Even if he does not commend her methods, he is compelled to reevaluate them in light of her goal.[66] Through his reevaluation, Judah concedes that the disguise was at least effective and essential to the achievement of the goal. Judah may also demonstrate that the levirate obligation took precedence over his choice to protect his son from Tamar. It is an acknowledgment that in situations of social obligation the rights of the individual may be subject to the larger social obligations. Thus, Tamar's right to a child is the overarching concern because it dictates the rights and social obligations of all involved.[67] Perhaps in her case the decisive factors are that her rights were denied, and that she has the fewest alternatives in securing the rights. Consequently, in sustaining the obligation, the domain allows her a measure of power and protection while suggesting certain parameters for using deception to achieve personal gain.

Parameters of Disguise

EVALUATING THE USE

Onan's case suggests that no disguise or deception should be used to achieve personal gain if the personal goal violates an overarching social obligation. In contrast, Tamar's case suggests that she is justified in her use of a disguise. If Tamar's disguise represents an unethical method, then the text suggests that it does not destroy another person's rights or access to them. Rather, it may suggest or at least leave open the possibility that finding a way to fulfill one's rights is commendable. The issue is not whether she is a prostitute; that issue tends to blur the distinctions between function and essence. What defines her as a prostitute is her behavior, whether occasional or ongoing. If accepting compensation in exchange for sexual involvement constitutes an act of prostitution, Tamar acts like a prostitute. Yet she is not alone in the act of prostitution. Judah is also implicated in the prostitution, yet he dares to condemn her for her

65. Cf. Elizabeth S. Anderson, "What Is the Point of Equality?" *Ethics* 109 (1999): 312–21. She examines aspects of universal moral equality as well as capabilities and approaches to equality. In the latter the societal structures and one's place in them contribute to the understanding of equality; and equality is considered within the conceptual framework of freedom.

66. Andrew ("Moving from Death to Life," 267) discusses the occurrence of *ṣdq* "righteousness" in Gen. 38:26. He notes that the commendation relates specifically to "the institution of levirate marriage" and not exclusively to a "single moral action." Cf. Hamilton (*Genesis 18–50*, 443), who commends Tamar as well as Esther and Naomi for their efforts in achieving their goals.

67. Cf. Coats, "Widow's Rights," 465.

involvement. His disguise is to withhold information that would present him as being as culpable in prostitution as Tamar. Furthermore, in the use of her disguise, Tamar trusts Judah to return with the compensation, knowing that he has been untrustworthy in other matters. She is confident because she has links to his social identity that can be used as collateral. If for no other reason, he would be concerned to protect his behavior from public scrutiny and possible ridicule (Gen. 38:23).

Judah's deception is for personal gratification rather than to secure unrealized rights. His confidence in participating in prostitution may come from leadership in the community and choice of a foreign and anonymous partner. Thus he is ready to condemn Tamar for her use of unsanctioned means in securing her right to an heir, not realizing that his unsanctioned behavior is directly responsible for her pregnancy. His involvement with a prostitute may have been unconventional, and he does not readily reveal it to his community. Rather, Judah's deception illustrates his perpetual concealment of his role in Tamar's pregnancy and his effort to avoid public humiliation for his involvement with a prostitute. Even his acknowledgment of his failure to fulfill the levirate responsibility falls short of a full confession of his other contributions to Tamar's plight. Further, while Onan's behavior of destroying his semen transforms procreative sex into nonprocreative sex, Tamar's behavior and goal transform nonmarital sex and Judah's licentious sex into procreative sex. Judah may have been gratified temporarily, but she permanently redefines her status in the family by securing a legacy.

Nonetheless, Judah's concealed functional identity depicts several evaluative elements. First, as a leader who conceals his identity, he creates conflict in fulfilling the rights of others who are dependent on him. The sum total of his behavior shows a distorted evaluation of situations. While withholding Shelah may be reprehensible, one cannot deny his parental concern for his son. His status within the domain defines the extent of his power to affect others, but he behaves as if the effects of his behaviors are confined to him. Hence his concern for his son is not simply that of a father for a child but as a leader whose decisions alter the viability of the social obligation and his family structure.

Second, Judah conceals his motive through normal behavior. To postpone the union of Tamar and Shelah would be normal, but his motive is a perpetual rather than a temporary withholding. Apparently, Judah uses Shelah's youth as a logical argument and plausible reason for asking Tamar to wait.[68] Yet Tamar's willingness to accept the rationale is due to her own myopia concerning her situation and the options available to her. She may also have been persuaded because Judah had given Onan

---

68. Cf. Andrew, "Moving from Death to Life," 262.

to her. But how realistic is her waiting since she is already of marital age while Shelah is not? Along with Judah's lack of integrity in fulfilling this obligation to give Shelah to Tamar, Tamar is persuaded to wait because of his disguised motive and her assumptions about him.

VALIDATING THE USE OF DISGUISE

Does societal neglect of personal rights validate the use of any method to secure one's rights? The text suggests that the apparent absence of viable means does not automatically validate the use of an otherwise reprehensible method (e.g., Onan). Yet Judah's response to Tamar's method reflects his understanding of the parameters for acceptable behavior, including her relationship with her brother-in-law, her waiting for Shelah, and her return to her father's house. Likewise, the domain also defines some behaviors as unacceptable, namely, Tamar's prostitution. Tamar's pregnancy would have been welcomed if it had come about through acceptable circumstances. While the pregnancy is not offensive, the apparent circumstances in which she became pregnant are.

A woman's fertility is usually accepted as normal. Thus in Genesis infertile women attempt to become mothers through surrogacy (e.g., Sarah, Rachel). Tamar's lack of progeny is due to the actions of men and not to a congenital problem; but when she finally conceives, the news is met with consternation rather than jubilation. Clearly, even conception is subject to normative parameters that define some pregnancies as more socially acceptable than others. The criterion of acceptability appears to be the relational status of the expectant mother. An unmarried woman, therefore, is not to conceive because she has not been authorized by her domain to engage in sex. Consequently, nonmarital sex would define the ensuing pregnancy as socially unacceptable. Likewise, the pregnancy of a widow would be unacceptable apart from the parameters of appropriate sexual encounters, namely, levirate obligation or remarriage. She may engage in nonmarital sex only with the levir and for the sole purpose of procreation. A female prostitute is acting against the norms for an unmarried woman by consenting to sexual encounters. Ironically, her behavior also has social expectations that a prostitute could manage her own behavior. It is expected that prostitutes would not conform to the rules for unmarried women, namely, to expect marriage to follow a sexual encounter. Rather than an adult male guardian giving his consent, prostitutes give their own consent to their sexual availability and behavior. This consent process is normative to the functional identity of a prostitute.

In other cases where an unauthorized male consents for a woman, it is usually categorized as sexual violation or a situational norm, for example, women captives of war who are taken as the captors' wives

(Deut. 21:10–14), or Dinah and seduced women (Gen. 34; Exod. 22:15–16 [NRSV 22:16–17]; Deut. 22:28–29). In the latter cases, the normalization of the violation is achieved through the potential or subsequent marriage to the violator.[69] In Tamar's case, the normalization is achieved by identifying the male who impregnated her and by removing the punishment and the social stigma of her prostitution. Most importantly, the role that her unborn sons would potentially play in furthering the family line also normalizes her status and validates her behavior in her domain.

Conclusion

The many dimensions of disguised identity represented above lead to several concluding observations.

First, close familial relationships and intragroup elements and alliances do not deter deception but may facilitate deception. In Onan and Tamar's case, he behaves as if he has her best interest at heart but does not. The trust factor conceals his identity as one who impedes her rights. Judah and Tamar's case also illustrates that intragroup identity itself may facilitate unmerited trust. Because Judah had intimated that he would give her his son, Tamar waits on her father-in-law to do so. When he communicates with Tamar, Judah does not indicate the conditions of giving or withholding his son. His behavior and Naomi's are comparable in that they both are in positions to regulate the marriage of an in-law. While Judah withholds his intent as a mode of persuading Tamar to remain a widow, Naomi discloses her dire situation to dissuade Ruth and Orpah from waiting. Like Laban, who may have concealed his motive in agreeing to a seven-year term of labor as a bride-price for Rachel, Judah conceals a lack of commitment in his actions. The insidious nature of the deceit is that one is persuaded to blindly follow a course of behavior that does not lead to the goal that one perceives. In all these instances, trust increases the likelihood of deceit within the relationships. Tamar has no reason to distrust Judah's sincerity and efforts to fulfill his obligation toward her. Unfortunately for her, the effectiveness of the deception is that it fosters connections between entities (events, persons, actions) that are perceived to be real, even if they are not.

Second, the one whose rights are denied may persuade others to fulfill those rights through the subversive use of power. Yet in achieving what is otherwise denied, one may violate ethical principles and generate perpetual suspicion among all who are involved.

69. Jacobs, "Love, Honor, and Violence," 17–19, 22.

Third, one may mask one's shortcomings in a readiness to see condemnable behavior in others. In such cases, one may publicly condemn another and pronounce judgment for the same undisclosed behavior in one's past. Judah pronounces punishment on Tamar for prostitution but conceals his involvement with her in the act of prostitution.

Fourth, the power of perception is a vital part of being persuaded. Judah's actions are shaped by his misperception of several situations in which he may have behaved otherwise had his perception been different. Likewise, Tamar's persuasion about the viability of her choice to wait is altered by her perception. She then manifests her power by reevaluating her circumstances and altering her perception of what it would take to secure her rights. In both cases, perception persuades someone to sustain or alter her/his behaviors.

Excursus

Aspects of the Law in the Genesis Narratives

Within the narratives so far discussed, the legal ethos is evident in the language and the primary concerns. This excursus is an overview of the legal instances, for example, of adultery, polygyny, levirate responsibilities, marriage to siblings, inheritance, and premeditated murder. While these are all examples of the laws that regulate male-female relationships, other legal issues may be included. I make no effort here to explain any competing perspectives observed between practices noted in the Genesis narratives and the relevant legal prohibitions and stipulations. The correlation between the narratives and the legal tradition is highlighted as a point for further consideration rather than an entry into comparative analysis of the conceptual affinities between the narratives and the law.

Table 3: Legal Inferences in the Genesis Narratives

Issue		Genesis Narratives	Legal Texts
Levirate marriage	Gen. 38	Tamar and Onan	Deut. 25:5–10
Firstborn's inheritance	Gen. 27	Jacob and Esau	Deut. 21:15–17
	Gen. 29–30	Reuben—firstborn of the hated wife	
Murder	Gen. 27	Esau's threat against Jacob	Exod. 20:13; 21:12–14
Adultery	Gen. 12; 20	Sarah and rulers	Exod. 20:14; Lev. 20:10; Deut. 5:18

Issue	Genesis Narratives		Legal Texts
Polygyny	Gen. 26:34	Esau—Judith and Basemath	Lev. 18:18
	Gen. 29–30	Jacob—Rachel and Leah	
Polyandry	Gen. 12; 20	Sarah with Pharaoh	—
Exogamy	Gen. 16:3	Abraham—Hagar	Num. 36:8; Deut. 7:1–6
	Gen. 26:34; 36:2	Esau—Judith, Basemath, Adah, Oholibamah	
	Gen. 38:2	Judah—Shua's daughter	

Proscribed sexual partners

Father and daughter-in-law	Gen. 38	Judah and Tamar	Lev. 18:15; 20:12
Uncle-niece	Gen. 11:29	Nahor and Milcah (?)	—
Brother-sister	Gen. 20	Abraham and Sarah	Lev. 18:9
Brother and sister-in-law	Gen. 38	Onan and Tamar	Lev. 18:16

Proscribed marital unions

Brother-sister	Gen. 12; 20	Abraham and Sarah	Lev. 20:17
Brother and sister-in-law	Gen. 38	Onan and Tamar	Lev. 20:21

PART 3

Female-Male Dynamics in Contemporary Contexts

I ssues of gender and power constitute one of the frontiers in which equity has yet to be achieved. Part of the challenge is a basic under-standing of gender within the relationship parameters of the public vis-à-vis the private domains. Cultural and religious ideologies have formed commitments and thus have defined the basic understandings about gender, even among those who do not claim a religious affilia-tion. Consequently, gender and gender differentials are decisive for the structure and cohesion of the domains and the functional identities therein. The conceptual framework therefore evidences the collective cultural or segmental persuasion about gender and power issues. Often, the framework includes ideologies of male dominance and female in-feriority as the norm, and the typical female and male relationship as intimate or an opportunity for intimacy. I reaffirm in part 3 that the biblical narratives discussed in parts 1 and 2 function as a mirror of today's challenges and reflect conceptual frameworks defined by gender, power, and persuasion.

While part 3 of the book is not a sociological analysis, in it I explore insights for understanding gender in power and persuasion dynamics. Accordingly, in this section I note that the Judeo-Christian understand-ings of Gen. 1–3 have informed the collective cultural and segmental framework about female-male relationships in both the private and the public domain and have sustained many attitudes about women's and men's abilities and places within society. In parts 1 and 2, I analyzed selected biblical narratives through the conceptual frameworks of gender as it is manifested in power and persuasion. First, I established that the conceptual domain of the narratives show human relationships as part of a larger reality influenced and controlled by God. Consequently, basic to any discussion of these narratives is the tension between human power and the Deity's power, and by implication the issue of powerlessness as an inherent attribute of all humans in a system where the Deity's will dominates. Second, parts 1 and 2 explored various configurations of the female-male dynamics as modes of manifestation (functional identity) rather than differences inherent in the gender identity of the participants. These configurations include female-male, male-male, and female-female. Finally, I concluded each chapter in parts 1 and 2 with observations about issues of gender, power, and persuasion exhibited in the behavioral and relational dynamics of the various narratives.

In part 3 of this book I use the concluding observations from the preceding chapters as a starting place for exploring female-male dynamics in contemporary domains. In chapters 8 and 9 I build on the proposal that all situations in which human beings are involved constitute a relationship. The question is not whether a relationship exists in any given domain but rather what is the nature of the relationship as defined by the domain and vice versa. While it is not my goal in part 3 to discuss the nature of all domain configurations, the goal is to explore further the noted observations about the behavioral and relational parameters that constitute various contemporary domains, and to present brief situation and character analyses that exemplify these observations. Accordingly, in chapter 8 I explore observations relating to gender and power, and in chapter 9 I explore observations relating to gender and persuasion.

8

Gender and Power Differentials

The main goal of this chapter is to explore aspects of gender and power with reference to the contemporary domains of family and work. The exploration takes the form of situation and character analyses beginning with the biblical scene and proceeding to the contemporary. I propose that power is domain-specific and manifested through functional identity and parameters. This exploration identifies insights into the relational dynamics and exposes rather than suggests patterns that are to be emulated.

Since the discussion assumes the domains as the manifestations of the relational dynamics, I begin with an overview of a contemporary conflict of domains. While the intersection of the domains is a fact of existence, the nature and extent of the overlap varies. The health of both domains requires that one transfer from the private domain only those characteristics that are appropriate to the functional and relational viability within the public domain. On the other side of the balance transfer is the risk of excessive compartmentalization by which the disconnection between the private and the public persona results in disintegration in one or both domains. Accordingly, the healthy workplace in which men and women coexist is defined by lines of authority manifested through functional identity. While harmonious relationships are integral to healthy environments, blurred boundaries often foster negative and unhealthy relationships.

The relationship danger in the workplace is to redefine the parameters of the public relationship by presuming the characteristics of the more

intimate private ones. Conflict of domains exists where the roles and ideologies of one domain clash with those of another domain. For example,
the conflict is seen in males who attempt to transfer this power from their
private domain to public ones. The result may be countertransference
of the spouse or daughter's characteristics onto their female colleagues.
One manifestation of this is the male expectation to be appreciated by
female colleagues in ways reserved for intimate familial relationships.
Thus the male may expect to be complimented or nurtured by his female
colleagues and to be praised for all his efforts—whether or not these
efforts are praiseworthy. Likewise, the male may expect to be treated
as the superior in terms of ability—whether or not he is more skilled or
intelligent than his female counterpart. If in his home the females cater
to his needs and accept his perspective as decisive, he may also expect
that of his female colleagues. Such males often do well with functional
subordinates but feel uncomfortable with their female superiors, peers,
or functional counterparts. In such situations, the male may attempt to
gain superiority by various means, including patronizing or intimidat-
ing his colleagues.

In response to this type of male power, some females may choose to
perform below their potential if that potential would equal or surpass
the male colleague. The female inclination to downplay her ability and
to spare the male ego highlights a behavioral transfer from her private
domain. The symbiosis of the male and female powers may be further
nourished by males who expect female inferiority, function well with
females who behave as inferiors, but resist females of equal or superior abilities. On the contrary, males and females may generate another
symbiosis defined by valuing ability and functional competence over
perceived gender inferiority, and by nurturing the female-male power
dynamics as potentially mutually affirming.

The conflict of domains is also evident in females who succumb to
countertransference of characteristics from the private domain into the
public domain. Some females deem themselves inferior to males while
others assert their superiority. In the case of female countertransference, she may transfer her father or husband's characteristics onto her
male colleagues. One manifestation is the expectation to be affirmed
as a woman (gender identity) when the relationship is otherwise constituted (functional identity). In such situations, the female tends to be
overly dependent on the advice of male colleagues and less inclined to
be assertive for fear of punishment or lack of affirmation. In contrast,
some females may have had negative experiences with their father or
husband and therefore a priori attribute these negative traits to their
colleagues. The tendency may include several configurations of the following aspects: to assume an infantile or juvenile disposition, to become

a maternal figure, or to vilify the male while victimizing oneself. None of these is appropriate for a healthy functional identity in the public domain. Transferring the expectations from their private to their public domain allows the boundaries of one domain to exceed the boundaries of the other and muddles the nature of power and its manifestation. On the basis of this overview, in this chapter I explore three aspects of gender and power.

The Nature of Power

Power Is Domain Specific in Its Manifestation and Influence

Power is not abstract from interaction, behavior, and thought, but is manifested in a domain and by particular agents. Power is therefore defined here as the ability to effect change and exercise choice. It is manifested in different ways and because of this may be characterized as different types. Nonetheless, power is not determined by positional status or socially sanctioned behaviors. Rather, it is possible to have significant power in one domain and limited power in another. For example, as mistress over Hagar, Sarah wields a power that she does not demonstrate in her publicly manifested relationship with Abraham in Egypt and Gerar, where he pretends that she is his sister.

Power Is Defined by Function, Not by the Essence of the Being Who Manifests It

The implication of this is challenging to the extent that one overlooks the persuasive power of the relatively weak by presupposing that their status makes them inferior and powerless. Such presumptions may surround the understanding of the challenge for power as depicted in Gen. 3. In this respect, the narrative power is the depiction of the cunning serpent as powerful in its ability to influence the humans. By seeing naming as an act of dominance, the serpent, a named creature, is usually designated to the category of the subordinate. The error of this interpretation is to assess a being's power based on group identity. Whether or not it is an animal, the serpent exercises a power that alters the humans' perception of their reality and their willingness to explore the boundaries of that reality. Similarly, the woman is often viewed negatively as a seductress or as weak for succumbing to the serpent's challenge. Instead, one may also see her as innovative and courageous in her attempt to achieve another form of actualization despite the limitations imposed on her by the prohibition. She is also audacious in her attempt to defend the Creator, even presuming to speak for the Deity. Whatever the results, the exercise of her ability to discern options is part of her power, as is her and her husband's choice between the alternatives.

Even Hagar exhibits the power to change her oppressive circumstances and does so by removing herself from them. Hers is the power to perceive the nature of her situation and to choose between the present situation and the unknown and potentially dangerous wilderness. Likewise, her power is seen in her ability to make a choice to leave rather than to remain in the oppression. Even the decision to remain is an exercise of her power of choice. Her ultimate challenge is to surrender her power of choice to the wishes of the Deity and thus act against her better judgment by returning to the oppressive situation.

Female Relationships Are Often the By-Product of Male-Implemented Systems

Relationships are usually defined by internal and external parameters, assume the existence of other relationships, and show the power of humans over one another. They are usually systems that define people's behavior toward one another. Out of their sense of control, Laban and Jacob foster circumstances in which Rachel and Leah are placed in competition, or at least placed at odds with each other. For Rachel the quandary may be represented by a question about whom to love: her husband, who has declared his love for her, her sister, who is her co-wife through deceit, or her father, who orchestrated the deceit. If Leah is innocent of the ruse and just a pawn in Laban's machinations, to Rachel she is still evidence of the ruse and the problematic point of reference. One can easily see the connections to modern female relationships in various domains. In a blended family the wife and ex-wife are often at odds with each other because of the nature of their relationship to the man. An ex-wife who has been replaced by a younger woman may resent the new wife, thus seeing her as "other"—the other woman. In this situation, it is often difficult for either woman to recognize herself in the other person and to acknowledge that they both want to be loved and respected. Parents may use their children as channels to vent their anger against the ex-spouse or the new spouse. In some cases, the stepparent may also resent the current spouse's relationship with her/his biological children. As in the case of Jacob's relationship to Leah's children, the parent may be distant from the children because of the negative relationship with the other parent.

Leah was not responsible for becoming a co-wife or for being more fertile than Rachel. Yet Rachel, with all her advantages, was still jealous of Leah. Neither created the circumstances that defined their relationship as co-wives, yet both facilitated and maintained the dynamics of that relationship through their competition and quest to become like the other. The other side of this is that they blamed each other for their perceived deficiency. Thus Leah believed that Rachel took Jacob from her even though he never expressed any desire to be her husband or to love her (Leah). In the work domain the female dynamics may also be shaped by the system implemented and sustained by men. In this respect, the system may recognize the achievements of women but still reward the woman deemed to be the most attractive while showing little regard for those deemed average or unattractive. Consequently, women may compete with one another for acceptance by the men in their work domain while actively contributing to the negative view of other women in that domain. Some women who may have worked hard to achieve their positions may harbor resentment toward men who create challenges for them along the way. While they may not retaliate against the men, they would readily retaliate against other women and perpetuate what was done to them rather than seek to break the cycle.

On the other side are the men, who because of their competition with one another create environments that are fraught with suspicion and mistrust. They may do anything to be seen as the best or the most powerful, including deceiving one another. Their concern is not the climate of the work domain as much as their place within it. Surely, Laban knew that it would not be the best situation to pawn off Leah to a man who made no indication that he wanted her. He thus created a bad situation for Leah and everyone involved and then appeared to solve it by giving Rachel to Jacob. Rather than resolving it, Laban constructed a family dynamic defined by deception and competition for resources. The deceit also set the stage for the strained relationship between Jacob and Laban and between Jacob and Leah. Laban's motive may have been to secure a husband for Leah, but his effort focused more on his accomplishment of that goal than on her well-being as an unloved wife. He also displayed the tendency to seek control of his domain, as head of household. While this shows his sense of responsibility and the power to fulfill it, in its mode of execution he also showed his willfulness to exercise that control, even to the detriment of others. While part of this control was endemic to his ethos and functional identity, other aspects were particular to him, namely, his use of deceit and manipulation of his family to advance his concerns. In this respect, Laban is like the male who creates conflict so he can resolve it and be seen as one who is adept at problem solving. Similarly, he is like the man who withholds vital information from his colleagues, then later presents it as a way of being helpful or of saving the project.

In keeping with the characterization of the person who generates tension by placing others at odds with one another, Jacob's polygyny is classic. He married two sisters and persisted in having sexual encounters with both, one of whom he did not love. Here he symbolizes the male who pits women against each other by entangling them in a relationship with him. A married man who maintains a relationship with his mistress with the intermittent suggestion that he will leave his wife may not intend to divorce his wife to marry the mistress, but may continue to entangle her through sex and emotional ties. For the single man, it may be that he is dating multiple women until he finds "Ms. Right," but prefers to tell the "good-enough-for-now" women that he is not ready.

Positional Authority and Power Are Not the Same

The choice of behavior—ethical or otherwise—is a function of personhood, not simply of status or gender. Thus the idea that unethical behavior is the first choice of the underprivileged is a fallacy. Power is not solely the product of noble character, nor is it restricted by status or authority. Like other people, those of high status are just as likely to deceive. Abraham consistently and knowingly compromises his wife yet has the power to do otherwise. He enjoys the protection of his father's house for much of his adulthood. He is told that he is specially chosen by God to father a nation and to take land that is already occupied. He has wealth yet convinces himself that he is more vulnerable than Sarah and uses Sarah as a shield. Whatever aspects of his character are displayed in relation to Sarah, Abraham is the source of her problem while they are in Egypt and Gerar. How a man of his power and privilege could envision himself as vulnerable illustrates the danger of privilege and its inherent power. Like the underprivileged, the privileged may be unable to understand one's power and allow that misconception to dictate behavior. Abraham is not vulnerable for the reasons that he articulates. His sense of vulnerability comes from the misconception of being in a social domain where he is among other privileged persons, and where he is not the most powerful in that domain. Much like the situation of the underprivileged, who are not powerless but may view themselves as powerless because of their place within the social hierarchy, Abraham's relative status among rulers does not make him powerless. He knows power and how to be the most powerful in his family domain, but he appears uncomfortable when he is not the most powerful.[1]

The balance of power is the challenge that is observed in this male-male dynamic. He devises a way of protecting himself, yet not a way of protecting his wife, Sarah. Once he deceives a ruler and Sarah is taken to be another man's wife, Abraham receives possessions, possibly as a

---

1. This balance of power is also the root of Abimelech's action to expel Isaac from Gerar. He perceived that Isaac had become more powerful than the Gerarites and tried to get rid of him (Gen. 26).

bride-price for Sarah. A nation is punished for Abraham's behavior, yet he repeats the behavior and claims that this is part of his strategy when traveling to a foreign region (Gen. 12:10–20; 20:11–13). What first appears as vulnerability is a propensity to do what works for him without careful consideration of the consequences for Sarah. What looks like an error in judgment the first time looks like a habit the second.

As a man of power, Abraham does not understand how to function within a system where he is just one of many privileged persons. Abraham's actions are based on a bias against foreigners. He epitomizes a person whose perception is dwarfed or stunted by his privilege and power. Nevertheless, the privileged group to which he belongs would be much smaller than the citizens of modest means. With an entourage, a man of wealth would be noticed. Even so, his misconception is a by-product of his bias against the unknown, and his vulnerability is more perceived than real. How could one who has the support of the Deity be vulnerable? Abraham's behavior also illustrates the quality of needing parental rescue when, because of a lack of judgment, one has created a mess. The parent comes in and rescues the child while in the process implicating others and affirming the relational bonds with the child. The child receives reinforcement for the behavior and thus is likely to repeat it. Abraham, like those who have known such privilege and little else, tends to function well only in situations where he is privileged. Such people tend to seek ways of gaining an advantage when they perceive that their power has been restricted.

Gender Does Not Determine Abuse of Power

Since power is not distinctive to either gender, neither is the abuse of power. It is not the magnitude of the power that determines whether it may be abused, but rather the existence of power itself. For anyone who possesses power the possibility exists that she/he may abuse it. Because the domain defines power, it also defines the particular abuse, including the persons who will be affected. Given the dynamics of behavior to transcend the immediate context, one can no more control the effects of the abuse than one can control the effects of any other behavior. One notable pattern observed relative to the access to and use of power is that those who have been subordinated and marginalized may perpetuate the behavior to which they had been subjected. This depicts the truism that people learn from life—they do as they have experienced (whether through observation or participation). People learn from their experience how to view themselves and how to view and treat others. In time, the abused may become the abuser, and within the same situation, the abused may be the abuser. Consequently, multiple roles and functions of one individual may be defined by do-main-specific attributes.[2]

For instance, in the family domain, the abused child grows up to abuse her/his spouse or child, and the abused wife may abuse her children. Within the historical-social context, the examples are prominent—the marginalized woman who has a measure of power in her domain mar-ginalizes others within her influence. She may silently assent to the abuse of other women either because she feels powerless to help or because she believes that others deserve the abuse. In some cases, she may believe that since she "made it" through the abuse others (if they are worthy of their status) should be able to "make it" on their own. In her experience of abuse she may have suffered as the silenced "other" in one domain while being the norm and having a voice in another, therefore living two existences as one person. The previously muted female may silence others when she gains a voice. Likewise, women, the classic "other" in the male domain, may also classify persons on the basis of various phys-ical and social attributes and use that classification to mistreat them. For example, by using her status and power to oppress Hagar, Sarah marginalizes her just as Sarah had been marginalized. Just as she was given to the pharaoh, she gives Hagar to Abraham. Sarah's consent in the ruse is nowhere noted, thus suggesting her compliance due to the lack of a viable option to alter the situation. Likewise, she is responsible for Hagar's imposed compliance.

Another part of this situation analysis regards the power shift within a domain. Hagar's recognition of her change in status may have resulted in the devaluation of Sarah in Hagar's eyes. The narrator is clearly sym-pathetic toward Sarah, showing that Sarah's response to Hagar is the result of Hagar's disregard for Sarah after Sarah had given her status as a wife.[3] Their situation suggests that the one who fosters the shift of the subordinate's power and the relational dynamics (whatever the motive) opens the possibility that the former subordinate may become one's functional equal or superior. The power shift creates the possibility that the former subordinate may contribute to the demise of the former functional superior. Although that is the most readily perceived abuse resulting from the power shift, it is not simply a matter of the former subordinate actively abusing the superior. Another more pervasive and equally harmful dynamic is the animosity toward the one whose role has been elevated. This is the classic teacher's envy of a former student, or parent's envy of the successful child, where the elevated person's ac-

2. See chap. 5 regarding layered relational and functional identities.
3. Cf. Code of Hammurabi §146 (*ANET*, 172) regarding the attitude of the surrogate mother.

tions are perceived as an affront to the former functional or relational superior. As in Sarah's case, part of the animosity may be born out of grief over the loss of opportunity or even envy of the other for achieving where she had not.

This situation also reflects the classic younger/older person dynamic in many professions. In this way, it also epitomizes the female pattern of competition in the work domain, where in many instances women are still perceived as "other" while the male is the functional norm. One aspect in particular of the female pattern is the use of the system to pit women against each other. For additional power to support her actions against Hagar, Sarah appeals to the system that defined her first as wife and then as mistress over Hagar. When she gives Hagar to Abraham, she allows Hagar to become wife and to conceive; yet she envies Hagar for being pregnant and subsequently banishes her and her son, Ishmael. Rather than resolving the situation on her own, Sarah enlists Abraham's help. Thus for all her functional advancement from servant to wife, Hagar remains a functional subordinate to Sarah, who uses the status differential to her advantage. In this, Sarah displays the tendency to project animosity toward another for one's own shortcomings. While she may have envied Hagar at one point, once she becomes a mother Sarah facilitates a solution to her problem by readily disposing of Hagar and Ishmael. Her treatment of Ishmael—the prior solution to her infertility—also displays her assertiveness in another aspect of the co-wife and stepparent relationship, namely, the dispensability of the "other."

The expiration of Hagar's usefulness for Sarah's purposes defines the terms of the dispensability. Within that system, Hagar is still restricted by her relationship to Sarah as surrogate and maid. Thus Hagar is both useful and devalued. Yet the system works for Sarah and against Hagar such that she is as much marginalized as "other" by the Deity as by Sarah and Abraham. When the Deity asks her to return to the oppressive situation, this is an indication of her limited significance to the Deity's plan and a sign that Sarah is functionally more important to the Deity than Hagar. Even so, both Sarah and Hagar are in subsidiary or supporting roles that are important to the extent that they maintain the focus on someone else (i.e., Abraham, Isaac).

Sarah is therefore like the woman of positional authority in her job who is acclaimed from the outside but who is marginalized within her work domain. Inside she may be objectified and silenced by the status quo. Others represent her voice, and even then her voice is rarely heard. She may even use her power to subject her subordinates to the oppression to which she had been subjected. Often unwittingly, she becomes the female antagonist who insidiously creates and sustains difficulties for other women. She may also be involved in situations much like Sarah's, where her entourage is silent. On their trips to Egypt and Gerar, no one spoke on Sarah's behalf to prevent the deception or the compromise of her character. Of course, that would have meant going against Abraham. Why would Sarah not speak for herself when given the opportunity? For the sake of her husband, Sarah exhibits loyalty; but Abimelech defends her honor after the ruse is uncovered. Evidently, those who are subordinate in a relationship do not speak for a superior. Instead, the one in authority speaks for the subordinate—Abimelech for Sarah and God for Sarah.

It is therefore not surprising that given their shared experiences Sarah functions with her subordinates as one privileged rather than bonding with them. Sarah is like the compartmentalized woman, the marginalized, privileged person whose status is the vehicle for her marginalization. She often does not even recognize her marginalization, or when she does, she keeps the facade and becomes part of her own muted existence. She is the submissive wife whose husband's demands have stifled her into compliance. Her privilege may explain the rift between her and others who share her experience and may be willing and able to help her.

Power and Choice

Power and choice are domain-specific and regulated by the domain. Within the purpose domain governed by God's plan, the choices of the individual may be defined and limited by the plan.

God Defines the Agents in God's Plan

The Genesis narratives depict the women as both privileged and marginalized, namely, as the matriarchs of a nation but disregarded in the day-to-day reality; and as women of status, who from the perspective of the outsider are privileged. In the domain of the plan, they are women of status, but in their family domain and interaction with their husbands, they have been marginalized and muted. The irony is that Sarah is set aside as the exclusive choice for birthing Abraham's heir. That choice, however, represents a life course with specified and limited possibilities. Even Abraham must conform to the Deity's plans for him, but Sarah's options are even more restricted. Sarah's experience, particularly involving the wife-sister ruse, illustrates some of the fallacies of her privilege.

Abraham is selected as the vehicle through which to fulfill the plan, and as such, his actions in his domains (private and public) are not evaluated as reprehensible nor is any punishment directed at him. Rather, part of his power is that he is a selected agent, favored as essential to the Deity's plan. One cannot escape the narrative's view of Abraham as one who compels the Deity's favor and protection. Abraham's existence displays the difference between being essential and being dispensable.

To be essential is to have the plans cohere around him and be executed through his circumstances, without consideration of replacing him if his circumstances are challenging. In contrast, to be dispensable is to have a limited contribution to the Deity's plan and be replaceable based on one's usefulness. In this case, the criterion for usefulness is one's ability to contribute to the goals or the stages in the plan. Consequently, if the goal of the plan is to have a child and the child is already born, one's usefulness has been fulfilled, making one dispensable unless one contributes to another aspect of the plan. Here the plan itself constitutes a domain. Even so, to be essential or dispensable is relative to the function rather than the essence of the person. Thus Sarah's role was not always considered essential due in part to her infertility and Abraham's perspective of his reality.

Further, to be essential is a power in and of itself. Those regarded as essential persons usually attempt to structure the environment around their needs and concerns. This will involve treating others as incidental to one's plans and replacing them to fulfill particular perceived needs and agendas—all with the protection of the domain. Just like Abraham, who was willing to make choices to preserve his status within the domain, others also make such choices. The choice to sacrifice the well-being of his wife to protect himself against a perceived but unsubstantiated threat mirrors a contemporary choice to protect one's status at another's expense. In this respect, essential persons may be insulated. However, they may also be fearful of losing their prescribed status and dwarfed in their ability to negotiate their domain. In them one may perceive, as in Abraham, persons who are rescued from challenging situations and thus do not exhibit the skill to devise other viable alternatives. Additionally, essential persons are characterized by their conformity to another's agenda, being persuaded of their significance to that agenda and lack of significance apart from it. Their power is the security of being primary to a plan or purpose.

Selecting Agents Reveals the Deity's Character

The characterization of Abraham's power as that which is constituted by privilege also illustrates the character of his God. The Deity's power is depicted as orchestrating events toward a particular outcome. As such, the Deity displays a purpose that incorporates both temporal and spatial dimensions. To the extent that the Deity's plan is defined and the roles of the agents within are prescribed, the Deity is portrayed as one who is functionally if not essentially biased. Certainly, the Deity does not regard all persons as equal agents within the domain, but sets up a system in which there are functional superiors and subordinates. Consequently, the character of the selected agents is not a criterion for their selection but appears as a capricious aspect that eventuates in distinctive traits. Additionally, the Deity is the controlling power within the domain and by its purpose defines the viability of all other plans. Within the domain, the plan is essential; to remain viable, however, essential agents must adjust to the plan. Fundamentally, being selected to participate as a specific agent in the Deity's plan may be defined as a privilege, namely, the advantage and option of being assigned significance within the domain.

Being selected and having significance in a plan does not make one honorable or ensure that one's behaviors are honorable. Thus a situation is not honorable because an allegedly honorable person instigates it. Likewise, it is not dishonorable because an allegedly dishonorable person is involved. The misconception about Pharaoh and Abimelech shows that perceived dishonor is not a function of status, the Deity's favor, or nationality. Clearly, the Deity's chosen behaved in a dishonorable way, while the foreign rulers displayed honor in their behavior. Abraham's concern about his safety put Sarah's well-being at risk and did not constitute an honorable act. Conversely, both Abimelech and Pharaoh resolved the potential harm to Sarah by restoring her to Abraham. Because they were deceived, they inadvertently took another man's wife and consequently suffered. While hurting another may be unacceptable, the Deity determines whose hurt is unacceptable and for what reason. The Deity vehemently defends persons as long as those persons are instrumental to the advancement of the divine plan. Thus the Deity responds to humans but is not controlled by them. In this way, the Deity is predictable and unpredictable—predictable in sustaining the divine plans and in maintaining the status quo; yet unpredictable in disregarding various facets of the status quo, speaking to whomever and ignoring others.[4] The Deity is predictable in being committed to the chosen yet unpredictable in who that may be. There are some consistent favorites, but one may be chosen for an alternate plan rather than the primary one. The Deity may persuade the chosen to participate and to remain compliant to the Deity's plan as the dominant reality in their lives. For them their power is in choosing whether to embrace the Deity's plan.

Using Power Includes Persuading Others

Sarah persuades Abraham to participate in her mistreatment of Hagar, but before she does she persuades herself to use Hagar as a surrogate.

4. Humphreys, *Character of God*.

Subsequently, she also persuades herself that it is in her best interest to get rid of Hagar and Ishmael. Quite apart from the prudence of her behavior, her power to act comes from her power to persuade herself to do so. Her choice to use Hagar as a surrogate also demonstrates that she is part of a domain and is persuaded by the ideologies within that domain about the social viability of using a surrogate. When she manifests that choice, she is demonstrating the domain's choice for her and her consent to that choice. Whether the issue is surrogacy, fashion, career, or family, part of the power of choice is consulting the domain to ascertain the parameters of viability. Since everyone lives in a domain, everyone is subject to interaction with the domain as a precondition for exercising choice. Part of the power is also to evaluate the domain and to respond in ways that are conducive to effectiveness within it. Thus Sarah's choice to persuade Abraham to take Hagar as a wife is a valid choice without social shame attached to it. Therefore, surrogacy is used as a conducive and efficient mode of motherhood.

In contrast, Leah is the unloved spouse who, like the unloved child or disfavored worker, does what she believes will win her favor, but to no avail. She persists in her efforts to win that favor while being in a mode of self-persuasion that reinforces itself rather than being reinforced by the accomplishment of a goal. Leah is the wife who bears children to keep her family together only to realize in the end that children do not bring love to spouses who do not already love each other. Self-persuasion facilitates one's use of power even when that use does not yield the desired results.

The Use of Power to Determine the Future Is Not Exclusive to Humans

For the narrative, this point is bad news for Hagar and her descendants. Her effort to escape her situation is redirected by the Deity. She is asked to accept a consolation prize and to acquiesce to her marginalization and oppression. In accepting the promised future, she is plagued by the residue of her oppression.

Yet one must realize that being the favorite does not guarantee the absence of adversity; it is not always the case that the Deity opposes the marginalized. Clearly, the disfavored Leah was blessed with children while Rachel was temporarily infertile. One sees in this that the Deity may attempt to equalize the situation of inequity so that the favored also has a taste of disfavor (cf. Jacob and Laban). Most often, however, the reversal of fortunes is portrayed primarily under human control and apart from divine intervention (Jacob-Laban and to a lesser extent Joseph and his brothers). Again, this characterization is juxtaposed to the Deity, who participates in the oppression of the disfavored and thus sides with the oppressor to actualize the Deity's plan.

Part of the genius of the narratives is that they create a mosaic of the Deity as one who allows human participation in the course of history to the extent of altering that history and creating apparent alternatives. Yet humans do not control the Deity. The power of the text is the ability to persuade the reader of the multiple perspectives about the same Deity, persons, and events. It allows an understanding into human experience of both adversity and blessing, suggesting that no person exists without challenges. Part of the Deity's power is to ensure a type of equilibrium of the collective human experience—one achieved through distribution of adversity among all but without reciprocal distribution of blessings. Thus, Rachel and Hannah are made to endure infertility although they are loved, and Leah is made fertile though she is unloved. They are similar to the man who has a great job, family, home, and community and thus appears to have it all. One day he awakes to the news that he has a life-threatening illness. He and his family are then forced into a period of struggle that seems to erase the ease of the past. They struggle to understand why, without entertaining the notion of "why not them." On the other side is the woman like Rachel, who is loved by her husband, financially secure, and the envy of other women, but all her friends and sisters have children while she does not. Since she defines her existence in terms of her ability to be a mother, she constantly struggles to appreciate the other aspects of her life and continually envies her friends, even those pained by divorce and abuse. She agonizes over her infertility and efforts to conceive while her friends and sisters have several successful pregnancies. Whether or not these situations were specifically designed by the Deity to equalize human experience, there is a suggestion that pain touches humans in various forms—some humans more than others. Although the form of the suffering may differ from person to person, in suffering each human shares a common bond.

Power, Privilege, and Character

The third and final element of the gender-power differences looks at issues of character. As with the other two elements, several observations address the dynamics of power and privilege.

The Ideal Life Is a Construction from an External Perspective

The irony of privilege is that the outside perspective idealizes it and makes it into what it may not be. For many privileged persons, how they are perceived often does not cohere with the reality of their lives. Some types of privilege usually exacerbate the disparity between perception and reality that is basic to human existence. Those who are central to the formation of a group's identity, as its pioneers, fall into this category of privilege. Others include those of high visibility in their domain, where the public persona is equated with the private reality and professional expertise is assumed as evidence of refined life skills. There are numerous examples of the successful professional whose personal life is plagued by struggles, from addiction, to family problems, to depression.

Abraham is an example of the power of privilege. Sarah is an example of the liability of privilege. In today's society, she would be in a domain that other women only dream about. She has access to people of high status and in her family she is the wife of a man of status. Yet her privilege marginalizes her from those like her husband and likewise from those of socially marginalized status who may be more acquainted with her plight than she is able to articulate. Consequently, she does not affiliate with those who share her experiences because they are socially differentiated and in separate domains. Ironically, she may be experientially differentiated from those in her social domain and thus separated from them. Within her social and public domain, she is not at the lowest level. Relative to her maids she has power, but relative to her husband she is treated as a subordinate. Her entire existence is defined by her relational identity to her family. Yet, that relational identity is her privilege and her problem.

Another fallacy is that privilege is pervasive in the lives of those of that status. Privilege is a manifestation of favor but does not necessarily mean favor in every domain of one's life. Where disfavor and privilege coincide a paradox is fostered. Privilege may mean being selected for a particular role not available to others. The benefit itself is being selected, but the disadvantage is the role to which one has been selected. The woman who marries an abuser is an example. Rachel exemplifies this in that she is selected and favored but is subsequently disfavored by God and marginalized from her sister and husband. The woman executive who is persistently harassed by her colleagues is another example. Any leader of a community may have the privilege of such leadership at the cost of her/his time and privacy. In short, every privilege has a counterprivilege that is often merged with it and prohibits problem-free existence.

One fallacy of privilege is that it is somehow better than being underprivileged. The basic part of this fallacy is the failure to understand that experience and observation have different relationships to reality. The fallacy assigns value based on observation of the reality and usually out of a preference for the perceived privilege. The availability of alternatives is one aspect of privilege, but so is the experience of choosing among the alternatives. The preference for the privilege often does not take into account that there are degrees of being underprivileged just as there are degrees of being privileged. Sarah's privilege and her underprivileged status coalesce. As a woman with the challenge of being married to a man of privilege, her life course has already been defined; however, her status as wife is her liability. She is at once valuable to Abraham as a way of protecting himself but dispensable precisely because she is used to curry favor. Likewise, she is valuable as the designated mother of his children, but devalued because of her infertility. Many contemporary women find themselves in Sarah. They are the women whom others envy for any one of several aspects, including a successful husband, children, a good career, and a beautiful home. These women of privilege enjoy aspects of life others only dream of. Nonetheless, these women often live with the reality of being marginalized within their homes or careers. This is the class of useful yet nonessential persons.

Humans Tend to Prefer and to Desire to Be the Privileged "Other"

The examples of Rachel and Leah may also be instructive in understanding the reality of their lives and the tendency to envy others. As with Sarah, they are extolled in the history of Israel's development and existence as matriarchs. However, this contribution came at a great cost to them. These women are like any pioneer who is admired for paving the way into unexplored territories—geographical, social, or professional. To the public eye the achievement is visible, but the sacrifices and struggles are often de-emphasized, ignored, or treated as invisible.

Rachel is the beloved wife who is unfulfilled in her life and blames her husband. She is like the person who displaces her anger onto others in an attempt to cope with her challenges. Rachel is also the type who has just about everything except the one thing that she wants. Despite having so much, she wants to be what she is not. She wants what someone else has but is not being realistic about the entire picture of what they endured to acquire it. Leah is the other side of Rachel, wanting what Rachel has and failing to see the full picture of what she already has. Further, both fail to see themselves in the other and thus are at odds rather than supporting each other.

Rachel and Leah exemplify the desires fostered by many to be rich, famous, or powerful. In that desire they perceive the visible aspects of the desired privilege without a clear perception of the realities within the privilege. Included in this misperception is the idea that acquisition of the privilege would make one's life better and happy. This perception equates happiness and fulfillment with privilege, but it fails to see that there are challenges within each domain. There is no problem-free existence, just different types of problems and challenges. Clearly, it is not the presence or absence of the challenges that define one's contentment but one's perception of what one needs to be content.

Privilege Does Not Necessarily Exclude Adversity

Adversity may be a by-product of one's privilege, a facet of one's dispensability. In connection with the previous observation, I further note that Sarah is remarkably passive in both accounts of her acting as Abraham's sister. With Abimelech, she is implicated in the ruse and perhaps for this reason needs to be exonerated in the eyes of those closest to her. She is portrayed as a woman who is central only as an object of concern to someone else. Furthermore, she is valuable but perhaps not as essential as Abraham in the domain of the Deity's plan. Within the domain, her status as Abraham's wife is one fundamental factor to her detriment as well as her preservation. Thus the Deity intervenes on her behalf but does not speak to her. Abraham implicates her and yet does not consult her when he makes his defense to Abimelech. He implicates her only to the extent that his claim would buttress his defense. In his perception she is clearly dispensable as wife and thus as a potential mother of his children. Both her value and dispensability are measured by the contribution to his preservation, namely, that her presence does not lead to his harm.

In the public domain, Abimelech, the foreign ruler from whom her husband claims to be protecting her, tries to clear Sarah's name. He speaks to her on multiple occasions even after he is punished because of her participation in the ruse. By presenting Abimelech in all other aspects as reliable and honorable, the narrative allows the validity of his claim that she participates in the ruse. Even so, he assists in caring for her when she is neglected by her husband and left open to criticism. The power dynamic of the ruler and the neglected wife does not deter him from speaking to her. From the dynamic of the situation, Abimelech, the ruler, has every reason to rid himself of the person who is the immediate cause of his adversity. Instead, he exhibits care for her and does not subject her to further adversity. Care for her well-being comes not from the most expected sources but from the least expected. The narrative further suggests that the greatest danger comes from the one closest to her and the ones who have made her central to their plan and a casualty of her own existence. Sarah is both the valuable instrument and the devalued person. She is the embodiment of the basic anomaly of every functional identity—its dispensability.

Consequently, while privilege is power, it may also be a liability. The power of privilege is often the opportunities that it allows. As a privileged woman, Sarah has access to wealth and to persons in a way that others may not. She meets rulers of nations and gains access to their personal domain as their wives. Yet her access is fostered by deceit and alienation from her husband. She is much like the maid in a wealthy family who, in the company of the wealthy, participates in maintaining the domain but does not have a voice among those in charge of the domain.

Sarah's situation of repeatedly being used by her husband in ways that compromise her well-being and honor epitomizes a woman as both privileged and marginalized. Like Sarah, many women who have status find themselves marginalized because of the flaws within their domain, and experience unspoken horror and humiliation while being admired from the outside. In their adversity, they hope for persons like Abimelech who challenge the offender to be accountable for his actions and who relate to the woman as a person rather than as an object. Such persons are protectors within the system whose power and understanding of it allows them to offer a measure of protection that shields the woman from perceived dishonor and perpetual harm.

Privilege Does Not Define Character

A person's character and other domain-specific aspects will determine how privilege is manifested. Abraham's character pales in comparison to the rulers he encounters. He bases his behavior on a misconceived notion about others; even when his misconception is disaffirmed, he sustains his behavior. His notion is that foreigners display a lack of hospitality to those who come into their domain. The reality is that he creates a situation that fosters an opportunity for the foreigners to display the behavior he attributes to them. Even so, their behavior does not conform to his preconceived and misconceived notions about them. Nonetheless, Abraham has a tendency to become entrenched in a pattern of thought that shapes his behaviors and is fueled by the pattern itself rather than the competing realities. As in Abraham's case, an otherwise viable disposition is often used to sustain a misconceived notion. Thus he equates the "fear of God" with hospitality. The implication is that if the foreigners "feared God" they would be hospitable by honoring his relationship with his wife. Ironically, the foreigners do not behave as he expects. He also demonstrates the tendency to apply a principle to others but not to himself. Abraham perceives the foreigners to be without the fear of God and therefore malevolent. This correlation would suggest that in having the "fear of God" one would be benevolent. Yet Abraham, the one who presumably fears God, exhibits the malevolence he projects onto others. The foreigners display a sense of decorum that honors the relational bond between husband and wife rather than violating it as

Abraham thought they would. In this respect, he displays the negative behavior while the others display the positive traits. Nonetheless, when presented with another similar situation with foreigners, Abraham clings to his misconceived notions. They do not mistreat him because he is a stranger or because of his attractive wife but respond based on his self-representation.

One cannot miss the connections between his behavior and those who adhere to various prejudices. They share several tendencies. First, the tendency is to misconceive by generalizing the behavior of some to all within a particular subgroup. In this case, the expectations of the subgroup are defined by membership in the group rather than any other concerns or traits. Second, the tendency is to reinforce misconceptions even when cases disconfirm them. In the latter instance the tendency is to see the disconfirmations as exceptions rather than the rule and fail to realize that by virtue of the disconfirmation the rule has ceased to apply. Third, the tendency is to be selectively blind to one's display of the negative traits attributed to others. In this way, one tends to seek ways of addressing someone else's faults while ignoring one's own shortcomings (see chapter 7).

9

Persuasion in Functional and Relational Domains

The relational dynamics within modern contexts are facilitated by communication. Every act of communication is part of a persuasion process, including those that are inherent to life and relationship and those that are salient because of their heightened scope (effect or effort). Consequently, the texts are instruments of persuasion to convince of events, attitudes, and effects and thereby to foster perceptions and beliefs. In this chapter I examine persuasion as part of the functional and relational domains. I build on concluding observations from parts 1 and 2 and expand the analysis through brief situation and character analyses.

Persuasion Process

The success of persuasion depends on the readiness of those who are persuaded. This readiness is constituted by their disposition to be convinced and to change their behavior as prescribed by the persuasion process. Persuasion exists as part of a larger system that makes sense of the alternatives presented or suggested by the process.

Persuasion Is a Function of Preconditions

There are several preconditions for persuasion. First, in cases of the assumed trust among strangers, persuasion is built on the unknown—

unknown persons and relational identity. When one is among strangers, some aspects of one's relational identity are easily concealed via a
simple assertion. In these situations, persuasion happens because one is
inclined to think that people are truthful about their relational identity.
Because the Egyptians and the Gerarites had no prior knowledge of
his relational identity to Sarah, Abraham claimed that Sarah was his
sister and thus deceived them. Similarly, a man may have a different
functional identity than the one he claims and pose as a financially
successful businessman while he is unemployed. Because he dresses,
spends, and behaves according to the expectations for businessmen,
those around him may be persuaded that he is what he claims and may
treat him accordingly. In this instance, as in many involving strangers,
persuasion is as effective as the expectation that the one making the
claim is trustworthy in representing her/his relational and functional
identity.

Second, Abraham and Sarah's situation epitomizes the circumstances
in many modern settings where a person conceals her/his marital status
in order to gain a perceived advantage. In some cases, the perceived
advantage is to secure an extramarital relationship with someone who
may not have otherwise conceded to the relationship. Since the marital
relation is not acknowledged, the second party does nothing to investigate
the relational status of her/his partner. For example, a woman may learn
that her current companion is already married. The relational status may
be discovered when someone who knows about it discloses it to her, the
unsuspecting party. In this case, the man may deny his relational identity
as husband by sticking to the deception or may acknowledge his marital
status but justify the affair. Abraham displays both types of adaptation
when his deception concerning Sarah is discovered.

Third, a precondition of persuasion is usually the trust facilitated
by relational identity. In Tamar's case, the precondition is Judah's prior
behavior and his relationship status as her father-in-law. Since he had
given Onan to her for procreation purposes, it appeared to her that he
would act the same under similar circumstances. She is like Jacob,
whose relationship with Laban predisposed him to trust Laban. In both
instances, the precondition served as a filter through which the situations were viewed. Like Tamar, Jacob was given information that he
used as the basis of his decisions; meanwhile, Laban, the giver of that
information, planned to act contrary to his words. Thus Laban promised to give Rachel to Jacob at the end of his seven years of labor, and
Jacob believed him. With the suggestion that Judah would give her his
last son as her husband, Tamar was told to return home. Because the
giver of the information is a relative, in both instances trust facilitated
the persuasion.

Fourth, timing is key to the persuasion process, namely, the time between the communication introducing an event and the realization of an anticipated event. Notably, neither Tamar nor Jacob had any way of proving the viability of their relative's word to bring about the desired outcome in a timely manner. Both Judah and Laban made claims that could be verified only years later. The period of waiting allows for the one who imposes it to persist in his intention without any suspicion. Until the time comes to produce the event, the one persuaded to wait will continue to anticipate the event. Once the time frame is actualized, if the event does not happen, then the one who was persuaded to wait has the choice of continuing to wait or changing to adapt to an unanticipated outcome.

Both Tamar and Jacob exemplify those caught in a situation where they are persuaded of a pending event; however, the one who persuaded them does not intend to bring about the event. Consequently, these persons continue to wait, sustained by their convictions that a desired event is imminent. One finds such in families where a parent may promise a child to purchase a toy for a birthday or a graduation present but secretly hopes that the child will forget. Yet the child adapts his behavior to the promise, being persuaded that the parent will fulfill the promise. Similarly, some employees are led to believe that they will be promoted and wait for the promotion. Like Judah and Laban, the employers veil their intentions so as neither to explicitly promise nor to deny a promotion, but to give sufficient clues as to suggest that a promotion is pending within a particular time frame. When the time frame passes and the promotion is not forthcoming, the employees are forced to adapt to the new information and situation. Here the nature of the functional relationship allowed the employees to be persuaded of information that the employer crafted to be ambiguous, though skewed toward the perception of a favorable outcome.

Postponement as a means of persuading is also seen in many other situations, not the least of which is a romantic relationship between a man and a woman who have been dating for an extended period of time. The man in this relationship may allude to the prospect of marriage and so keep the woman hoping and waiting for a marital commitment. She does not seek out other prospects because she is convinced that she is in a lifelong relationship that is moving more slowly toward marriage than she anticipated. He may use the idea of a good job and financial stability as conditions to be fulfilled before marriage. Likewise, he may use youth and lack of readiness as a means of postponement, suggesting that the marriage will happen in the future. For women in these relationships, as with Tamar, the moment of truth is the realization that the condition has been fulfilled but that marriage has not taken place or that the man has opted to marry another.

Finally, vulnerability is often a component of persuasion. People are more likely to be persuaded when they are vulnerable. More basic, however, is the realization that certain vulnerabilities predispose a person to imprudent decisions. In Esau's case, he is hungry and wants some of the food that Jacob is cooking. Consequently, he uses his birthright to bargain with Jacob for food. By seeing food as more desirable than his birthright, Esau is persuaded to resolve a temporary problem with a solution that has permanent consequences. He is a caricature of one who gives away his home for a bottle of whiskey or a drug fix. After the moment is gone and the nature of the transaction is realized, one is awakened to the uneven exchange. Additionally, certain vulnerabilities construct a bond of trust between persons, for example, the physically impaired and her/his caregiver, an employer and an employee, a doctor and a patient, clergy and a parishioner, a parent and a child. In all these instances, it is usually presumed that the one in authority is trustworthy and would not violate the trust that is formed by the functional identities within the situations. In these instances those in authority may sustain the trust or violate it by devising alternative behaviors that abuse the trust yet maintain the relationship.

Persuasion Needs Viable Choices

Whether or not the persuasion process delineates the possibilities, the process itself suggests viable alternatives or choices. These choices may be most salient because of the norm and restrictions within the domain. Because of a lack of awareness, some may not perceive alternatives other than those revealed by the persuasion process. It is precisely because of the novelty of the alternatives that those alternatives may become more appealing than the typically available ones.

As portrayed in the Gen. 3 narrative, the shrewdness of the serpent is the skill to persuade the first humans to reconsider the alternatives available to them. By introducing alternatives outside their purview, the serpent shows the humans their previously restricted options. The genius of this exposure is that it casts doubt on the humans' perception as well as on the Deity, who offers the limited options. The doubt itself is then part of the process because it unearths new options. What is exposed may not be better than or more readily accessible than what is already perceived. While the presentation of alternatives may suggest that the proposed alternatives are better than others, that is a matter of perception and a conclusion designed by the persuasion process. The inherent fallacy in presupposing that the alternatives are better is to assume the benevolence of the one presenting them. Just as the serpent's attempts at persuasion may have been more about challenging the Deity's control and authority than looking out for the well-being of the humans, so other persuasion processes may be more about the ulterior motives than the perceived ones.

Another aspect of viable choices is seen in Rebekah's effort to persuade Jacob to deceive his father. Thus Rebekah persuades Jacob, and Jacob in turn appears to persuade Isaac. With regard to Rebekah, she does not introduce a new alternative to Jacob but rather suggests how to actualize an existing alternative. Jacob had already succeeded in securing Esau's birthright. Rebekah simply persuades Jacob that deception is a viable way of securing Isaac's blessing. She also convinces him that she would absorb any negative repercussions and that he would be left unscathed.

Similarly, the Deity persuades Hagar to return to her oppressive situation and to believe that long-range goals take precedence over present discomforts. The viable alternative presented to her is that she would be matriarch of a nation. Moreover, basic to her persuasion is the conviction that another's perspective on her reality is preferable to her perspective and choices. Concerning what is best for her, Hagar surrenders her discernment to the Deity. She is like many who surrender their discernment about their lives to a perceived authority, not realizing that the perspective of the authority figure is simply that—another perspective. Likewise, the perspective is formed by the authority figure's plans and commitments, and all else is secondary to those plans. This aspect of the persuasion also facilitates deception.

Deception and Persuasion

Deception Is a Manifestation of Persuasion

The act of persuasion does not define its goal. Rather, the goal regulates and qualifies the process as deceitful or otherwise. One may attempt to persuade another of something that is true or false. If one is attempting to persuade someone to believe a lie, the goal of the process is to deceive; if one is attempting to persuade someone to believe the truth, the goal of the process is not to deceive. In both instances, the goal of the process is to alter another's perception of and adherence to a belief. Accordingly, Judah persuades Tamar to remain a widow and to return to her father's house until Shelah grows up. The deception is that he had already decided that regardless of Shelah's age he would not give him to Tamar. Meanwhile, Tamar is made to believe that she has a viable option by waiting (Gen. 38). The deception is achieved through omitting vital information necessary for the particular decision but giving enough information to sustain a perception of truthfulness.

Similarly, in responding to her father about whether she stole the household gods, Rachel alludes to her menstrual cycle as the reason for not rising from her saddle. She thus ties two unrelated elements together to persuade her father of her cooperation in locating the household gods that she had hidden in her saddle. Whether she is menstruating at the time is beside the point.[1] The effectiveness of the persuasion lies in creating a particular perception. Had she subjected herself to a search, she would have been found out and possibly put to death in accordance with Jacob's oath (Gen. 31:33–35).[2] Certainly, she does not confirm or deny taking the gods. Instead, she diverts attention from that issue and focuses on a more delicate one. In this way, she evades a response to the question at hand and refrains from verbalizing her deception.

How many persons have performed a similar maneuver to avoid telling the truth about a matter? For example, take the wife who is suspected of having an affair and who responds by saying that she cannot believe that her husband does not trust her. She may continue to say that she is hurt that he never trusts her. A husband may use the same maneuver to evade the issue of his infidelity.[3] In these instances, if the deception is uncovered the deceiver may argue that she/he never denied having an affair. This, of course, is a matter of perception, whereby one is persuaded to discount a central issue because an irrelevant one is highlighted. The deception accomplished by diverting attention from a central to a peripheral issue exemplifies a skillful act of persuasion.

Persuasion May Blur the Line between the Deceived and the Deceiver

The process of persuasion is multidimensional, including the use of vulnerability, predisposition, and sanctioned animosity to secure one's wish. In some situations, the deceiver is deceived by virtue of her/his apparent success in deceiving another person. Isaac's impaired vision constitutes a physical vulnerability that his family uses to deceive him (Gen. 27). Yet Isaac may also have used his impairment to persuade others about the extent of his vulnerability. In so doing, he conforms to the expectation that he is deceived. Meanwhile, he uses his vulnerability to conceal his own attempt to deceive. The dynamics of the deceived and the deceiver suggest that one may pretend to be deceived as a way of explaining or defending uncharacteristic behavior. Both the pretense

1. Cf. Fuchs, "Way of Women."
2. He swore that he did not take the household gods. Furthermore he declared that anyone who had them should not live (Gen. 31:32)
3. Cf. Garcia ("Lies") regarding the selective disclosure of information or giving "excessive detail" as ways of deceiving others.

and the uncharacteristic behavior are modes of deception. Since being deceived usually indicates unconscious consent to a particular action or belief, the status of being deceived constitutes one's defense against any blame or responsibility. It presumes that one would act otherwise given other information.

Being in a domain may also facilitate some forms of deception because a domain perpetuates stereotypes that guide behaviors and beliefs. For example, while it may have been characteristic of the domain to harbor animosity toward foreigners, the relational dynamics of Rebekah and Esau's foreign wives are probably not defined solely by their nationality. By juxtaposing their nationality and the negative relationship with Rebekah and Isaac, the narrator fosters the notion of inherent animosity between persons of different national origins. Consequently, since the animosity may have been perpetuated within the domain, it would be easy for Rebekah to utilize it to make her case to Isaac. Thus she argues that the foreign women are making her life difficult and that she would die if Jacob were to marry one of them (Gen. 28:46). This prejudicial attitude resonates with Isaac and persuades him to guard against the perceived danger. In this respect, Rebekah does not persuade because of any set of reasoned propositions but on the basis of a prejudice against others. Perhaps she does not consider that individuals from different nations could share a harmonious relationship. She thus uses her animosity to persuade Isaac to send Jacob away from home.

In many instances a bias against a group of people is used to make a decision or to persuade someone to make a decision. Notably, the biases against women have been manifested in various issues: women in the workplace, women as functional superiors over men, women's right to vote, and women clergy. The issue is usually gender appropriateness for the role. In some situations, women are persuaded of their "place" in the private domain, and work environments are created that undermine their ability to function effectively in the public domain.[4] Similarly, the question of interracial marriage is not so much an issue of relational compatibility as a perception of racial inequality. Fundamentally, such perception may lead to animosity against a group of persons because of their natural identity. The inherent danger of the animosity is that it ignores the fact that characteristics that define "otherness" may also define "essence." Nonetheless, the influence of the domain on relational and behavioral dynamics may persuade one to have and use animosity.

4. Bernard, *Female World*, 87–88. She observes that various strategies have been used to convince women that their place is in the home, including religious ideology and rewards and punishments within the social structure.

Family Relationships May Facilitate Deception

Given the intimate resources allowed by close familial relationships and intragroup alliances, these relational contexts facilitate deception. As seen in Isaac's case, the family domain may facilitate deception because it gives family members access to one's vulnerabilities. For example, Rebekah and Jacob are willing to fulfill their wishes by taking advantage of Isaac's visual impairment (Gen. 27). Similarly, Onan behaves as if he has Tamar's best interest at heart (Gen. 38), but the trust factor conceals his action that impedes her rights. In addition, Judah and Tamar illustrate that intragroup identity may facilitate unmerited trust. Tamar waits for her father-in-law to give her his son as he had intimated, but he fails in his responsibility toward her. Tamar has no reason to distrust Judah's sincerity and effort to fulfill his obligation toward her; subsequently, she realizes that she has misplaced her trust. Just as he has deceived her, she tricks him into fulfilling his obligations toward her.

The trust fostered in a parent-child relationship and a family system allows the family members greater access to one another. Who would assume that a parent would deliberately risk his daughter's future by subjecting her to an unwanted marriage? Yet Laban puts Leah in a situation that disadvantages her from the start. Leah's many vulnerabilities include her father's action of giving her to Jacob, her desire to be loved, and her belief that she could secure her husband's love by having his children. Her desire to be loved leads her to bear seven children for a man who does not love her. Even so, Leah's situation pales in comparison to women who are raped by their husbands, or children who are sexually violated by their parents or an adult. In most cases, they are deceived into believing that they caused the abuse or that their disclosure of it would ruin the family and the chance to be loved. The further tragedy of such violations may be the shattered trust and unhealthy quest for love, including the inability to free oneself from the loop of ineffective or self-destructive behaviors and relationships.

Such shattered trust is also evident in the clergy who use private information shared by parishioners as the basis of sermon illustrations, revealing every detail except the names of the parishioners. The psychological abuse of the parishioners who hear their problems trumpeted from the pulpit have caused some to distrust clergy and, by extension, many in the healing professions. Furthermore, in the public domain vulnerability may be fostered by functional status. In cases where a functional superior uses the work relationship to abuse a subordinate, the risks to the subordinate may include the loss of a sense of self.

Persuasion and Behavioral Patterns

Self-Persuasion and Maintaining Behaviors

Leah's perception that she could win love through favorable behavior was in opposition to the reality of her existence. She courted that dissonance in her life as a way of dealing with being unloved, yet she remained stagnant in a way that further entrenched her in her self-delusion (Gen. 29–30). After bearing numerous children, she should have realized the futility of her plan to secure love. Instead, she added resources to further her plan (30:9–13). Leah epitomizes women who in both the private and the public domain of their lives tailor their behavior toward the goal of being loved by the men around them. This may mean having sex with a man to secure a relationship with him, becoming pregnant to get a man to marry her, or having a child to keep a husband in a marriage. In the public domain, some women may seek inappropriate attention from their male colleagues or allow inappropriate behavior in order to be accepted. Like Leah, some fail to realize that they do not control people's emotions. Especially for those seeking love through children and sexual favors, the insight is that love cannot be bought using any currency—children, sex, and so on. Yet many get stuck in unhealthy self-persuasion, not realizing their power to change their perception and behavior. This change is illustrated in Tamar's move from waiting to seizing an opportunity to fulfill her rights (Gen. 38). Once she changed her perception of her reality, she changed her actions accordingly.

Persuasion and Prejudice

The domain's ideology is a basic precondition of persuasion. Because persuasion assumes a perceived viability of alternatives, it builds on a basic ability to discern and choose among actions, thoughts, and so on. Prejudice is a product of ideology and a form of persuasion. It is evident in the animosity or bias against foreigners in Abraham and Rebekah's behavior, for example, in Rebekah's bias against the foreign women and in Abraham's misconception about the way that the people of Egypt and Gerar would behave toward him. While of a different sort, Judah's bias against Tamar may also be categorized as a form of prejudice. It is formed by an observation of events and a predisposition to misperceive the nature of the correlation between events. Judah did not overlook or conjure up connections; rather, he misunderstood the nature of the connections. He believed that there was a direct connection between his sons' relationship with Tamar and their deaths, but he did not realize that this connection was channeled through a more primary one—their behavior while they were in a relationship with Tamar. Er was evil and

Onan behaved contrary to his levirate responsibilities. In both cases, the Deity was the one who evaluated the men's actions as unacceptable and meted out punishment. Through circumstantial evidence, Tamar was implicated in their deaths. Judah's bias against her was therefore fostered by his perception of the cause-effect patterns. People perceive the patterns differently, hence aspects of the pattern may be misconstrued. Consequently, Judah's deceitful actions toward Tamar show the persuasive force of circumstantial evidence to lead someone to a conclusion that may be contrary to fact. Apart from Judah's act of giving or withholding a son, there was perhaps no way of verifying his perception. Yet to give his son he would have to risk his son's life and his own legacy.

The power of perception is a vital part of being persuaded and deceived. Judah's actions were shaped by his misperception of several situations in which he may have behaved otherwise had his perception been different, for example, when he condemned Tamar for her prostitution. In Judah's case, perception persuaded him to sustain his behaviors toward her, yet he tended to be highly selective in his perception. Accordingly, Mary Shields asserts: "The humor of the story relies on Judah's ability to see only what he wants to see, or the literary strategy of narrative irony, and on the timeless folk tale form of the comeuppance of the hero. Judah . . . is forced to accord her the quality given only to two others in Genesis, Noah and Abraham—righteousness."[5]

Other aspects of prejudice include the inherent danger of assigning value to persons solely on the basis of their group identity or historical place. Those who are perceived to be outside the norm and the valued group are usually assigned negative worth. The narratives appear to address situations of functional value rather than inherent value (Gen. 12; 16; 20). Even so, they suggest that relational parameters define and regulate functional value and result in the assignment of positive or negative value to the same person. For example, the maid may become a wife and her children legitimate heirs to their father's fortune and legacy, but to some she will always be a maid and an inferior being (Gen. 16; 29–30). Furthermore, the woman, like the foreigner, is often treated as the "other." Many who would not think of speaking disparagingly of a woman may do so regarding the foreigner. Why should anyone be surprised by a Canaanite's righteousness (38:26)? The power of the narrative is its depictions of the foreigner as "other" and as a source of character. In Abraham's ruse in Egypt and Gerar, the foreigner is commendable; likewise, in Tamar's case she is deemed righteous.

As in the narratives, still today the danger of biases is to use the social or functional value to create permanent relational identity and behav-

5. Shields, "More Righteous Than I?" 33.

ioral parameters. Ishmael is isolated for reasons governed by Sarah's insecurity about the status of her biological son over her stepson. The isolation is perpetuated in order to maintain the larger plan for a particular future for Abraham, and the values within that plan are assigned to his offspring (Gen. 16; 21). Consequently, Ishmael's usefulness to Sarah expires; he is still defined as "other" than Isaac in his usefulness and place in the Deity's plan. Similarly, various domains assign values that are defined by racial and gender inequity. For example, the sale and enslavement of human beings was supported on the basis of the Bible in much the same way that Gen. 2–3 is used to sustain the subjugation of women as a divinely approved value. As a function of its domain, the ideology often dictates women's roles even in contexts where they are active contributors. Even so, in societies where maintaining the family necessitates women's contribution to the family's economic viability, there is seldom a question of her appropriate domain and value. In these domains, women's contribution to the family is not restricted to the home because neither male nor female can survive without the other.[6] Curiously, necessity often redefines attributed value and the nature and extent of the ideological bias. There may also be a more equitable distribution of resources and use of power.

Persuasion and Abuse of Power

The use and abuse of power are products of persuasion; consequently, complying with abuse is a matter of persuasion and a manifestation of one's power of choice. Thus, while people have slowly come to recognize the various forms of abuse in the private domain (family), they minimize its manifestations in the public domain. On the job, the abuse usually takes the form of verbal assaults through sarcasm, satire, the proverbial backhanded compliment, belittling, or suggestive comments. Like Abraham, the male abuser is usually successful and privileged, sometimes insecure in his status or driven by fears. While others admire him in the public domain, he may use his wife to conceal his perceived inadequacies, for example, as a scapegoat for whatever he feels unable to express publicly. Because he does not feel as in control of his public domain as he desires, he may attempt to tightly control his private domain. A woman in this situation is not powerless, but with the conditioning of her domain, she may be persuaded that she is. The success of the abuse has been to limit her choices and awareness and thus to control her function within her domain. The conviction is usually reinforced every time she endures abuse.

6. Bernard, *Female World*, 87. She discusses the "cult of domesticity" as a creation to maintain a social structure in which women are viewed and treated as nonessential beings (cf. Prov. 31:10–27).

Ironically, her compliance is a manifestation of her power of choice, thus contradicting her domain's perception that she is powerless. She will be transformed when she perceives her choice as a power and exercises that power by choosing different behaviors. Nonetheless, the abused may function quite proficiently outside the domain in which she is being abused—that is, unless she is persuaded that the domain-specific abuse represents her essence and is thus appropriate to all domains of her life. Yet the paradox is that persuasion can transform and limit her power of choice. This process is exemplified in Abraham's claim that Sarah agreed to participate in his plan to deceive (Gen. 20:11–14). In this claim is the tendency of an abuser to assert that the abused accepts the way that she/he is treated. This is usually the abuser's attempt to justify the abuse; it may also be an insidious way of reinforcing the choices of the abused, namely, to survive within the abusive situation or to thrive apart from it.

Persuasion as the Basis for Change

Judah's behavior toward Tamar leads her to wait to marry Shelah. When she eventually realizes that Judah has deceived her, she takes matters into her own hands. While one may be tempted to see her method as a last resort to gain her rights, there may be no such thing as a last resort. Rather, she may have foreclosed on alternatives because she perceived them as nonviable. Having foreclosed on the nonviable alternatives, one opts for an alternative that is deemed viable for that situation, whether for its immediate or for long-term effects. Whether conscious or unconscious, foreclosure is a necessary part of choice. In this respect, using deception is a choice and a manifestation of one's power rather than one's powerlessness. Since choosing is itself an exercise of power, wherever there is the power of choice powerlessness is only a matter of perception. Accordingly, the language and attitude of "last resort" and powerlessness belong to the realm of persuasion and demonstrate that one has been convinced to act or think in a particular way. Whatever its extent—be it family, job, society, or historical legacy reinforced by current circumstances—the domain has participated in persuading some that they are powerless.

Tamar's power was in reevaluating her situation and thus convincing herself that there were other alternatives to remaining a widow. In her case, she saw Shelah as the final option for marriage and procreation. When this perception was shattered, she became aware of options outside her domain of consideration. In this way, she is like many women who lock themselves into options that restrict their consideration of other alternatives for their lives. In Tamar, one glimpses the widow who sees her life as over and thus does not explore options for growth and fulfillment. In some Christian contexts, divorced persons are persuaded that they must remain divorced or risk God's wrath. Like Tamar, any change in their behavior will come from a transformed perception. By contrast, Leah retained her perception and remained entrenched in her effort to use her children to purchase love. Leah continued with ineffective behaviors while expecting different results. She failed to see that multiplying the futile behavior will not change the outcome. Perception is clearly fundamental to persuasion and to the exercise of power in all domains. The nature of the perception also defines one's awareness and use of power.

Conclusion

Many aspects of modern life are analogous to the characters and situations in the biblical narratives. Even so, the narrative portrayals are not necessarily prescriptive of behaviors, relationships, or beliefs. Rather they are windows that offer perspectives into the type of relationships and situations and by implication into general human-human and divine-human dynamics. Clearly, some interpretations and applications of these narratives to the modern context may be uplifting—equality for all humans, God's protection, and so on. Conversely, some interpretations may be detrimental to the well-being of persons and community, including the idea of male superiority, the concept of powerlessness, the appeal to a greater authority to introduce or sustain abuse, and devaluing the "other." I propose that these are issues of personhood rather than gender, status, or reliance on the Deity's power or plan.

People of faith are compelled yet challenged by the faith commitments in their quest for methodological and intellectual clarity about female-male dynamics of power and persuasion. Fundamentally, the issue is to develop and adhere to sound methodological practices while dealing with inherited understandings of the Deity and personhood as presented in traditional interpretive trends. With the glimpse into the terrain of challenges presented in this book, one may note the richness of the biblical tradition and its valuable insights for any who are willing to investigate, resignify, and value the role of the biblical narratives in modern life.

Bibliography

Adams, Robert M. "Self-Love and the Vices of Self-Preference." *Faith and Philosophy* 15.4 (1998): 500–513.

Adar, Zvi. *The Book of Genesis: An Introduction to the Biblical World*. Jerusalem: Magnes, 1990.

Aichele, George, ed. *Culture, Entertainment, and the Bible*. Journal for the Study of the Old Testament: Supplement Series 309. Sheffield: Sheffield Academic Press, 2000.

Alexander, T. D. "Are the Wife/Sister Incidents of Genesis Literary Compositional Variants?" *Vetus Testamentum* 42 (1992): 145–53.

Allison, Julie A., and Lawrence S. Wrightsman. *Rape: The Misunderstood Crime*. Newbury Park, CA: Sage, 1993.

Alter, Robert. *Art of Biblical Narrative*. New York: Basic Books, 1981.

———. *Genesis: Translation and Commentary*. New York: Norton, 1996.

Anderson, Bernhard W. *From Creation to New Creation: Old Testament Perspectives*. Overtures to Biblical Theology. Minneapolis: Fortress, 1994.

Anderson, Elizabeth S. "What Is the Point of Equality?" *Ethics* 109 (1999): 287–337.

Anderson, Rosemarie. "A Tent Full of Bedouin Women: Tamar in Gen. 38." *Daughters of Sarah* 19 (1993): 34–35.

Andrew, Maurice E. "Moving from Death to Life: Verbs of Motion in the Story of Judah and Tamar in Gen. 38." *Zeitschrift für die alttestamentliche Wissenschaft* 105.2 (1993): 262–69.

Arbeitman, Yoël L. "Tamar's Name or Is It? (Gen. 38)." *Zeitschrift für die alttestamentliche Wissenschaft* 112.3 (2000): 341–55.

Astour, Michael C. "Tamar the Hierodule: An Essay in the Method of Vestigial Motifs." *Journal of Biblical Literature* 85 (1966): 185–96.

Bach, Alice, ed. *The Pleasure of Her Text: Feminist Readings of Biblical and Historical Texts*. Philadelphia: Trinity Press International, 1990.

———. *Women, Seduction, and Betrayal in Biblical Narrative*. Cambridge: Cambridge University Press, 1997.

Baker, James. *Women's Rights in Old Testament Times*. Salt Lake City: Signature, 1992.

Bal, Mieke, ed. *Anti-Covenant: Counter-Reading Women's Lives in the Hebrew Bible*. Journal for the Study of the Old Testament: Supplement Series 81. Sheffield: Sheffield Academic Press; Decatur, GA: Almond Press, 1989.

———. *Lethal Love: Feminist Literary Readings of Biblical Love Stories*. Bloomington: Indiana University Press, 1987.

———. "Tricky Thematics." *Semeia* 42 (1988): 133–55.

Barr, James. *The Garden of Eden and the Hope of Immortality*. Minneapolis: Fortress, 1993.

Beattie, D. R. G. "What Is Genesis 2–3 About?" *Expository Times* 92 (1980): 8–10.

Bechtel, Lyn M. "Rethinking the Interpretation of Genesis 2:4b–3:24." In *A Feminist Companion to Genesis*, edited by Athalya Brenner, 77–117. Sheffield: Sheffield Academic Press, 1993.

———. "What If Dinah Is Not Raped? (Genesis 34)." *Journal for the Study of the Old Testament* 62 (1994): 19–36.

Bellis, Alice O. *Helpmates, Harlots, Heroes: Women's Stories in the Hebrew Bible*. Louisville: Westminster John Knox, 1994.

Ben Isaiah, Abraham, and Benjamin Sharfman. *The Pentateuch and Rashi's Commentary: A Linear Translation into English*. Vol. 1, *Genesis*. Brooklyn, NY: S. S. & R., 1949.

Berlin, Adele. *Poetics and Interpretation of Biblical Narrative*. Sheffield: Almond Press, 1983.

Bernard, Jessie. *The Female World: A Brilliant Exploration of a Previously Uncharted Region—the Special World of Women*. New York: Free Press, 1981.

Bettinghaus, Erwin P., and Michael J. Cody. *Persuasive Communication*. 5th ed. New York: Harcourt Brace, 1994.

Bilezikian, Gilbert. *Beyond Sex Roles: A Guide for the Study of Female Roles in the Bible*. Grand Rapids: Baker Academic, 1985.

Bird, Phyllis A. "The Harlot as Heroine: Narrative Art and Social Presupposition in Three Old Testament Texts." *Semeia* 46 (1989): 119–39.

———. "'Male and Female He Created Them': Gen. 1:27b in the Context of the Priestly Account of Creation." *Harvard Theological Review* 74 (1981): 129–49.

Bledstein, Adrien J. "Binder, Trickster, Heel and Hairy-Man: Rereading Genesis 27 as a Trickster Tale Told by a Woman." In *A Feminist Companion to Genesis*, edited by Athalya Brenner, 282–95. Sheffield: Sheffield Academic Press, 1993.

Bos, Johanna W. H. "Out of the Shadows: Genesis 38; Judges 4:17–22; Ruth 3." *Semeia* 42 (1988): 37–67.

Brenner, Athalya, ed. *A Feminist Companion to Genesis*. Sheffield: Sheffield Academic Press, 1993.

———. *The Israelite Woman: Social Role and Literary Type in Biblical Narrative*. Sheffield: JSOT Press, 1985.

Brenner, Athalya, and Fokkelien van Dijk-Hemmes, eds. *On Gendering Texts: Female and Male Voices in the Hebrew Bible*. Biblical Interpretation Series 1. Leiden: Brill, 1993.

Brett, Mark. "Self-Criticism, Cretan Liars, and the Sly Redactors of Genesis." In *Autobiographical Biblical Criticism: Between Text and Self*, edited by Ingrid Rosa Kitzberger, 114–32. Leiden: Deo, 2002.

Bruckner, James K. *Implied Law in the Abraham Narrative: A Literary and Theological Analysis*. Journal for the Study of the Old Testament: Supplement Series 335. Sheffield: Sheffield Academic Press, 2001.

Brueggemann, Walter. *Genesis*. Interpretation: A Commentary for Teaching and Preaching. Atlanta: John Knox, 1982.

———. "Of the Same Flesh and Bone." *Catholic Biblical Quarterly* 32 (1970): 532–42.

Camp, Claudia V. *Wise, Strange, and Holy: The Strange Woman and the Making of the Bible*. Journal for the Study of the Old Testament: Supplement Series 320. Sheffield: Sheffield Academic Press, 2000.

Carmichael, Calum M. "Forbidden Mixtures." *Vetus Testamentum* 32 (1982): 394–415.

———. *Law and Narrative in the Bible: The Evidence of the Deuteronomic Laws and the Decalogue*. Ithaca, NY: Cornell University Press, 1985.

———. *Law, Legend, and Incest in the Bible: Leviticus 18–20*. Ithaca, NY: Cornell University Press, 1997.

Carr, David. "The Politics of Textual Subversion: A Diachronic Perspective on the Garden of Eden Story." *Journal of Biblical Literature* 112 (1993): 577–95.

———. *Reading the Fractures of Genesis*. Louisville: Westminster John Knox, 1996.

Cassuto, Umberto. *A Commentary on the Book of Genesis*. Translated by Israel Abrahams. Jerusalem: Magnes and Hebrew University, 1978.

Chafetz, Janet Saltzman. *Gender Equity: An Integrated Theory of Stability and Change*. Sage Library of Social Research 176. Newbury Park, CA: Sage, 1990.

Childs, Brevard S. *The Book of Exodus: A Critical Theological Commentary*. Old Testament Library. Philadelphia: Westminster, 1974.

Chisholm, Robert B., Jr. "Does God Deceive?" *Bibliotheca Sacra* 155 (1998): 11–28.

Clines, David J. A. *What Does Eve Do to Help? and Other Readerly Questions to the Old Testament*. Journal for the Study of the Old Testament: Supplement Series 94. Sheffield: JSOT Press, 1990.

Coats, George W. *Genesis*. Forms of the Old Testament Literature 1. Grand Rapids: Eerdmans, 1982.

————. "The God of Death: Power and Obedience in the Primeval History." *Interpretation* 29 (1975): 227–39.

————. "Widow's Rights: A Crux in the Structure of Genesis 38." *Catholic Biblical Quarterly* 34 (1972): 461–66.

Coggins, Richard J. "On Kings and Disguises." *Journal for the Study of the Old Testament* 50 (1991): 55–62.

Cohen, Norman J. *Self, Struggle, and Change: Family Conflict Stories in Genesis and Their Healing Insights for Our Lives*. Woodstock, VT: Jewish Lights, 1995.

Cole, William G. *Sex and Love in the Bible*. New York: Association Press, 1959.

Constable, Pamela. "In Pakistan, Women Pay the Price of 'Honor'; Maiming, Killing Accepted Response to Perceived Sins." *Washington Post*, May 8, 2000, A01.

Davies, Eryl W. "Inheritance Rights and the Hebrew Levirate Marriage." *Vetus Testamentum* 31 (1981): 138–44, 257–68.

Davies, Philip R. "Women, Men, Gods, Sex, and Power: The Birth of a Biblical Myth." In *Feminist Companion to Genesis*, edited by Athalya Brenner, 194–201. Sheffield: Sheffield Academic Press, 1993.

Davies, Philip R., and David J. A. Clines, eds. *The World of Genesis: Persons, Places, Perspectives*. Journal for the Study of the Old Testament: Supplement Series 257. Sheffield: Sheffield Academic Press, 1998.

Dennis, Trevor. *Sarah Laughed*. Nashville: Abingdon, 1994.

Dragga, Sam. "Genesis 2–3: A Story of Liberation." *Journal for the Study of the Old Testament* 55 (1992): 3–13.

Dreifuss, Gustav, and Judith Riemer. *Abraham, the Man and the Symbol: A Jungian Interpretation of the Biblical Story*. Translated by Naphtali Greenwood. Wilmette, IL: Chiron, 1995.

Dresner, Samuel H. *Rachel*. Minneapolis: Fortress, 1994.

Elazar, Daniel J. "Jacob and Esau and the Emergence of the Jewish People." *Judaism* 43.3 (1994): 294–301.

Ellis, Lee. *Theories of Rape: Inquiries into the Causes of Sexual Aggression*. New York: Hemisphere, 1989.

Elshtain, Jean Bethke. "Beyond Consent." *New Republic*, May 4, 1998, 8.2.

Emerton, John A. "Examination of a Recent Structuralist Interpretation of Genesis 38." *Vetus Testamentum* 26 (1976): 79–98.

————. "Judah and Tamar." *Vetus Testamentum* 29 (1979): 403–15.

————. "Some Problems in Genesis 38." *Vetus Testamentum* 25 (1975): 338–61.

Ess, Charles. "Reading Adam and Eve: Re-visions of the Myth of Woman's Subordination to Man." In *Violence against Women and Children: A Christian Theological Sourcebook*, edited by Carol J. Adams and Marie M. Fortune, 92–120. New York: Continuum, 1995.

Exum, J. Cheryl. *Fragmented Women: Feminist (sub)Versions of Biblical Narratives*. Journal for the Study of the Old Testament: Supplement Series 163. Sheffield: JSOT Press; Philadelphia: Trinity Press International, 1993.

————. *Plotted, Shot, and Painted: Cultural Representations of Biblical Women*. Journal for the Study of the Old Testament: Supplement Series 215. Sheffield: JSOT Press, 1996.

Falk, Ze'ev W. *Hebrew Law in Biblical Times*. Jerusalem: Wahrmann, 1964.

Feldner, Yotam. "'Honor' Murders—Why the Perps Get Off Easy (1)." *Middle East Quarterly* 7.4 (2000): 41.

Fewell, Danna N., and David M. Gunn. *Compromising Redemption: Relating Characters in the Book of Ruth*. Louisville: Westminster John Knox, 1990.

————. *Gender, Power, and Promise: The Subject of the Bible's First Story*. Nashville: Abingdon, 1993.

————. "Tipping the Balance: Sternberg's Reader and the Rape of Dinah." *Journal of Biblical Literature* 110.2 (1991): 193–211.

Frymer-Kensky, Tikva. "Virginity in the Bible." In *Gender and Law in the Hebrew Bible and the Ancient Near East*, edited by Victor H. Matthews, Bernard M. Levinson, and Tikva Frymer-Kensky, 79–96. Journal for the Study of the Old Testament: Supplement Series 262. Sheffield: Sheffield Academic Press, 1998.

Fuchs, Esther. "'For I Have the Way of Women': Deception, Gender, and Ideology in Biblical Narrative." *Semeia* 42 (1988): 68–83.

————. *Sexual Politics in the Biblical Narrative: Reading the Hebrew Bible as a Woman*. Journal for the Study of the Old Testament: Supplement Series 310. Sheffield: Sheffield Academic Press, 2000.

————. "Who Is Hiding the Truth? Deceptive Women and Biblical Androcentrism." In *Feminist Perspectives on Biblical Scholarship*, edited by Adela Yarbro Collins, 137–44. Chico, CA: Scholars Press, 1985.

Fulkerton, M. McClintock. *Changing the Subject: Women's Discourse and Feminist Theology*. Philadelphia: Fortress, 1994.

Furman, Nelly. "His Story versus Her Story: Male Genealogy and Female Strategy in the Jacob Cycle." *Semeia* 46 (1989): 141–49.

Garcia, J. L. A. "Lies and the Vices of Deception." *Faith and Philosophy* 15.4 (1998): 514–37.

Goldin, Judah. "The Youngest Son or Where Does Genesis 38 Belong." *Journal of Biblical Literature* 96 (1977): 27–44.

Goldman, Shalom. *The Wiles of Women/The Wiles of Men: Joseph and Potiphar's Wife in Ancient Near Eastern, Jewish, and Islamic Folklore*. Albany: State University of New York Press, 1995.

Good, Edwin M. "Deception and Women: A Response." *Semeia* 42 (1988): 116–32.

Goodfriend, Elaine A. "Adultery." In *Anchor Bible Dictionary*, edited by David Noel Freedman. 6 vols., 1:82–86. New York: Doubleday, 1992.

Gordon, Cynthia. "Hagar: A Throw-Away Character among the Matriarchs?" In *Society of Biblical Literature Seminar Papers* 24, edited by Kent Harold Richards, 271–77. Atlanta: Scholars Press, 1985.

Graetz, Naomi. "Dinah the Daughter." In *A Feminist Companion to Genesis*, edited by Athalya Brenner, 306–17. Sheffield: Sheffield Academic Press, 1993.

Grayson, A. K., and J. Van Seters. "The Childless Wife in Assyria and the Stories of Genesis." *Orientalia* 44 (1975): 485–86.

Greengus, S. "Sisterhood Adoption at Nuzi and the 'Wife-Sister' in Genesis." *Hebrew Union College Annual* 46 (1975): 5–31.

Grice, Geoffrey Russell. *The Grounds of Moral Judgement*. Cambridge: Cambridge University Press, 1967.

Grice, H. Paul. *Studies in the Way of Words*. Cambridge, MA: Harvard University Press, 1989.

Guest, Deryn. "Hiding Behind the Naked Women in Lamentations: A Recriminative Response." *Biblical Interpretation* 7.4 (1999): 413–48.

Gunn, David M., ed. *Narrative and Novella in Samuel: Studies by Hugo Gressmann and Other Scholars, 1906–1923*. Translated by David E. Orton. Journal for the Study of the Old Testament: Supplement Series 116. Sheffield: Almond, 1991.

Hamilton, Victor P. *The Book of Genesis: Chapters 1–17*. New International Commentary on the Old Testament. Grand Rapids: Eerdmans, 1990.

———. *The Book of Genesis: Chapters 18–50*. New International Commentary on the Old Testament. Grand Rapids: Eerdmans, 1995.

Harris, Kevin. *Sex, Ideology, and Religion: The Representation of Women in the Bible*. Totowa, NJ: Barnes & Noble Books, 1984.

Harris, R. Laird, Gleason L. Archer Jr., and Bruce K. Waltke, eds. *Theological Wordbook of the Old Testament*. 2 vols. Chicago: Moody, 1980.

Hartley, John E. *Leviticus*. Word Biblical Commentary 4. Dallas: Word, 1992.

Hayes, C. E. "The Midrashic Career of the Confession of Judah (Genesis xxxviii 26)." *Vetus Testamentum* 45 (1995): 62–81.

Higgins, J. M. "The Myth of Eve: The Temptress." *Journal of the American Academy of Religion* 44 (1976): 639–47.

Ho, Craig Y. S. "The Stories of the Family Troubles of Judah and David: A Study of Their Literary Links." *Vetus Testamentum* 49 (1999): 514–31.

Humphreys, W. Lee. *The Character of God in the Book of Genesis: A Narrative Appraisal*. Louisville: Westminster John Knox, 2001.

Ireland, Mardy S. *Reconceiving Women: Separating Motherhood from Female Identity*. New York: Guilford, 1993.

Jacobs, Mignon R. "Comparative Analysis of 11QTS66, Lev. 18:6–18, and Related Texts: An Examination of Their Conceptualities." Paper presented in Reading Biblical Law in the Qumran Era, AAR/SBL Annual Meeting, Toronto, November 2002.

———. "The Conceptual Dynamics of Good and Evil in the Joseph Story." *Journal for the Study of the Old Testament* 27.3 (2003): 309–38.

———. "Family or Freedom: Conceptual Tensions in the Law of Release in Exod. 21:2–6." Paper presented in Biblical Law Group, AAR/SBL Annual Meeting, Nashville, November 2000.

———. "Love, Honor, and Violence." In *Pregnant Passion: Gender, Sex, and Violence in the Bible*, edited by Cheryl A. Kirk-Duggan, 11–35. Semeia Studies 44. Atlanta: Society of Biblical Literature, 2003.

———. "Methodological Challenges and Necessities of Diaspora Studies: Some Preliminary Observations." In *Institute for the Study of Religion and Culture in Africa and the African Diaspora*, edited by Carol Duncan and Hugh Page, 23–25. South Bend, IN: University of Notre Dame, 2005.

Janzen, J. Gerald. *Abraham and All the Families of the Earth: A Commentary on the Book of Genesis 12–50*. International Theological Commentary. Grand Rapids: Eerdmans; Edinburgh: Handsel, 1993.

Jenni, Ernst, and Claus Westermann, eds. *Theological Lexicon of the Old Testament*. Translated by Mark E. Biddle. 3 vols. Peabody, MA: Hendrickson, 1997.

Joines, Karen R. "The Serpent in Gen. 3." *Zeitschrift für die alttestamentliche Wissenschaft* 87 (1975): 1–11.

Jongsma-Tielman, P. E. "The Creation of Eve and the Ambivalence between the Sexes." In *The Creation of Man and Woman: Interpretations of the Biblical Narratives in Jewish and Christian Traditions*, edited by Gerard P. Luttikhuizen, 172–86. Leiden: Brill, 2000.

Keefe, Alice A. "Rape of Women/Wars of Men." *Semeia* 61 (1993): 79–97.

Kimelman, Reuven. "The Seduction of Eve and the Exegetical Politics of Gender." *Biblical Interpretation* 4.1 (1996): 1–39.

Kunin, Seth Daniel. *The Logic of Incest: A Structuralist Analysis of Hebrew Mythology*. Journal for the Study of the Old Testament: Supplement Series 185. Sheffield: Sheffield Academic Press, 1995.

Lacocque, André. *The Feminine Unconventional: Four Subversive Figures in Israel's Tradition*. Overtures to Biblical Theology. Minneapolis: Fortress, 1990.

Langland, Elizabeth, and Walter Gove, eds. *A Feminist Perspective in the Academy: The Difference It Makes*. Chicago: University of Chicago Press, 1981.

Lanser, Susan. "(Feminist) Criticism in the Garden: Inferring Genesis 2–3." *Semeia* 41 (1988): 67–84.

Leggett, Donald A. *The Levirate and Goel Institutions in the Old Testament: With Special Attention to the Book of Ruth*. Cherry Hill, NJ: Mack, 1974.

Leneman, Helen. "Portrayals of Power in the Stories of Delilah and Bathsheba: Seduction in Song." In *Culture, Entertainment, and the Bible*, edited by George Aichele, 139–55. Journal for the Study of the Old Testament: Supplement Series 309. Sheffield: Sheffield Academic Press, 2000.

Levy, Shimon. "The Performance of Creation, Creation in Performance." In *The Creation of Man and Woman: Interpretations of the Biblical Narratives in Jewish and Christian Traditions*, edited by Gerard P. Luttikhuizen, 187–205. Leiden: Brill, 2000.

Ljung, Inger. *Silence or Suppression: Attitudes towards Women in the Old Testament.* Uppsala: S. Academiae Ubsaliensis, 1989.

Lockwood, Peter F. "Tamar's Place in the Joseph Cycle." *Lutheran Theological Journal* 26 (1992): 35–43.

Luttikhuizen, Gerard P., ed. *The Creation of Man and Woman: Interpretations of the Biblical Narratives in Jewish and Christian Traditions.* Leiden: Brill, 2000.

Maddox, Randy L. "Damned If You Do and Damned If You Don't: Tamar—A Feminist Foremother, Genesis 38:6–26." *Daughters of Sarah* 13 (1987): 14–17.

Magonet, Jonathan. "The Themes of Genesis 2–3." In *A Walk in the Garden: Biblical, Iconographical, and Literary Images of Eden,* edited by Paul Morris and Deborah Sawyer, 39–46. Journal for the Study of the Old Testament: Supplement Series 136. Sheffield: JSOT Press, 1992.

Makiya, Kanan. "State Rape: Violation of Iraqi Women." *New Statesman and Society* 6.251 (May 7, 1993): 16.

Malcolm, Clark W. "A Legal Background to the Yahwist's Use of 'Good and Evil' in Genesis 2–3." *Journal of Biblical Literature* 88 (1969): 266–78.

Manor, Dale W. "A Brief History of Levirate Marriage as It Relates to the Bible." *Restoration Quarterly* 27.3 (1984): 129–42.

Mars, L. "What Was Onan's Crime?" *Journal of the Society for Comparative Study of Society and History* 26 (1984): 429–39.

Marsman, Hennie J. *Women in Ugarit and Israel: Their Social and Religious Position in the Context of the Ancient Near East.* Oudtestamentische Studiën 49. Boston: Brill, 2003.

Masters, Carlos. *Eden, Golden Age or Goad to Action?* Translated by Patrick J. Leonard. Maryknoll, NY: Orbis, 1974.

Mathewson, Steven D. "An Exegetical Study of Genesis 38." *Bibliotheca Sacra* 146 (1989): 373–92.

Matthews, Victor H., and Don C. Benjamin, eds. "Honor and Shame in the World of the Bible." Special issue, *Semeia* 68 (1994).

———. *Old Testament Parallels: Laws and Stories from the Ancient Near East.* New York: Paulist Press, 1991.

Matthews, Victor H., Bernard M. Levinson, and Tikva Frymer-Kensky, eds. *Gender and Law in the Hebrew Bible and the Ancient Near East.* Journal for the Study of the Old Testament: Supplement Series 262. Sheffield: Sheffield Academic Press, 1998.

McCord, James N., Jr. "Politics and Honor in Early-Nineteenth-Century England: The Dukes' Duel." *Huntington Library Quarterly* 62 (2000): 88–114.

McEntire, Mark Harold. *The Blood of Abel: The Violent Plot in the Hebrew Bible.* Macon, GA: Mercer University Press, 1999.

Menn, Esther Marie. *Judah and Tamar (Genesis 38) in Ancient Jewish Exegesis: Studies in Literary Form and Hermeneutics.* Journal of the Study of Judaism Supplement Series 51. Leiden: Brill, 1997.

Meyers, Carol. *Discovering Eve: Ancient Israelite Women in Context*. New York: Oxford University Press, 1988.

Miscall, Peter D. "Literary Unity in Old Testament Narrative." *Semeia* 15 (1979): 27–44.

Morriss, Peter. *Power: A Philosophical Analysis*. New York: St. Martin's Press, 1987.

Murphy, Roland E. *The Tree of Life: An Exploration of Biblical Wisdom Literature*. 2nd ed. Grand Rapids: Eerdmans, 1996.

Nicol, George G. "The Alleged Rape of Bathsheba: Some Observations on Ambiguity in Biblical Narrative." *Journal for the Study of the Old Testament* 73 (1997): 43–54.

Niditch, Susan. *Chaos to Cosmos: Studies in Biblical Patterns of Creation*. Chico, CA: Scholars Press, 1985.

———. *War in the Hebrew Bible: A Study in the Ethics of Violence*. New York: Oxford University Press, 1993.

———. "War, Woman, and Defilement in Numbers 31." *Semeia* 61 (1993): 39–57.

———. "The Wronged Woman Righted: An Analysis of Genesis 38." *Harvard Theological Review* 72 (1979): 143–49.

Noble, Paul. "A 'Balanced' Reading of the Rape of Dinah: Some Exegetical and Methodological Observations." *Biblical Interpretation* 4 (1996): 173–204.

Noort, Ed. "The Creation of Man and Woman in Biblical and Ancient Near Eastern Traditions." In *The Creation of Man and Woman: Interpretations of the Biblical Narratives in Jewish and Christian Traditions*, edited by Gerard P. Luttikhuizen, 1–18. Leiden: Brill, 2000.

Nowell, Irene. *Women in the Old Testament*. Collegeville, MN: Liturgical Press, 1997.

Patte, Daniel. *Ethics of Biblical Interpretation: Reevaluation*. Louisville: Westminster John Knox, 1995.

Petersen, John. *Reading Women's Stories: Female Characters in the Hebrew Bible*. Philadelphia: Fortress, 2004.

Phipps, William E. *Assertive Biblical Women*. Westport, CT: Greenwood, 1992.

Pitt-Rivers, Julian. "The Fate of Shechem or the Politics of Sex." In *The Fate of Shechem, or, The Politics of Sex: Essays in the Anthropology of the Mediterranean*, 126–71, 182–86. Cambridge Studies in Social Anthropology 19. Cambridge: Cambridge University Press, 1977.

Polaski, Donald C. "On Taming Tamar: Amram's Rhetoric and Women's Roles in Pseudo-Philo's *Liber Antiquitatum Biblicarum* 9." *Journal for the Study of the Pseudepigrapha* 13 (1995): 79–99.

Pressler, Carolyn. *The View of Women Found in the Deuteronomic Family Laws*. Beihefte zur Zeitschrift für die alttestamentliche Wissenschaft 216. Berlin: de Gruyter, 1993.

Pritchard, James B., ed. *Ancient Near Eastern Texts Relating to the Old Testament*. 3rd ed. Princeton, NJ: Princeton University Press, 1969.

Prouser, O. Horn. "The Truth about Women and Lying." *Journal for the Study of the Old Testament* 61 (1994): 15–28.

Quinones, Ricardo J. *The Changes of Cain: Violence and the Lost Brother in Cain and Abel Literature*. Princeton, NJ: Princeton University Press, 1991.

Rackman, Joseph. "Was Isaac Deceived?" *Judaism* 43.1 (1994): 37–45.

Rand, Herbert. "Judah and Joseph: A Study in Contrasts [The Judah-Tamar Incident, Gen. 38]." *Jewish Bible Quarterly* 21 (1993): 127–28.

Reardon, Kathleen Kelly. *Persuasion in Practice*. Newbury Park, CA: Sage, 1991.

Rendsburg, Gary A. "David and His Circle in Genesis 38." *Vetus Testamentum* 36.4 (1986): 438–46.

Robbins, Gregory Allen, ed. *Genesis 1–3 in the History of Exegesis: Intrigue in the Garden*. Lewiston, NY: Mellen, 1988.

Rogerson, John W., Margaret Davies, and M. Daniel Carroll R., eds. *The Bible in Ethics: The Second Sheffield Colloquium*. Journal for the Study of the Old Testament: Supplement Series 207. Sheffield: Sheffield Academic Press, 1995.

Rook, John. "Making Widows: The Patriarchal Guardian at Work." *Biblical Theology Bulletin* 27 (1997): 10–15.

Rowlett, Lori L. *Joshua and the Rhetoric of Violence: A New Historicist Analysis*. Journal for the Study of the Old Testament: Supplement Series 226. Sheffield: Sheffield Academic Press, 1996.

Sakenfeld, Katharine Doob. *Just Wives? Stories of Power and Survival in the Old Testament and Today*. Louisville: Westminster John Knox, 2003.

Sarna, Nahum M. *Genesis*. Jewish Publication Society Torah Commentary. Philadelphia: Jewish Publication Society, 1989.

Satlow, Michael L. *Jewish Marriage in Antiquity*. Princeton, NJ: Princeton University Press, 2001.

———. *Tasting the Dish: Rabbinic Rhetorics of Sexuality*. Brown Judaic Studies 303. Atlanta: Scholars Press, 1995.

Schmitt, John J. "Like Eve, Like Adam: *mšl* in Gen. 3, 16." *Biblica* 72 (1991): 1–22.

Scholz, Susanne. *Rape Plots: A Feminist Cultural Study of Genesis 34*. Studies in Biblical Literature 13. New York: Peter Lang, 2000.

———. "Was It Really Rape in Genesis 34? Biblical Scholarship as a Reflection of Cultural Assumptions." In *Escaping Eden: New Feminist Perspectives on the Bible*, edited by Harold C. Washington, Susan Lochrie Graham, and Pamela Thimmes, 182–98. New York: New York University Press, 1999.

Schottroff, Luise, Silvia Schroer, and Marie-Theres Wacker. *Feminist Interpretation: The Bible in Women's Perspective*. Translated by Martin and Barbara Rumscheidt. Minneapolis: Fortress, 1998.

Schüngel-Straumann, Helen. "On the Creation of the Man and the Woman in Genesis 1–3: The History and Reception of the Texts Reconsidered." In *A Feminist Companion to Genesis*, edited by Athalya Brenner, 53–76. Sheffield: Sheffield Academic Press, 1993.

Schwartz, Regina M. *The Curse of Cain: The Violent Legacy of Monotheism*. Chicago: University of Chicago Press, 1997.

Schwendinger, Julia R., and Herman Schwendinger. *Rape and Inequality*. Sage Library of Social Research 148. Beverly Hills, CA: Sage, 1983.

Selvidge, Marla J. *Woman, Violence, and the Bible*. Lewiston, NY: Mellen, 1996.

Shavitt, Sharon, and Timothy C. Brock, eds. *Persuasion: Psychological Insights and Perspectives*. Boston: Allyn & Bacon, 1994.

Sheres, Ita. *Dinah's Rebellion: A Biblical Parable for Our Time*. New York: Crossroad, 1990.

Shields, Mary E. "'More Righteous Than I': The Comeuppance of the Trickster in Genesis 38." In *Are We Amused? Humour about Women in the Biblical Worlds*, edited by Athalya Brenner, 31–51. Journal for the Study of the Old Testament: Supplement Series 383. London: T&T Clark, 2003.

Smith, Carol. "Samson and Delilah: A Parable of Power?" *Journal for the Study of the Old Testament* 76 (1997): 45–57.

———. "The Story of Tamar: A Power-Filled Challenge to the Structures of Power." In *Women in the Biblical Tradition*, edited by George J. Brooke, 16–28. Studies in Women and Religion 31. Lewiston, NY: Mellen, 1992.

Soggin, J. Alberto. "Judah and Tamar (Genesis 38)." In *Of Prophets' Visions and the Wisdom of Sages: Essays in Honour of R. Norman Whybray on His Seventieth Birthday*, edited by Heather A. McKay and David J. A. Clines, 282–306. Journal for the Study of the Old Testament: Supplement Series 162. Sheffield: JSOT Press, 1993.

Sölle, Dorothee. *Great Women of the Bible in Art and Literature*. Translated by Joe H. Kirchberger. Grand Rapids: Eerdmans, 1994.

Speiser, E. A. *Genesis*. Anchor Bible Commentary 1. Garden City, NY: Doubleday, 1964.

———. "The Wife-Sister Motif in the Patriarchal Narratives." In *Biblical and Other Studies*, edited by A. Altmann, 15–28. Cambridge, MA: Harvard University Press, 1963.

Sternberg, Meir. "Biblical Poetics and Sexual Politics: From Reading to Counter-Reading." *Journal of Biblical Literature* 111.3 (1992): 463–88.

———. *The Poetics of Biblical Narrative: Ideological Literature and the Drama of Reading*. Bloomington: Indiana University Press, 1985.

Stordalen, Terge. "Man, Soil, Garden: Basic Plot in Genesis 2–3 Reconsidered." *Journal for the Study of the Old Testament* 53 (1992): 3–26.

Stratton, Beverly J. *Out of Eden: Reading, Rhetoric, and Ideology in Genesis 2–3*. Journal for the Study of the Old Testament: Supplement Series 208. Sheffield: Sheffield Academic Press, 1995.

Streete, Gail C. *The Strange Woman: Power and Sex in the Bible*. Louisville: Westminster John Knox, 1997.

Tarlin, Jan William. "Tamar's Veil: Ideology at the Entrance to Enaim." In *Culture, Entertainment, and the Bible*, edited by George Aichele, 174–81. Journal for the Study of the Old Testament: Supplement Series 309. Sheffield: Sheffield Academic Press, 2000.

Teubal, Savina J. *Hagar the Egyptian: The Lost Tradition of the Matriarchs*. San Francisco: Harper & Row, 1990.

Thistlethwaite, Susan Brooks. "'You May Enjoy the Spoil of Your Enemies': Rape as a Biblical Metaphor for War." *Semeia* 61 (1993): 59–75.

Thompson, Thomas L. *The Historicity of the Patriarchal Narratives: The Quest for the Historical Abraham*. Beihefte zur Zeitschrift für die alttestamentliche Wissenschaft 133. Berlin: de Gruyter, 1974.

Tigay, Jeffrey H. *Deuteronomy*. Jewish Publication Society Torah Commentary. Philadelphia: Jewish Publication Society, 1996.

Tomes, Roger. "A Father's Anxieties (Sirach 42:9–11)." In *Women in the Biblical Tradition*, edited by George J. Brooke, 71–91. Studies in Women and Religion 31. Lewiston, NY: Mellen, 1992.

Trible, Phyllis. "Depatriarchalizing in Biblical Interpretation." *Journal of the American Academy of Religion* 41 (1973): 30–48.

———. *God and the Rhetoric of Sexuality*. Overtures to Biblical Theology. Philadelphia: Fortress, 1978.

———. *Texts of Terror: Literary-Feminist Readings of Biblical Narratives*. Overtures to Biblical Theology. Philadelphia: Fortress, 1984.

Ullendorff, E. "The Bawdy Bible." *Bulletin of the School of Oriental and African Studies* 42 (1979): 434.

Van Dijk-Hemmes, Fokkelien. "Tamar and the Limits of Patriarchy: Between Rape and Seduction (2 Samuel 13 and Genesis 38)." In *Anti-Covenant: Counter-Reading Women's Lives in the Hebrew Bible*, edited by Mieke Bal, 135–56. Journal for the Study of the Old Testament: Supplement Series 81. Sheffield: Sheffield Academic Press, 1989.

Van Seters, John. *Abraham in History and Tradition*. New Haven: Yale University Press, 1975.

———. "The Creation of Man and the Creation of the King." *Zeitschrift für die alttestamentliche Wissenschaft* 101 (1989): 335–41.

Vawter, Bruce. *On Genesis: A New Reading*. Garden City, NY: Doubleday, 1977.

von Rad, Gerhard. *Genesis*. Translated by John H. Marks. Rev. ed. Old Testament Library. Philadelphia: Westminster, 1972.

von Wolde, E. J. *A Semiotic Analysis of Genesis 2–3: A Semiotic Theory and Method of Analysis Applied to the Story of the Garden of Eden*. Studia Semitica Neerlandica 25. Assen: Van Gorcum, 1989.

———. "Texts in Dialogue with Texts: Intertextuality in the Ruth and Tamar Narratives." *Biblical Interpretation* 5.1 (1997): 1–28.

Wallace, Howard N. *The Eden Narrative*. Harvard Semitic Monographs 32. Atlanta: Scholars Press, 1985.

Walsh, Jerome T. "Genesis 2:4b–3:24: A Synchronic Approach." *Journal of Biblical Literature* 96 (1977): 161–77.

Washington, Harold C. "Violence and the Construction of Gender in the Hebrew Bible: A New Historical Approach." *Biblical Interpretation* 5.4 (1997):
324–63.

Washington, Harold C., Susan Lochrie Graham, and Pamela Thimmes, eds.
Escaping Eden: New Feminist Perspectives on the Bible. New York: New York
University Press, 1999.

Watson, Francis. "Strategies of Recovery and Resistance: Hermeneutical Reflections on Genesis 1–3 and Its Pauline Reception." *Journal for the Study of the
New Testament* 45 (1992): 79–103.

Wenham, Gordon J. *Genesis 1–15*. Word Biblical Commentary 1. Waco: Word,
1987.

———. *Genesis 16–50*. Word Biblical Commentary 2. Waco: Word, 1987.

———. "Why Does Sexual Intercourse Defile (Lev. 15:18)?" *Zeitschrift für die
alttestamentliche Wissenschaft* 95 (1983): 432–34.

Westbrook, Raymond. *Property and the Family in Biblical Law*. Journal for the
Study of the Old Testament: Supplement Series 113. Sheffield: JSOT Press,
1991.

Westenholz, Joan Goodnick. "Tamar, *Qĕdēša, Qadištu*, and Sacred Prostitution
in Mesopotamia." *Harvard Theological Review* 82.3 (1989): 245–65.

Westermann, Claus. *Genesis 1–11: A Commentary*. Translated by John J. Scullion.
Minneapolis: Augsburg, 1984.

———. *Genesis 12–36: A Commentary*. Translated by John J. Scullion. Minneapolis: Augsburg, 1986.

———. *Genesis 37–50: A Commentary*. Translated by John J. Scullion. Minneapolis: Augsburg, 1986.

Whybray, R. N. "The Immorality of God: Reflections on Some Passages in Genesis, Job, Exodus and Numbers." *Journal for the Study of the Old Testament*
72 (1996): 89–102.

Wildavsky, Aaron. "Survival Must Not Be Gained through Sin: The Moral of the
Joseph Stories Prefigured through Judah and Tamar." *Journal for the Study
of the Old Testament* 62 (1994): 37–48.

Williams, James G. *The Bible, Violence, and the Sacred: Liberation from the Myth
of Sanctioned Violence*. San Francisco: HarperSanFrancisco, 1991.

———. *Women Recounted: Narrative Thinking and the God of Israel*. Sheffield:
Almond Press, 1982.

Wright, George R. H. "The Positioning of Genesis 38." *Zeitschrift für die alttestamentliche Wissenschaft* 94 (1982): 523–29.

Young-Bruehl, Elisabeth. *The Anatomy of Prejudices*. Cambridge, MA: Harvard
University Press, 1996.

Scripture Index

Subject Index